"*My All in All* is rich with insight, reminding us of God's all-consuming love and His concern for all the details of our lives. Robert Morgan's books always bless me!"
— *Terri Blackstock,* Author, *Last Light* and *Cape Refuge*

"This book of daily devotionals reflects how God's Word is relevant to issues that most of us have faced. Rob Morgan's transparent and applicable style makes the book a favorite."
— *Judy Comstock,* Executive Director
International Network of Children's Ministry

"*My All in All* applies inviting prose and insightful illustrations to inspired texts. These devotions will help you grow in grace and knowledge."
— *Timothy W. Eaton,* President
Hillsdale College, Moore, Oklahoma

"In reading this powerful new book, I am reminded why Robert Morgan has become a favorite author of our '100 Huntley Street' TV viewers. His poignant illustrations and penetrating scriptural insights are a breath of fresh air to the soul!"
— *Ron Mainse,* Host, "100 Huntley Street"
President, Crossroads Christian Communications Inc.

"Everyone of Rob Morgan's previous books . . . has taken me to greater depths of faith and obedience in my personal walk with the Lord. This daily devotional book is no exception. Its profound simplicity will stir your heart to love God more deeply and serve Him more faithfully as you discover all that He wants to do for you and all that He wants to do through you. . . . As a family, read one page of *My All in All* every day, then pray about what you read. Each day's entry is brief and can be easily understood by both adults and children."
— *Dr. George W. Murray,* Chancellor
Columbia International University

"Rob Morgan has penned this unique devotional for daily encouragement and enrichment. I am sure *My All in All* will

be a blessing to 'all' who read it carefully and prayerfully. The blending of personal reflections, vivid illustrations, and devotional insights adorn beautifully the biblical truths that are foundational to this creative volume. This volume will take you on a fresh devotional journey providing assurance and challenge as you walk in the grace of God."
— *David Olford,* Stephen Olford Professor
of Expository Preaching, Union University

"Robert Morgan brilliantly uses his God-given abilities to inspire and challenge all of us as he shares about 'the largest little word in the world': *all. My All in All* will daily show you through God's Word how to find comfort, peace, and assurance through God's promises and truths. Familiar Scriptures will have new meaning as one reads this collection of verses and sees things like they have never seen them before."
— *Warren Peek,* President and CEO
The Southern Baptist Foundation

"Of all of the writers I have read throughout all of my life, Rob Morgan is the best biblical illustrator of them all. With practical creativity and pastoral compassion, *My All in All* illustrates 365 scriptural passages so you'll have food for the soul all the days of the year."
— *Morris Proctor,* Morris Proctor Seminars

"Rob Morgan has done it again—encouragement on steroids! Here is true documentation of Rob's daily walk poured out in expressions of overflow, wisdom, love, and reverence to a God who knows all, loves all, and understands all. Rob allows us to look into his soul and enjoy the journey with him. His words are succinct, profound, and passionate. His stories are personal, penetrating, and practical. I am certain that my life will be richer, my walk with God sweeter, my worship deeper, and my relationships with others more personal, as I make reading these gems a daily habit. I look forward to using *My All in All* for many years."
— *Vernon M. Whaley,* Director
The Center for Worship, Liberty University

MY ALL
IN ALL

DAILY ASSURANCE OF GOD'S GRACE

My All in All

ROBERT J. MORGAN

B&H
PUBLISHING GROUP
Nashville, Tennessee

ISBN: 978-0-8054-4663-0

Published by B&H Publishing Group (Nashville, Tennessee)

Dewey Decimal Classification: 242.2
Subject Heading: DEVOTIONAL LITERATURE \ GOD—PROMISES

Often throughout this book the author italicizes text for emphasis.

1 2 3 4 5 6 7 8 9 10 11 12 13 14 15   12 11 10 09 08

TO

Ava Grace

Acknowledgments

It's an honor to work with Thomas Walters, my editor and friend, and the team of professionals at B&H Publishing Group.

Dittos to Yates and Yates, my literary agents, especially to Chris Ferebee, who has unfailingly given me wise counsel and timely assistance.

Just as I was finishing this manuscript, my computer crashed like a freight train. Sherry Anderson, my co-worker at The Donelson Fellowship, sprinted into crisis mode, recovered the files, and "fixed things."

Most of all, my dear wife Katrina has given me honest insight for every page and tireless support for every step. May the Lord fulfill for her the words of Thomas Olivers's great hymn echoing the theme of this book:

> The God of Abraham praise, whose all sufficient grace
> Shall guide me all my happy days, in all my ways. . . .
> I shall behold His face; I shall His power adore,
> And sing the wonders of His grace forevermore.

He is all in all to me,
And my song of songs shall be,
Hallelujah, O My Savior,
I am trusting only Thee.
Fanny Crosby

*I*ntroduction

One evening several years ago when troubled about a particular matter, I sat at the dining room table and picked up my Bible. I turned to a little book near the back and read through 1 Peter, thinking the old fisherman might have an encouraging word for me. When I got to the last chapter, I came across verse 7: "casting all your care upon Him, because He cares about you." It was a verse I knew well, indeed had memorized it; but now I saw something I'd never seen before. It said: "casting *ALL* your care upon Him."

The Divine Author could easily have omitted the word *all* without hindering the flow or force of the text: *casting your care upon Him*. But the Lord deliberately dropped that little *all* into the sentence like a pearl in the pathway, and I had overlooked it for years.

But what a word! The "all" indicated this was an all-inclusive promise. Nothing is excluded from the invitation. No problem is too small for His notice, none too large for His power. He's concerned about each and every problem I have or would ever have, public or personal, large or little. He can handle them, and I should give them all to Him in total trust.

Then a thought came to me. I wondered if there were other "alls" in the Bible that I'd missed. Continuing my reading, I noticed three verses later that God is "the God of *all* grace." Four verses later: "Peace to *all* of you." Three verses down the column, in

1

2 Peter 1:3, I read, "His divine power has given to us *all* things that pertain to life and godliness, through the knowledge of Him who called us" (NKJV).

Looking up the word in a concordance, I was amazed to find 5,675 "alls" in the Bible. This word shows up in a remarkable number of verses, and it amplifies many of our greatest truths, commands, and promises:

- "*All* things work together for the good of those who love God" (Rom. 8:28).
- "You have thrown *all* my sins behind Your back" (Isa. 38:17).
- "Even the hairs of your head have *all* been counted" (Matt. 10:30).
- "Love the Lord your God with *all* your heart" (Matt. 22:37).
- "Trust in the Lord with *all* your heart" (Prov. 3:5–6).
- "Come to Me, *all* you who are weary and burdened" (Matt. 11:28).
- "Goodness and mercy will follow me *all* the days of my life" (Ps. 23:6 NIV).
- "Seek first the kingdom of God and His righteousness, and *all* these things will be provided for you" (Matt. 6:33).

The Lord doesn't waste words in His Book. In the verses above, the *alls* could easily have been left out; yet there they are. Seems it's one of God's favorite words. He used it thousands of times, often in passages that would have read nicely without it; yet the *all* maximizes the meaning to the absolute. It's the largest little word in the world, taking already-strong statements and broadening their applications to virtual infinity, which, after all, is what one would expect from an omnipotent Father.

The frequency of this word in Scripture speaks to the all-sufficient grace of our Almighty Savior. It highlights the infinite omniqualities of God, and the complete devotion we should afford

Him. He is the Lord of All, our All-in-All, our Almighty God, our All-Sufficient Savior from whom All blessings flow; and He is All we need.

Looking up all these *alls* was the simplest Bible study I've ever done, but one of the most bolstering to the soul, because *all* Scripture is given by inspiration of God—even the thousands of occurrences of this little monosyllabic term.

So for each day of the year, I've selected an "all" from Scripture—365 of them, *all* told.

The other 5,310 occurrences you'll have to dig out for yourself.[1]

January 1

*God is able to make **all** grace abound toward you;*
*that ye, always having **all** sufficiency in **all** things,*
may abound to every good work.

2 Corinthians 9:8 (KJV)

Missionary Amy Carmichael attended a meeting featuring the renowned preacher Dr. Andrew Bonar. "He was very old and could not speak very plainly or strongly," she recalled. "The hall was full, and I was near the back. I could not catch a single word he said, except this word *all*. He read 2 Corinthians 9:8 and he put every bit of strength he had into it, so that the one word rang out—*all—always—all—all*. I have forgotten thousands of great sermons, but that 'all' I have never forgotten, and it has helped me countless times."[2]

The context of this verse involves giving to the Lord's work, yet the promise is larger than its context. The words *God is able* represent a recurring divine promise:

- He is able to establish us (Rom. 16:25).
- He is able to do immeasurably more than we ask or think (Eph. 3:20).
- He is able to keep what we have committed to Him (2 Tim. 1:12).
- He is able to aid us in temptation (Heb. 2:18).
- He is able to keep us from falling (Jude 24).
- He is able to deliver us (Dan. 3:17).
- And He is able to make *all* grace abound to us in *all* ways at *all* times for *all* things.

Our God is able! Throughout this year, He isn't going to impart *some* grace or *some* sufficiency in *some* things for *some* good works. It's *all—all—all—all!*

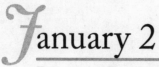

January 2

*Trust in the Lord with **all** your heart,*
and do not rely on your own understanding.

Proverbs 3:5

Many times I've preached this verse to myself, repeating over and over: "Trust in the Lord with all your heart, . . . Trust in the Lord with all your heart, . . ." Recently I dug a little deeper into that word *trust*. According to the *Theological Wordbook of the Old Testament*, the original term here in Proverbs 3:5 is *batucha*, which literally means to "trust in, feel safe, be confident, careless."

Careless—care-less, as in carefree.

The *TWOT* goes on to explain that this word expresses the sense of well-being and security that results from having something or someone in whom to place confidence. The basic idea behind "trust" goes beyond intellectual belief; it emphasizes an attitude or emotion of feeling safe and secure, unconcerned—being confident to the point of being care-less or carefree.[3]

That doesn't preclude a healthy concern for things we've entrusted to the Lord. It does mean that the Proverbs 3:5-variety of trust liberates us from toxic anxiety, fear, worry, and crippling concern. The old French mystic, Jean Nicolas Grou, said, "Give yourself to Him, trust Him, fix your eye upon Him, listen to His voice, and then go on bravely and cheerfully."

Don't trust Him with *some* of your heart, which taps into *some* of His peace. Abide with total trust. That's His desire and His command for you today: "Trust in the Lord with *all* your heart."

> 'Tis so sweet to trust in Jesus,
> Just to take Him at His word;
> Just to rest upon His promise,
> Just to know "Thus saith the Lord."
>
> —*Louisa M. R. Stead, 1882*

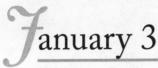

January 3

*Think about Him in **all** your ways,*
and He will guide you on the right paths.

Proverbs 3:6

Recently I spoke to students of Bryan College in Tennessee about God's guidance over matters large and small in our lives. Afterward I was bombarded with questions. Another speaker had suggested that God establishes certain parameters for our lives but doesn't involve Himself in specifics, that He doesn't specifically know or ordain our steps. But I believe God's guidance is detailed, daily, personal, unfailing, and preplanned, as Psalm 139:16 says: "*All* my days were written in Your book and planned before a single one of them began."

If He has planned *all my days,* I should acknowledge Him in *all my ways.* That means developing the habit of deliberately pausing to ask God's will before making a purchase, giving an answer, writing a letter, making a decision, or taking an action. Acknowledge Him as Lord of that matter.

This was Nehemiah's habit, as we see in chapter 2 of his book: "Then the king asked me, 'What is your request?' So I prayed to the God of heaven and answered the king." In the royal palace in Susa that day, no one noticed the slight pause in the conversation. But during that strategic second of silence, Nehemiah shot an arrow of prayer heavenward and consulted God, quietly asking: "Lord, give me wisdom and grant me favor!"

Strategic pauses like that throughout the day would save us from many a mistake.

*In **all** your ways acknowledge Him,*
and He shall direct your paths.

NKJV

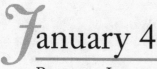anuary 4

*Lord, You know **all** things.*
John 21:17 (NKJV)

One day while perusing A. W. Tozer's *The Knowledge of the Holy*, I came across a peculiar idea. Tozer asserted that God has never learned anything. He cannot learn; it is impossible. Imagine the lifted eyebrows if a pastor started Sunday's sermon with that declaration. But Tozer was right. Because God is omniscient, He possesses perfect knowledge and therefore has no need to learn.[4] There isn't a scrap of information, a byte of data, or a spark of genius that He hasn't known from eternity past. He compasses and surpasses all facts; He comprehends and transcends all reality; and in Him are the treasures of wisdom and knowledge.

That means all truth is God's truth, and true science will never contradict the realities of Scripture. It means He knows the future as well as the past, and He is guiding His creation toward pre-appointed ends. Yet it means more. As Peter acknowledged in John 21, Jesus also knows the world within us.

He knows my strengths, so He can use me for His purpose. He knows my weaknesses, so He can perfect what concerns me. He knows my anxieties, so He can reassure me with His promises. He knows my hurts, so He can apply His salve. He knows my sins, so He can cleanse my soul. He knows my failures, so He can work all things for my good. He knows my past, so He can lead me toward maturity. And He knows my future, so He can lead me all the way.

All wise, all good, almighty Lord,
Jesus, by highest Heav'n adored.

—Charles Wesley, 1745

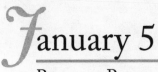

January 5

*Let **all** who take refuge in You rejoice;*
let them shout for joy forever.

Psalm 5:11

During two periods of my life I've suffered bouts of depression, so I know something of its perils. According to the World Health Organization, major depression is the fourth-leading cause of disability in the world, and it's on its way to becoming the second-leading cause, just behind heart disease.[5]

It's a complex illness, and I don't want to oversimplify it. Yet our depression, anxiety, anger, or fear is often the by-product of discounting the unfailing promises of God. Israel's King David suffered periodic depression, as revealed in some of his psalms. He often brought his heavy heart to the Lord and replenished his emotions in the endless reservoirs of God's grace. In so doing, he developed this formula in Psalm 5:11—

Relying on the Lord → Rejoicing in the Lord.

That's simple enough for a wall plaque, yet it's one of the most profound equations for emotional health ever discovered: "Let all those rejoice who put their trust in You" (NKJV). The word *all* signifies that this truth is applicable to everyone on earth. We can all learn to *rely*, and thereby to *rejoice*.

My daughter Grace once gave me a figurine of a lazy frog with his hands behind his head, resting on a rock, legs folded leisurely. Knowing my penchant for worry, she thought it a good reminder of the acronym FROG: Fully Rely On God. It's hard to be depressed when there's a frog on your desk; and it's hard not to rejoice when you're fully relying on Him.

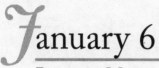

January 6

READING: MATTHEW 6:25–34

*After **all** these things the Gentiles seek.*
*For your heavenly Father knows that you need **all** these things.*
But seek first the kingdom of God and His righteousness,
*and **all** these things will be added to you.*

Matthew 6:32–33 (NKJV)

England's Queen Elizabeth I once asked a British merchant to undertake a mission for the crown. "But your Highness," said the man, "such a long absence will be fatal to my business." To which the queen replied: "You take care of my business, and I will take care of yours." When the man returned, he found that the queen's patronage had enlarged his company immeasurably.[6]

Alice Taylor was a missionary to China whose four children were captured by the Japanese and interned in a concentration camp during World War II. Alice suffered galloping anxiety. But she recalled her pastor once putting Matthew 6:33 like this: "If you take care of the things that are dear to God, He will take care of the things that are dear to you." Alice forced herself to focus on the Lord's work while trusting Him with her cares. In time her children came home safely to the glory of God.[7]

What's our greatest need today? Whatever it is—financial, relational, physical, or emotional—it's included in that universal *all*. Jesus said, "All these things . . . all these things . . . all these things."

Those who seek the Lord
will not lack any good thing.

Psalm 34:10

January 7

*Thus Noah did; according to **all***
that God commanded him, so he did.

Genesis 6:22 (NKJV)

Total trust results in total obedience. Hebrews 11:7 says, "By faith Noah, after being warned about what was not yet seen, in reverence built an ark."

By *faith* Noah *obeyed*.

Some scholars believe no rain had fallen to earth prior to that time. Genesis 1:7 speaks of the waters above the expanse of the sky, perhaps indicating that a vast thermal shield of vapor encased Earth and maintained a greenhouse effect. This blanket of moisture filtered the sun's destructive rays and may have contributed to the long life spans listed in Genesis. When the vapor canopy collapsed, torrential rains lasted forty days and nights. So in an age in which people knew nothing of rain, God told Noah to build an enormous ship, and Noah obeyed completely, down to the last nail.

To measure your faith, pull out the dipstick of obedience. Does God tell us to build up others with our words? To be kind to one another, tenderhearted, forgiving one another? To do the work of an evangelist? To avoid sexual immorality? To keep our eyes from vanity? To meditate on Scripture?

Scottish novelist George MacDonald said, "You can begin at once to be a disciple of the Living One—by obeying Him in the first thing you can think of in which you are not obeying Him. We must learn to obey Him in everything, and so must begin somewhere. Let it be at once, and in the very next thing that lies at the door of our conscience."[8]

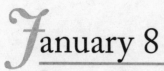

January 8

Till heaven and earth pass away,
one jot or one tittle will by no means pass from the law
*till **all** is fulfilled.*

Matthew 5:18 (NKJV)

A jot is the Hebrew letter *yodh*, the tiniest of the twenty-two letters of the Hebrew alphabet, about the size of an English apostrophe. Charles Ryrie said, "Though it is the smallest of the Hebrew letters it is as important as any other letter, for letters spell words, and words compose sentences, and sentences make promises. . . . Every promise will be fulfilled just as it was spelled out."[9]

A tittle is even smaller than a jot. It's a slight pen stroke that comprises part of a letter. Jesus claimed that the Word of God is inspired, accurate, authoritative, infallible, unerring, and trustworthy down to its smallest elements.

Years ago in Palm Beach, Florida, my wife Katrina was mentored by a woman named Antoinette Johnson, a devoted Christian and Bible student. Katrina eventually moved away, but the two women stayed in touch periodically. Last year while in Florida, we tracked down Mrs. J.

She was ninety-one, alert, and sporting bright oversized glasses. During our visit she told us that her diminished vision has yielded an unexpected blessing. "I use a magnifying glass now to study the Bible," she said. "I can only read one word at a time, so I put the glass on each word and study out that word before going to the next. It's taught me afresh that every single word in the Bible is precious."

Read the Bible slowly and treasure every word; not one jot or tittle will fail.

January 9

*Above **all**, fear the LORD*
*and worship Him faithfully with **all** your heart,*
considering the great things He has done for you.

1 Samuel 12:24

Above all . . . with all . . . .
What a slogan for life! This verse comes at the close of one of the greatest speeches in recorded history, the farewell message of Samuel, who was bowing out after a lifetime as Israel's leader. His farewell address is the whole of 1 Samuel 12, and at one point he even called down thunder and rain from heaven—talk about visuals!—warning the people that everything depended on their serving God with *all* their hearts.

Someone once said that partial obedience is total disobedience. Too many of us have an unspoken idea that the stresses of life justify a little fudging of the rules. Life is hard, so we deserve a break—a little sinning here and there provides relief from the pressures we bear.

But little sins can cause big problems. After all, germs are little things, yet deadly. A spark is a little thing, but it can consume a forest. The Bible warns about the little foxes that spoil the vines, and Paul wrote that a little yeast leavens the whole lump.

On the other hand, obedience in little things is a big thing.

Is there a little sin in your heart that needs to be confessed and corrected? Some seemingly small area of obedience that should be embraced? "Above all, fear the LORD and worship Him faithfully with all your heart, considering the great things He has done for you."

Live Thou within us, Lord. Thy mind and will be ours;
Be Thou beloved, adored, and served with all our powers.

—John Ellerton, 1889

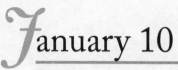anuary 10

*The glory of the LORD will appear, and **all** humanity
will see it together, for the mouth of the LORD has spoken.*

Isaiah 40:5

With these words Isaiah assured the Jews of the dispersion that
their warfare was over, their iniquities were pardoned, and
they had a divine mission: "Prepare the way of the LORD . . . make
a straight highway for our God . . . . Every valley will be lifted up,
and every mountain and hill will be leveled; . . . And the glory of
the LORD will appear, and all humanity will see it."

When John the Baptist arrived on the scene, he chose this as
his primary text.

In 1671, German hymnist Johannes Olearius rendered Isaiah 40 into resplendent verse: "Make ye straight what long was
crooked, Make the rougher places plain: / Let your hearts be true
and humble, as befits His holy reign."

In 1741, George Frederick Handel chose this passage to open
his oratorio, *Messiah*.

In 1963, Martin Luther King pealed out these words at the
Lincoln Memorial: "I have a dream that one day every valley shall
be exalted, and every hill and mountain shall be made low, the
rough places will be made plain, and the crooked places will be
made straight; and the glory of the Lord shall be revealed and all
flesh shall see it together."

For all that, the promise of Isaiah 40 has yet to be totally
fulfilled. A day is coming when the kingdoms of this world will
become the kingdoms of our Lord and of His Christ, and He will
reign forever and ever! Even so, come, Lord Jesus!

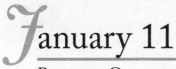

January 11

> ***All** the peoples on earth will be blessed through you.*
> **Genesis 12:3**

The transition between Genesis 11 and 12 is the Continental Divide of Scripture, even greater than the division between the Old and New Testaments. In the first eleven chapters of the Bible, God dealt with the world en masse; but in Genesis 12, He launched a far-reaching plan of redemption by choosing a man whose descendants would become a mighty nation. From that nation would come the Messiah from whom would come the church that, in turn, would take the gospel back to the whole world. This was outlined in advance in Genesis 12, given to Abraham and his "seed" or "offspring" (22:18).

There are seven promises in Genesis 12:1–3; and the *seventh* promise is repeated *seven* times in Scripture (Gen. 12:3, 18:18, 22:18, 26:4, 28:14; Acts 3:25–26; Gal. 3:8, 16). The seventh occurrence cuts straight to Calvary and is actually called "the gospel in advance" (Gal. 3:8 NIV).

> The Scripture [the Old Testament] foresaw that God
> would justify the Gentiles by faith and foretold the
> good news to Abraham, saying, *All the nations will be
> blessed in you. . . .* The promises were spoken to Abraham and to his seed. He does not say "and to seeds,"
> as though referring to many, but *and to your seed,*
> referring to one, who is Christ. (Gal. 3:8, 16)

Whenever tempted to doubt the gospel, I just go back to the Old Testament and notice how the unfolding plan of God was revealed in advance—preplanned, foreordained, and consistent from beginning to end.

January 12

A man's ways are before the LORD's eyes,
*and He considers **all** his paths.*

Proverbs 5:21

My friend Larry grew up in a dysfunctional home and was exposed to pornography early. After becoming a Christian and a husband, he still struggled with temptation. At Homestead Air Force Base, Larry's schedule kept him and his wife apart for stretches of time, and he developed a pattern. He would take a particular route to a part of town where he slipped into an adult store to rent movies. This became a ritual, and with it came a lessening sense of guilt.

One day in this store—June 20, 2001—Larry turned, and his eyes met those of a fellow church member. His breath left him. Here he was—husband, father, Sunday school teacher—caught in the act. The other man seemed amused, but for Larry, it was a pivotal moment. He went home in anguish, met with his pastor, confessed to his wife, and enrolled in a recovery program stressing daily Bible study, prayer, and holiness. "Since then," Larry said, "God has given me consistent victory, and the shock of that moment took from me all desire to return to my old ways."

It's sobering to realize the Lord knows the routes we take, and He sees every place we go, yet He finds ways of giving us victory and holiness. "I hid my sin for years," Larry said, "but the Lord saw all my paths and patterns, and in mercy led me out."

He'll do the same for you, so don't give up.

When temptation's darts assail us,
When in devious paths we stray,
Let Thy goodness never fail us,
Lead us in Thy perfect way.

—*Thomas Hastings, 1831*

January 13

*Not even Solomon in **all** his splendor*
was adorned like one of these!
Matthew 6:29

Imagine Solomon holding court. His surroundings accentu-
ated his glory, and visitors to the palace confessed the half had
never been told. The gilded walls, marble floors, rich tapestries,
golden furnishings, servants royally bedecked, the couriers and
courtiers—the glory that was Solomon's!—was like a fairy tale.

Yet King Solomon wasn't the best-dressed character in the
room.

Near the window, a lily grew in an exquisite pot. The richness
of its crimson petals outshone anything in Solomon's closet. Its
velvety feel was smoother than Solomon's silk, and the splash of
gold in its center was purer than his crown. The intricate design
of the flower surpassed the abilities of the royal tailors. Its tangle
of roots was superior to the shoes pinching the king's feet; and the
lily's fragrance was sweeter than Solomon's perfume.

It was the Lord's private joke—Solomon in all his glory
couldn't compare with a neglected flower in a nearby pot; yet for
a thousand years no one noticed the contrast till Jesus mentioned
it in His first sermon.

The same God who dresses the flowers and feeds the birds
knows our needs too. He knows when we're money-short and bone-
tired. He knows when we need food and raiment. So it's as simple
as this: "I tell you: Don't worry . . . . Why do you worry . . . ? So don't
worry . . . . Therefore don't worry" (Matt. 6:25, 28, 31, 34).

The billions of flowers blooming around the globe are preachers
with a single message: "Don't worry! God cares for our needs."

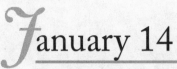
January 14

All this happened to King Nebuchadnezzar.
Daniel 4:28

Visitors to Berlin's Pergamon Museum are astounded by the Ishtar Gate, one of the most fabulous excavations from antiquity, built by King Nebuchadnezzar about 575 BC. It's covered with glazed bricks of rich blues and yellows, with stunning images of dragons, bulls, and daisies. It was one of eight entrances into the city, and Daniel himself entered Babylon through this gate.

In Daniel 4, Nebuchadnezzar boasted to himself about his great city, but the Lord cut him down to size, afflicting him with a humiliating mental illness known as zoanthropy in which he imagined he was an animal.

All this came upon Nebuchadnezzar as predicted, and for seven years he suffered bouts of insanity until he acknowledged that God's kingdom is an everlasting kingdom and His dominion endures from generation to generation. The Lord does as He pleases with the powers of heaven and earth. No one can hold back His hand.

Two words in Daniel 4 summarize the story of Nebuchadnezzar. In verse 26, Daniel told the king, "Your kingdom will be restored to you as soon as you acknowledge that *Heaven rules.*"

Those two words are simple enough to memorize and sloganize in our hearts. My candidate may lose the election, the globe may erupt in war, taxes may rise, culture may decay, plagues may come. And closer to home, my day may be ruined by things beyond my control. But heaven rules! The Most High oversees the universe, and "Jesus shall reign where'er the sun doth its successive journeys run."

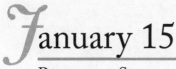

January 15

*Samuel judged Israel **all** the days of his life.*
1 Samuel 7:15 (NKJV)

The book of 1 Samuel is the Bible's leadership manual. The first portion of the book centers on Samuel himself, a *dedicated* leader; the middle part is about King Saul, a *defective* leader; and the last portion focuses on young David, a *developing* leader.

When it comes to Samuel, he was launched by a mother's prayers, and in childhood he learned to pray, "Speak, Lord, for Your servant is listening" (1 Sam. 3:9). As he grew, the Lord was with him and let none of his words fall to the ground. All Israel knew he had been established as the Lord's prophet (3:19–20).

All his days, Samuel dealt with aggravating people and problems while traveling a continuous circuit from town to town. He settled disputes, established order, and taught God's Word. Finally he announced his retirement and devoted his final years to a quiet ministry of prayer and teaching (12:23).

If Samuel ever had a midlife crisis, he weathered it. If he doubted his calling, he didn't show it. If he faced discouraging days, he overcame them. If he wanted to quit, he rested in the Lord and plunged back into the work. He served the Lord all the days of his life.

Are you going around in a circuit, dealing with aggravations? Feel like having a midlife crisis or nervous breakdown? God measures success by faithfulness, and He bestows fresh layers of mercy as we serve Him day by day, all the days of our lives.

So shall this and all our days,
Christ and God, show forth Thy praise.

—*William Bright, 1867*

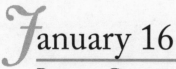

January 16

*And he gave him a tithe of **all**.*

Genesis 14:20 (NKJV)

The mysterious Melchizedek shows up at the beginning (Gen. 14), in the middle (Ps. 110), and at the end (Heb. 7) of Scripture, appearing out of nowhere, "without father or mother, without genealogy, without beginning of days or end of life." He's unique in Scripture, prefiguring Christ in a number of ways. In Genesis 14, he blessed Abraham, and in return Abraham gave him a tenth of all. This is the first reference to tithing in the Bible; but from this point, the Lord's people have been tithers.

Sometimes people ask me if we still have to tithe—is it a divine requirement? Well, in the Mosaic Law, tithing was commanded as part of Jewish national life; but Abraham tithed before the Law, and the New Testament simply tells us to give as God has prospered us (1 Cor. 16:2). I don't believe the tithe is a law to obey but a pattern to follow.

Richard Wurmbrand suffered in various Communist prisons because of his faith in Christ. The principle of tithing was so internalized in his heart that when he received a slice of bread a week and dirty soup every day, he faithfully tithed from it. Every tenth day he gave his soup to a weaker brother, and every tenth week he took his slice of bread and gave it to a fellow prisoner in Jesus' name.[10]

Can we not give a tithe of all?

> Whatever, Lord, we lend to Thee,
> Repaid a thousand-fold will be;
> Then gladly will we give to Thee
> Who givest all.

> *—Christopher Wordsworth, 1863*

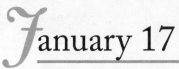# January 17

> *They were **all** filled with the Holy Spirit*
> *and began to speak in different languages,*
> *as the Spirit gave them ability for speech.*

Acts 2:4

"The mission of the church is missions," said Oswald J. Smith. That's the lesson of Acts 2:4. After the ascension of Christ, the disciples huddled in the Upper Room, waiting for Jesus to endow them with power as He had promised in Luke 24:49 and Acts 1:8. Then on the Day of Pentecost, the Holy Spirit burst into the room like a firestorm, flames licking every person and setting fire to every soul. It sounded like a tornado as the Spirit indwelt every heart. The Christians all tumbled into the streets, proclaiming Christ in the languages of those who had traveled to Jerusalem for the festival of Pentecost.

These momentary supernatural signs—fire, wind, tongues—signified the dawning of a new age. The Holy Spirit had been sent to indwell the church, commissioning every member as a missionary. In his *History of the Christian Church,* Philip Schaff wrote of those days: "Every congregation was a missionary society, and every Christian believer a missionary, inflamed by the love of Christ to convert his fellow-men. . . . Every Christian told his neighbor . . . the story of his conversion, as a mariner tells the story of the rescue from shipwreck."[11]

Every member a missionary is the slogan of Acts 2:4.

Is that true of your church?

Of you?

> If you take missions out of the Bible,
> you won't have anything left but the covers.
>
> —*Nina Gunter*

January 18

When they had prayed,
the place . . . was shaken,
*and they were **all** filled with the Holy Spirit*
and began to speak God's message with boldness.

Acts 4:31

If I'm filled with the Holy Spirit when I stand to preach, it means Jesus is controlling and empowering me, actually preaching the sermon *through* me. Being Spirit-filled means being Christ-used. At the Ascension our Lord went back to heaven, but at Pentecost He returned via the Holy Spirit to continue His ministry through us.

Paul and Barnabas told the Antioch church what God had done *through* them (Acts 14:27). Paul told the Judean leaders in Acts 21:19 what God had done *through* his ministry. In Romans 15:18, he wrote, "I would not dare say anything except what Christ has accomplished *through* me." In his final days, he testified that the Lord strengthened him, "so that the proclamation might be fully made *through* me" (2 Tim. 4:17). The Bible calls us ambassadors for Christ, as though God were making His appeal *through* us (2 Cor. 5:20).

When you share the gospel, teach the Bible, preach a sermon, quote a verse, encourage a friend, or write a note or article, remember—it's not what you're doing for Christ, but what He is doing through you.

Yes, sometimes it feels intimidating to share Christ—I still get nervous, and I've been doing it for years—but follow the Acts 4:31 model: Pray. Be shaken. Be filled with the Spirit. And speak the Word with boldness.

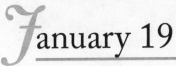anuary 19

*You have thrown **all** my sins behind Your back.*
Isaiah 38:17

I have a friend who sleeps fitfully, tormented by memories of what he did during the Vietnam War. Another friend struggles with forgiving himself for betraying his marriage, ruining his home, and destroying his career.

How do we forgive ourselves for moments in the past we can't change?

We must grasp vividly in our thoughts how the Lord throws all our sins behind His back. I've found it helpful to use biblical imagery as movie clips for the mind. For example, visualize approaching Christ with a foul-smelling sack containing all your rotten and decayed sins. He glances at the bag, takes it, and heaves it behind His back, saying, "There now, it's gone."

If the devil later tempts you toward guilt and shame, just replay that scene, quoting Isaiah 38:17: "You have thrown all my sins behind Your back."

If you need to strengthen the image, add Micah 7:19—the Lord tosses our sins into the depths of the sea.

If you need even greater imagery, picture the sea as filled with Christ's blood and quote 1 John 1:7: "The blood of Jesus His Son cleanses us from all sin."

Learn to use biblically based visualizations to change your thoughts and attitudes. This is biblical meditation, and it's a vital technique for mental and spiritual health.

PS: Never run back to recover the sack and start rummaging through all the filth again. If it's behind His back, it should be behind yours too.

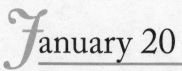

January 20

*The Lord be with **all** of you. . . .*
*The grace of our Lord Jesus Christ be with **all** of you.*
2 Thessalonians 3:16, 18

Are there books you've not yet read? Places not yet visited? In the same way, there are aspects of God's grace we've yet to experience. The word *grace* encompasses all the benefits God wants to pour into our lives today and tomorrow, on earth and in heaven. Even if we've been saved for years, there are aspects and applications of grace we've never even considered.

Anna Waring put it this way in one of her little verses:

> I thirst for springs of heavenly life,
> And here all day they rise—
> I seek the treasure of Thy love,
> And close at hand it lies.
>
> And a new song is in my mouth
> To long loved music set—
> Glory to Thee for all the grace
> I have not tasted yet.

When the apostle Paul wrote 2 Thessalonians, he began and ended his letter with words of grace and peace. In the introduction, he said, "Grace to you and peace from God our Father and the Lord Jesus Christ." Three chapters later, he concluded with, "May the Lord of peace Himself give you peace always in every way. . . . The grace of our Lord Jesus Christ be with all of you."

Thank the Lord today for His current blessings, and say: "Glory to Thee for all the grace I have not tasted yet."

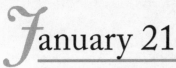

January 21

*This is a faithful saying and worthy of **all** acceptance,*
that Christ Jesus came into the world
to save sinners, of whom I am chief.

1 Timothy 1:15 (NKJV)

The *Christian Herald* once ran a story about London's Crystal Palace where, on October 7, 1857, Charles Spurgeon preached to 23,654 people. According to the paper, Spurgeon visited the hall the day before, fearing his voice wouldn't carry to all corners. Standing on stage, he quoted 1 Timothy 1:15.

Satisfied with the acoustics, Spurgeon left the building, unaware that a poor workman, battling depression, had been huddling behind one of the statues trying to pray. Suddenly a voice boomed into his ears: "This is a faithful saying and worthy of all acceptance, that Christ Jesus came into the world to save sinners, of whom I am chief."

From that moment, the man was converted to Christ.[12]

At the beginning of church history, the Lord deliberately transformed the angriest anti-Christian zealot on earth, Saul of Tarsus, as a token of His power to save anyone and everyone. "For that very reason I was shown mercy so that in me, the worst of sinners, Christ Jesus might display his unlimited patience as an example for those who would believe" (v. 16 NIV).

If you've given up on yourself or your loved one, don't! Jesus came to save the chief of sinners—the worst of the worst—and that's a statement deserving all acceptance.

> Chief of sinners though I be,
> Jesus shed His blood for me;
> Died that I might live on high,
> Died that I might never die.

—William McComb, 1864

January 22

All are going to the same place;
all come from dust, and all return to dust.

Ecclesiastes 3:20

There are many philosophies in the world; but really, only two: Hope and Despair. Without Jesus Christ and His Word, all other philosophies ultimately end in existential gloom. Swiss philosopher Henri-Frederic Amiel stated this honestly in 1864: "Melancholy is at the bottom of everything, just as at the end of all rivers is the sea. Can it be otherwise in a world where nothing lasts, where all that we have loved or shall love must die?"

The wisest philosopher in the Old Testament, Solomon, began and ended his career with piety; but during the middle of his life, drawn away by his vast wealth and many wives, he lost faith in God. The book of Ecclesiastes is a memoir of this period of his life.

Without God, Solomon realized, nothing lasts. All things perish and return to dust, and not even the dust endures. Given enough time, our planet will run down, our sun will burn out, the universe itself will fade, and all things will become as though nothing ever was. Life is ultimately meaningless without God.

But there's an old gospel song we used to sing up in the mountains that brightens the picture considerably:

> Time is filled with swift transition;
> Naught of earth unmoved can stand.
> Build your hopes on things eternal;
> Hold to God's unchanging hand!
>
> —*Jennie Wilson*

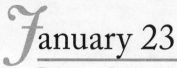

January 23

The Lord will save me;
*we will play stringed instruments **all** the days of our lives*
at the house of the LORD.

Isaiah 38:20

There's nothing that pleases God more than our songs of praise, whether played, sung, strummed, hummed, whistled, or yodeled. A hymn is emotionalized truth. It lifts our hearts to heaven and carries us with joy through all our lives.

Recently I received a letter from Liz Andress of Golden Valley, Minnesota, who wrote, "My mother tells me that when she was nursing me as an infant, she sang all the way through the Lutheran hymnal, start to finish. I've grown up very fond of the Lutheran hymnody, sang in college and church choir all the way through, and am now a member of our small but strong adult choir at church and direct the youth choir."[13]

Hezekiah had assumed the throne at age twenty-five. His reign had been peaceful and prosperous, and a great revival had swept the land. But right in the middle of everything, twin disasters struck. One was a national emergency—the Assyrian invasion—and the other was a terminal illness. Hezekiah, thirty-nine, collapsed physically at the very moment when his nation seemed doomed.

But he prayed and trusted and sang: "The Lord will save me; we will play stringed instruments all the days of our lives at the house of the Lord."

And the Lord delivered him.

The Lord will deliver us.

Let's sing all our days.

Now with singing and praise
Let us spend all the days
By our heavenly Father bestowed.

—*Charles Wesley, 1755*

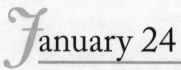# January 24

Don't be afraid.
*Even though you have committed **all** this evil,*
don't turn away from following the Lord.
*Instead, worship the Lord with **all** your heart.*

1 Samuel 12:20

In *Writing About Your Life,* William Zinsser tells of being stationed in Algeria during World War II. A huge map covered the façade of the post office in Algiers, and France was painted entirely in green. On D-Day (June 6, 1944) Zinsser joined the crowds in the square to watch workmen painting white stretches along the Normandy coast. Week after week, a white bulge spread south to Saint-Lô, and white ribbons ran north to Cherbourg. By August 21, the map was white all the way to the Seine, and eventually the whole of France was under Allied control, entirely white.[14]

Can you see yourself in that picture?

Before Jesus invades our lives, our hearts are under enemy occupation; but on our own personal Decision-Day, we receive Him as our Savior, and we're justified! A process of sanctification then begins as our thoughts, attitudes, and behaviors increasingly come under His control and we grow in the victorious Christian life.

Satan fights for every inch of territory, and we find ourselves in constant war with the world, the flesh, and the devil—but the victory of Jesus is unstoppable, and we are more than conquerors as we increasingly worship Him with all our hearts.

God paints in many colors,
but he never paints so gorgeously as when he paints in white.

—*G. K. Chesterton*

January 25

The promise is by faith, so that it may be according to grace,
*to guarantee it to **all** the descendants—*
not only to those who are of the law, but also to those
*who are of Abraham's faith. He is the father of us **all**.*

Romans 4:16

I'd probably get various answers if I asked, "Who's the father of the Christian faith?" But the apostle Paul cites Abraham as the father of *the Jewish nation* and of *the Christian church*.

That's an astounding assertion, but it's explained in Romans 4. We can't justify ourselves in God's sight, for His holiness is infinite and our sinfulness is undeniable. So God became a man who died in our stead. By placing our faith in His finished work, we're declared righteous in His sight. Abraham demonstrated this long ago when he was declared righteous through faith on the basis of grace alone (vv. 9–12).

The doctrine of justification wasn't a novelty invented by the apostles. It's always been God's plan. In both Old and New Testament days, everyone is saved by grace through faith. Abraham was saved on the basis of what Christ was going to do on Calvary. We are saved on the basis of what He has now done.

It is grace alone and faith alone; and thus Abraham, who first demonstrated this in Genesis 15:6, is the father of us all. "He did not waver in unbelief at God's promise, but was strengthened in his faith and gave glory to God," being fully persuaded that God could do what He has promised (Rom. 4:20–21).

Thy grace alone, dear Lord, I plead,
Thy death is now my life indeed,
For Thou hast paid my ransom.

—Paul Speratus, 1523

January 26

Lord, because of these promises people live,
*and in **all** of them is the life of my spirit as well.*

Isaiah 38:16

Isaiah 38 contains Hezekiah's hymn of praise after God had promised to heal him. Though not yet restored to health—that would happen at the end of the chapter—Hezekiah claimed God's promises and exulted in them as if already fulfilled.

Biblical promises are tightly wrapped, power-packed, portable capsules of Scripture, written by God and designed to meet our specific needs at specific times and in ways that correspond perfectly to His all-sufficient grace.

There's a promise in the Bible for every need we have and every crisis we face.

In the 1700s, Samuel Clarke compiled a list of promises for his congregation to study and memorize. The more he searched them out in Scripture, the more overwhelmed he felt by their sheer number and practicality. He organized them, and they were published as *Clarke's Scripture Promises*. In the introduction, Clarke wrote in his quaint Puritan style:

> A fixed, constant attention to the promises, and a firm belief in them, would prevent solicitude and anxiety about the concerns of this life. It would keep the mind quiet and composed in every change, and support and keep up our sinking spirits under the several troubles of life. . . . Christians deprive themselves of their most solid comforts by their unbelief and forgetfulness of God's promises. For there is no extremity so great but there are promises suitable to it, and abundantly sufficient for our relief in it.

January 27

"Vanity of vanities," says the Preacher;
*"Vanity of vanities, **all** is vanity."*

Ecclesiastes 1:2 (NKJV)

In his biography of Vincent van Gogh, D. M. Field points out that as a young man, Vincent longed to make a difference in the world. "I feel instinctively that I am good for something, that there is some point in existence," he wrote. "What use could I be . . . ? What service could I perform?" Choosing the ministry, Vincent poured himself into his Bible and longed to bring others to Christ. "Woe is me," he said, "if I do not preach the Gospel; if I did not aim at that and possess faith and hope in Christ, it would be bad for me indeed."[15]

Unfortunately, people didn't like Vincent's sermons, and he found little support among fellow preachers. Abandoning the ministry, he turned from the pulpit to the easel. His mental and emotional health declined, his art seemed unappreciated, and despair crept over him like a deepening dream until he shot and killed himself at age thirty-seven.

To me, Van Gogh is the most fascinating of the artists. Many theories have tried to explain his troubled life. But perhaps the best explanation is that of Solomon, another man who turned from God and found that without the Lord, there is no peace or purpose for which to live.

In Ecclesiastes, Solomon found that without God everything—hard work, pleasure, alcohol, sex, reading, and artistic endeavors—was vanity.

The ultimate philosophical truth is this: Without Christ, all is vanity even when it's easy; with Him, all is well even when it's hard.

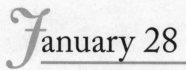anuary 28

Haman . . . set out to destroy
***all** of Mordecai's people, the Jews . . .*
*to destroy, kill, and annihilate **all** the Jewish people—*
young and old, women and children.

Esther 3:6, 13

King Frederick II of Prussia once asked his chaplain, "What proof exists that the Bible is true?" The chaplain responded by pointing to one of the king's advisors across the room, a man who was a Jew.

Nothing in recorded history matches the story of the Jews, and their survival is history's great miracle. From Haman to Hitler, they've been hated, hunted, expelled, executed, slandered, slain, and driven from their land; yet again and again deliverance has come in unexpected ways. No other people have been so reviled, or so resilient.

One political commentator noted that Israel is the only nation on earth that inhabits the same land, bears the same name, speaks the same language, and worships the same God as it did three thousand years ago. Yet even now powerful forces oppose them.

Christ's First and Second Comings are both connected with events surrounding Israel; and I believe the reestablishment of the state of Israel in 1948 has set the stage for the End Times. Though there are only about 14 million Jews on earth (half of them in Israel), the geopolitical headlines of our world are dominated by that tiny land.

Keep your eyes on the land of Israel, with a newspaper in one hand and a Bible in the other.

January 29

*Since you neglected **all** my counsel*
and did not accept my correction,
I, in turn, will laugh at your calamity.
I will mock when terror strikes you,
when terror strikes you like a storm
and your calamity comes like a whirlwind.
Proverbs 1:25–27

Never underestimate the power of Bible verses learned in childhood.

Case in point: During his earliest days, John Newton's mother instilled within him the Word of God; but she died when he was only six years old, and Newton grew up to become an immoral, blasphemous slave trader. One night aboard the *Greyhound,* he was awakened by a violent tempest that raged through the night. It was the most terrifying storm he'd ever experienced; there seemed little hope for survival. At one o'clock the next afternoon, Newton was tied to the helm where he steered the ship until midnight. As he pulled the wheel one way and the other, trying to keep the ship upright amid mighty swells, he came under deep conviction and felt he had sunk too low in immorality and wickedness to be forgiven.

Proverbs 1:24–33—verses from his childhood—flashed to mind, and Newton realized he had neglected all God's counsel. For years he had spurned God's correction. Now it seemed God was mocking him as terror came like a storm and calamity like a whirlwind.

Then and there, John Newton began making a series of decisions that would eventually lead him to become one of England's most powerful preachers and the author of the immortal words "Amazing Grace, how sweet the sound that saved a wretch like me."

January 30

*I acquired male and female servants and had slaves
who were born in my house. I also owned many herds of cattle
and flocks, more than **all** who were before me in Jerusalem.*

Ecclesiastes 2:7

In the history of Israel, no one rose to greater heights than
Solomon, yet fame and fortune filled him with emptiness.
He was the world's richest man—and its unhappiest.

Compare that with John Newton, the eighteenth-century
pastor who grew up at sea, escaped death again and again, and
became a deserter who was flogged at the gratings and then a
wretch who was sold to a slave in Africa.

After his conversion to Christ, he took a pastorate in the English village of Olney. One day when his parsonage was enlarged,
Newton thought of how thankful he was that his small congregation had expanded his quarters. In his journal, he wrote: "I am
a poor wretch that once wandered naked and barefoot, without
a home, without a friend; and now for me who once used to be
on the ground, and was treated as a dog by all around me, Thou
hast prepared a house suitable to the connection Thou has put
me into."[16]

Our satisfaction and contentment in life doesn't come from
riches but from righteousness. It isn't a matter of having servants,
flocks, herds, or money—it's a matter of being rich in God's amazing grace.

> More of Thy presence, Lord, impart,
> More of Thine image let me bear;
> Construct Thy throne within my heart,
> And reign without a rival there.
>
> —*John Newton*

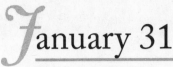

January 31

> *The LORD Most High is awe-inspiring,*
> *a great King over **all** the earth. . . .*
> *God is King of **all** the earth.*
>
> **Psalm 47:2, 7**

In 1682, Puritan writer Stephen Charnock published a book on the attributes of God in which he demonstrated the greatness of God's dominion by describing a map of the world. What is mighty old England except a spot you can cover with a finger? So, he said, is the whole world to God—simply a spot He can cover with one finger.

If we don't bear this in mind, we'll grow discouraged when our politicians are defeated, when terrorists strike our homeland, when our troops are in harm's way, when our church is persecuted, and when evil seems to triumph.

God is on His throne, providentially ruling and overruling, working out everything according to His will (Eph. 1:11). Psalm 47 takes that as a source of exuberance for us:

> *Clap your hands, all you peoples;*
> *shout to God with a jubilant cry.*
> *For the Lord Most High is awe-inspiring,*
> *a great King over all the earth.*
>
> **vv. 1–2**

When omniscience has lost its eyesight,
and omnipotence falls back impotent, and Jehovah
is driven from His throne, then the Church of Jesus Christ
can afford to be despondent, but never until then.
Despots may plan and armies may march, and the congresses
of the nations may seem to think they are adjusting all the
affairs of the world, but the mighty men of the earth are only
the dust of the chariot wheels of God's providence.

—*T. Dewitt Talmage*

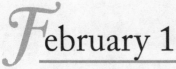

February 1

Turn Your face away from my sins
*and blot out **all** my guilt.*

Psalm 51:9

There is tremendous mental therapy in Psalm 51. Over the years, I've known a number of people who, following a great failure or setback, experienced remarkable emotional and mental healing by memorizing and meditating on this passage. I myself have found it so.

When we commit a horrible sin—all sin is horrible to God, but some sins are particularly painful for us—our self-respect is damaged, and a sense of shame and guilt undermines our morale and morality. Just as a slashing knife can sever an artery, falling into sin can inflict injuries that require treatment and time to heal.

Psalm 51 is a powerful medicine. King David wrote it when tormented by the guilt of adultery, murder, and cover-up following his sin with Bathsheba. Here in Psalm 51, he poured out his sincere confession and asked the Lord to blot out all his wrongdoing:

> Turn Your face away from my sins
> and blot out all my guilt.
> God, create a clean heart for me
> and renew a steadfast spirit within me.
> Do not banish me from Your presence
> or take Your Holy Spirit from me.
> Restore the joy of Your salvation to me,
> and give me a willing spirit.
> Then I will teach the rebellious Your ways,
> and sinners will return to You. (vv. 9–13)

Psalm 51 contains nineteen verses, so it may take a while to memorize; but if you read it over and over, it'll begin to settle down into your heart and soul, giving strength and healing from the Great Physician for past sins and harassing guilt.

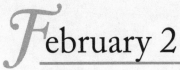

February 2

*Throughout **all** this Job did not sin
or blame God for anything.*
Job 1:22

There are 290 questions in the forty-two chapters of Job, and every chapter except Job 29 contains a question mark. The word *why* occurs twenty-eight times as Job struggled to make sense of his loss and pain. Yet five times in this book, Job affirmed his faith, refusing to give in to despair. It's because of these five declarations that the Bible later spoke of Job as a model of perseverance (James 5:11).

- Following his first series of problems, Job said, "The LORD gives, and the LORD takes away. Praise the name of the LORD" (Job 1:21).
- After his second set of problems, he asked his wife, "Should we accept only good from God and not adversity?" (Job 2:10).
- Responding to Zophar's criticism, Job said of God, "Even if He kills me, I will hope in Him. . . . This will result in my deliverance" (Job 13:15–16).
- He also declared, "I know my living Redeemer, and He will stand on the dust at last. Even after my skin has been destroyed, yet I will see God in my flesh" (Job 19:25–26).
- To Eliphaz, Job confessed, "He knows the way I have taken; when He has tested me, I will emerge as pure gold" (Job 23:10).

It helps us when we verbally declare that Jesus is Lord in the hard moments. Talk to yourself about the truths of God, and after He has tested you, you will emerge as gold.

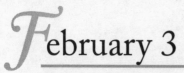

February 3

You will search for the LORD your God,
and you will find Him when you seek Him
*with **all** your heart and **all** your soul.*

Deuteronomy 4:29

The Bible nowhere allows partial devotion to the Lord. Instead it says:

> Seek Him with *all* your heart and *all* your soul. . . .
> Love the LORD your God with *all* your heart, with
> *all* your soul, and with *all* your strength. . . . What
> does the LORD your God ask of you except to fear the
> LORD your God by walking in *all* His ways . . . and to
> worship the LORD your God with *all* your heart and
> *all* your soul? . . .
>
> Return to the Lord your God and obey Him
> with *all* your heart. . . . Obey the LORD your God by
> keeping His commands and statutes that are written
> in this book of the law and return to Him with *all*
> your heart and *all* your soul. . . . Remain faithful to
> Him, and serve Him with *all* your heart and *all* your
> soul. . . . You know with *all* your heart and *all* your
> soul that none of the good promises the LORD your
> God made to you has failed. . . .
>
> If you are returning to the LORD with *all* your
> heart, get rid of the foreign gods and the Ashtoreths
> that are among you, dedicate yourselves to the LORD,
> and worship only Him. . . . Above all, fear the LORD
> and worship Him faithfully with *all* your heart, con-
> sidering the great things He has done for you. . . .
>
> Trust in the LORD with *all* your heart, . . . Think
> about Him in *all* your ways. . . .
>
> Believe with *all* your heart.[17]

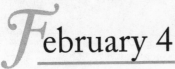# February 4

*Even the hairs of your head have **all** been counted.*
Matthew 10:30

In Matthew 10, Jesus ordained twelve disciples and commissioned them as apostles or missionaries. Verse 5 says, "Jesus sent out these 12 after giving them instructions," and the rest of the chapter contains His directives about their ministry.

As He spoke, He warned them of inevitable persecution. "Look," He said, "I'm sending you out like sheep among wolves. . . . Because people will hand you over to sanhedrins and flog you in their synagogues, beware of them. . . . When they persecute you in one town, escape to another."

But He assured them that in every condition the heavenly Father was deeply concerned, constantly mindful, and intimately acquainted with them and their challenges. He revealed that God even kept track of the hairs on their heads at any given moment.

According to experts, there are an estimated one hundred thousand hair follicles on the average scalp and about thirty thousand in a man's beard. Furthermore, most of us lose between fifty and one hundred hairs daily.

How remarkable that God constantly keeps track of the exact number! It's a function of His omniscience, of course, but it's also a token of His grace. If His love for us includes something so small, it's certain that nothing great will escape His attention either.

> Lo, their very hairs He numbers,
> And no daily care encumbers
> Them that share His every blessing
> And His help in woes distressing.
>
> —*Karolina W. Sandell-Berg, 1858*

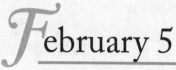

February 5

Yes, God is mighty, . . .
*He understands **all** things.*

Job 36:5

When we don't understand the sufferings of life, we lean on this
fact—God, being both loving and omniscient, understands
all. That's what comforted a nineteenth-century Christian named
Maxwell Cornelius.

Cornelius grew up in Pennsylvania farm country and became
a brick mason and contractor in Pittsburgh; but while working on
a house, his leg was broken and had to be amputated. Unable to
continue his trade, Cornelius enrolled in college. After graduating
with honors, he became a pastor; but because of his wife's health,
he moved to the milder climate of California, where he led a large
Presbyterian church in Pasadena through a building program.

Many who pledged money for the building went broke during an economic downturn, and Cornelius struggled to lead the
church through the crisis. Just as he emerged from this hardship,
his wife died. Cornelius preached the funeral sermon, and at the
end of it quoted a poem he had written, which later became a
well-known hymn:

> Not now, but in the coming years,
> It may be in the better land,
> We'll read the meaning of our tears,
> And there, some time, we'll understand.
>
> Then trust in God through all the days;
> Fear not, for He doth hold thy hand;
> Though dark thy way, still sing and praise,
> Some time, some time we'll understand.

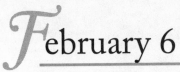

February 6

*Love the Lord your God with **all** your heart,*
*with **all** your soul, and with **all** your mind.*
This is the greatest and most important commandment.
The second is like it: Love your neighbor as yourself.
***All** the Law and the Prophets*
depend on these two commandments.

Matthew 22:37–40

This passage is a funnel through which the totality of God's character and requirements are narrowed down to a single word: *love.*

Let's begin with God's character. He is pure, holy, and blameless in all His thoughts, motives, attitudes, and actions. He expects us to reflect His character, so He gave us the Old Testament Law with its regulations and statutes. The Law is summarized in the Ten Commandments of Exodus 20.

The Ten Commandments, in turn, fall into two divisions. The first four concern our relationship with God, and the last six are about our relationships with others.

In Matthew 22, Jesus said that the entire Old Testament Law could be boiled down into two statements: Love God and love others. When we genuinely love God, we'll automatically keep the first four commandments. When we love others, we'll show it by observing the last six. If we love God, for example, we'll not take His name in vain or have anything in our lives that eclipses Him. If we love others, we'll not bear false witness, steal, or covet what they have.

These two commands summarize the Ten, which encapsulate the entire Law of God and reflect His holy character. And these two commandments are both summed up with the word *love.*

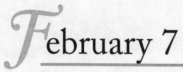

February 7

The torrential rains, His mighty torrential rains,
*serve as His signature to **all** mankind,*
*so that **all** men may know His work.*

Job 37:6–7

When my daughter Victoria was a little girl, a thunderstorm broke over our house one evening, and she was terrified. I pulled her up into my arms and said, "Don't be afraid. It's God's fireworks." We found a safe little spot where we could see the sky without being exposed to the lightning. The sky was popping with flashes of light, the rolling thunder came in waves, and the rain fell in bucketfuls. Victoria was still frightened, and she held on to me like a sailor clinging to timber. But she felt some security from being in her dad's arms, and she couldn't help being fascinated by the storm.

Now she's grown with little girls of her own. Recently I called to see how she was doing. "Oh, we're fine, Dad," she said. "There was a terrific thunderstorm earlier tonight, but we watched it from a safe place on the porch and I told the girls that it was God's fireworks. It was a great chance for me to talk to them about the Lord's power."

A friend recently gave me this definition of the so-called theory of evolution: It is believing that an explosion of nothing, instigated by no one, accidentally resulted in everything.

How foolish.

Thunder, lightning, and even the torrential rains are His signature, for the heavens declare the glory of the Lord and the earth displays His handiwork.

February 8

*We know that **all** things work together*
for the good of those who love God:
those who are called according to His purpose.

Romans 8:28

The word *all* in this verse is worth noticing. Not some things, a few things, a lot of things, select things, good things, bad things, sad things, or funny things—but all things. There is no asterisk on the word *all*. There are no exceptions or exemptions.

All means *all*; and when we realize that, it gives us a basis for lifelong optimism. Romans 8:28 is all-powerful, and always available. It is as omnipotent as the God who signed and sealed it. It's as loving as the Savior who died to unleash it. It can do anything God can do. It can touch any hurt and redeem any problem. It isn't a mere platitude, but a divine promise. It isn't a goal, but a guarantee. It isn't wishful thinking, but a shaft of almighty providence that lands squarely on our pathway each day and every moment.

The Lord moves heaven and earth to keep this promise. He puts His eye to the microscope of Providential Oversight and scans the smallest details of our lives, working them into a tapestry of blessing, making sure that goodness and mercy follow us all our days.

We can be optimists, for we know that every last detail of our lives works together for good to those who love the Lord and who are called according to His purpose.[18]

Praise God who works all things for good
for those who love His name.
His providential care shall turn
all burdens into gain.

—*RJM*

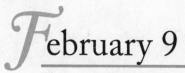# February 9

*My gracious favor is **all** you need.*
My power works best in your weakness.

2 Corinthians 12:9a (NLT)

Recently a woman in Minnesota told me that after her husband's death, she lost the family business. Leaving the foreclosure meeting, she collapsed into her car in tears, but mysteriously sitting on the seat was an old devotional magazine opened to 2 Corinthians 12:9: "My grace is sufficient for you." The sudden impact of that verse, she said, gave her supernatural strength for the moment; and many good things have since come from those events, including an opportunity to share Christ with her banker.

I believe 2 Corinthians 12:9 is one of the great understatements of Scripture. It's like a billionaire saying that his fortune is "sufficient" to cover a cup of coffee. It's like the ocean saying that its waters are "sufficient" to fill a thimble.

Whatever you're going through, His grace is more than sufficient.

When Dr. H. W. Webb-Peploe suffered the death of a beloved child, he cried in despair, "Lord, please make your grace sufficient." As he prayed he glanced up and noticed 2 Corinthians 12:9 inscribed in a framing over the fireplace. He also noticed for the first time that the word *is* was printed in capital letters: "My grace IS sufficient for thee."

"Lord, forgive me," he cried. "I have been asking Thee to make Thy grace sufficient for me, and all the time Thou hast been saying to me, 'My grace IS sufficient for thee.' I thank Thee for sufficient grace and I appropriate it now."

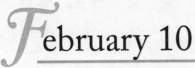

February 10

*He gives **all** the more grace;*
therefore it says, "God opposes the proud,
but gives grace to the humble."

James 4:6 (NRSV)

Not long after Annie Johnson was born on Christmas Eve, 1866, her mother died, and Annie and her sister went to live with the widow of a soldier killed in the Civil War. Neither girl felt loved in this home; but a nearby Christian family, the Flints, eventually adopted them.

Annie became a schoolteacher, but she contracted a severe form of arthritis that left her disabled. Her adoptive parents passed away, and Annie was left an invalid with no income. There was only one thing she could do, and she could barely do that—compose poetry. Annie Johnson Flint became a renowned writer across the Christian world, though her arthritic condition made it increasingly painful to record her compositions and her income was always meager. Yet her needs were met, and her income appeared just as she needed it.

One of her best-loved poems reminds us that God gives all the more grace as we need it, as we trust Him with yielded hearts whatever our circumstances:

> When we have exhausted our store of endurance,
> When our strength has failed ere the day is half done,
> When we reach the end of our hoarded resources,
> Our Father's full giving is only begun.
>
> His love has no limit; His grace has no measure.
> His pow'r has no boundary known unto men;
> For out of His infinite riches in Jesus,
> He giveth, and giveth, and giveth again!

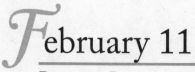# February 11

All *our days ebb away.*
Psalm 90:9

Psalm 90 has dual themes: God's eternity and the brevity of our lives. Verse 2 declares, "From eternity to eternity, You are God." But verse 10 confesses, "Our lives last seventy years or, if we are strong, eighty years. . . . They pass quickly and we fly away." Rather than being discouraged by that, we should pray, "Teach us to number our days carefully so that we may develop wisdom in our hearts" (v. 12).

We mortals need daily guidance from the Immortal One.

I've learned to start each day by praying, "Your agenda today, Lord!" Though I plan each day as carefully as I can, the Lord is the real planner of my days. Interruptions and opportunities come by His appointment.

Fenelon once wrote: "Cheered by the presence of God, I will do at each moment, without anxiety, according to the strength which He shall give me, the work that His Providence assigns me. I will leave the rest without concern; it is not my affair. I ought to consider the duty to which I am called each day, as the work that God has given me to do, and to apply myself to it in a manner worthy of His glory, that is to say, in exactness and peace."

Ask your King to take you wholly into His service,
and place all the hours of this day quite simply
at His disposal, and ask Him to make and keep you
ready to do just exactly what He appoints.
Never mind about tomorrow; one day at a time is enough.

—Frances Havergal[19]

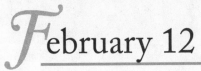

February 12

*You are exalted as head over **all**. . . .*
Now therefore, our God, we give You thanks.

1 Chronicles 29:11, 13

Christ rules over *all* and makes *all* work for good, so we can cast *all* our cares on Him and be thankful in *all* things. Thanksgiving is the most therapeutic of our attitudes. It's the best psychology for the soul and the most pleasant of our emotions. It's the opposite of grumbling, complaining, and hand-wringing.

In his classic book *A Serious Call to a Devout and Holy Life,* William Law writes:

> Would you know who is the greatest saint in the world? It is not he who prays most or fasts most; it is not he who gives most alms, or is most eminent for temperance, chastity, or justice; but it is he who is always thankful to God, who wills everything as God willeth, who receives everything as an instance of God's goodness, and has a heart always ready to praise God for it. . . .
>
> If anyone would tell you the shortest, surest way to all happiness and all perfection, he must tell you to make it a rule to yourself to thank and praise God for everything that happens to you. For it is certain that whatever seeming calamity happens to you, if you thank and praise God for it, you turn it into a blessing. Could you, therefore, work miracles, you could not do more for yourself than by this thankful spirit, for it heals with a word speaking, and turns all that it touches into happiness.[20]

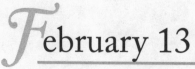

February 13

All things are lawful for me,
*but **all** things are not helpful.*
All things are lawful for me,
but I will not be brought under the power of any.

1 Corinthians 6:12 (NKJV)

My friend Dave Tosi is Vermont born-and-bred, and pastoring in the South has presented some interesting challenges for him. Once, he told me, a woman raised her hand in prayer meeting. She said in a rich Southern drawl, "I have an unspoken request."

This woman was a heavy smoker, and Dave thought she said, "I have a smokin' request."

"You're brave to confess it," exclaimed Dave in front of the whole crowd. "We all have vices we struggle with. You struggle with smoking, and others battle other things. But we can ask God to deliver you."

All the while, Dave's wife, Marilyn, was waving her arms, trying to get his attention. Finally, Marilyn blurted out, "She didn't say 'a smokin' request.' She said, 'an unspoken request.'"

Dave was horrified at his gaffe, but the woman was good-natured. "Well," she said in her Southern brogue, "I do have that problem, too, and I guess you can pray for me."

Do you have some addiction that can only be overcome with prayer? Our souls are weak and our sins are strong. If you need someone to pray for you, share your struggle in confidence and ask that person to pray for you along the lines of 1 Corinthians 6:12–20. Don't be overcome by sin. Remember—we were bought with a price. Let's glorify God in our body and spirit, which are His.

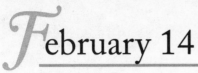

February 14

May he continue while the sun endures,
*and as long as the moon, throughout **all** generations.*

Psalm 72:5

Several years ago, in Edinburgh, I visited the famous Char-lotte Chapel and enjoyed some time with my friend Rev. Peter Grainger. He told me that the history of the church goes back two hundred years, having been established by a contemporary of missionary William Carey.

About fifty years after its founding, however, the congregation experienced hard times and attendance fell to about thirty people. They were on the verge of shutting down the church. But the clerk at that time was a man of vision and faith. Every Sunday he'd take his little boy to the services and say, "Can you see the crowds?"

The son would say, "Dad, there are no crowds. There's almost nobody here." But the man would say, "I can see the crowds." He believed that God would revive the church.

The church called a new pastor, Joseph Kemp, who had been touched by the Welsh Revival of 1904 and who called the church to prayer. Under his ministry a revival erupted like a volcano in Edinburgh, and Charlotte Chapel saw a thousand people converted to Christ each year.

Psalm 72, written by Solomon, is messianic in its sweep and describes the "greater-than-Solomon" kingship of Jesus. His reign will continue as long as sun and moon endure, throughout all generations. We never have to worry about Christianity being on its "last legs." There's always a new generation arising to worship and proclaim Him.

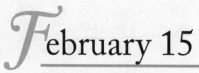

February 15

In Joppa there was a woman named Tabitha,
who was a believer . . . .
*She spent **all** her time doing good*
and helping the poor.

Acts 9:36 (GNB)

Tabitha is a biblical heroine whose life was devoted to small things. She made clothes for the poor a stitch at a time. She performed small tasks gladly, and her claim to fame wasn't in preaching great sermons or evangelizing vast multitudes. She just did what she could for the Lord.

The little things we do are bigger than the great things we do; and how wonderful to learn the importance of the sacred ordinary. Sometimes I grow weary of feeling I have to do "big" things—preparing a sermon, writing a book, or crafting an article. I often think I'd do better just to spend the afternoon baking a loaf of bread for my neighbor.

The Bible says, "Whatever you do, whether in word or deed, do it all in the name of the Lord Jesus, giving thanks to God the Father through Him" (Col. 3:17 NIV). And Peter said, "Each one should use whatever gift he has received to serve others, faithfully administering God's grace in its various forms" (1 Pet. 4:10 NIV).

As Henry Van Dyke said in his hymn, "Jesus, Thou Divine Companion":

> Every task, however simple, sets the soul that does it
>   free;
> Every deed of love and kindness done to the least is
>   done to Thee.
> Jesus, Thou Divine Companion, help us all to work our
>   best;
> Bless us in our daily labor, lead us to our Sabbath rest.

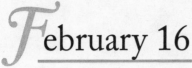

February 16

*We are **all** witnesses.*

Acts 2:32

We are all His witnesses, but sometimes we wonder if anyone's listening. We invite friends to church, insert our testimonies into daily conversation, give out Christian literature, and seek opportunities to share the gospel. But sometimes we wonder if our work's in vain.

It isn't.

Norman and Bessie Richards, retired missionaries who serve on our church staff, recently traveled to Arkansas for Norman's fiftieth high school reunion. "I was especially glad to see one of my best friends from high school days," said Norman. "The last time I saw him I tried to share the gospel with him, but that was fifty years ago. I wasn't even sure he was still alive. But there he was, and as we talked I again felt led to share a word for the Lord."

To Norman's amazement, the man said, "Why, Norman, I'm a Christian! I've known the Lord for fifty years! After you talked to me that day after school, I thought about your words. The next day I gave my life to the Lord. I should have told you, but somehow we lost contact. Your witness changed my life, and I'm still serving the Lord today."

Norman told me, "He's known Christ for fifty years because of my few words to him long ago, but I never knew it until last weekend. I've wondered about it all these years."

Only in heaven will we know how the Lord has used our words and testimonies, so don't be discouraged. We are all His witnesses.

Only one life, 'twill soon be past;
Only what's done for Christ will last.

February 17

The kingdom of heaven is like treasure hidden in a field.
When a man found it, he hid it again, and then in his joy
*went and sold **all** he had and bought that field.*

Matthew 13:44 (NIV)

My friend Fred Prouty of the Tennessee Historical Commission told me of a man during the Civil War with a large amount of money in gold coins. When Union forces entered the area in 1862, he was afraid they'd take his money, so he buried it in a field near his farm on the outskirts of Nashville. He made mental notes of the exact location of the treasure, using trees and rocks as markers, then fled the area.

The occupying Union soldiers cut down trees for firewood. They gathered rocks to form chimneys for their barracks and campfire pits. When the war ended, the man returned; but everything was different, and he was unable to locate the spot where he'd buried his fortune. He spent the rest of his life trying to find the lost coins.

In Matthew 13, Jesus told of a man who found such a treasure while working as a farm hand. According to the laws of the land, the treasure would be his if he owned the field; so he reburied the treasure and in joy he sold all he had and bought the field.

In losing all he had, he gained all he needed.

We might lose everything for His sake, but with Christ comes a treasure that never fades away.

> What is the world to me,
> With all its vaunted pleasure
> When Thou, and Thou alone,
> Lord Jesus, art my Treasure!
>
> —*Georg Pfefferkorn, 1667*

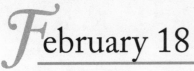# February 18

Whenever a round of banqueting was over,
Job would send for his children and purify them,
*rising early in the morning to offer burnt offerings for **all** of them. . . .*
This was Job's regular practice.

Job 1:5

Researchers at the University of Newcastle upon Tyne in Great Britain are on the verge of creating sperm cells from bone marrow, making it possible for women to conceive children without men. That would essentially make men optional at best, obsolete at worst, prompting some pundits to ask, "Who needs dads anyway?"

The Bible takes a different view. Job, for example, was a dad earnestly concerned about the welfare of his children. He provided for them financially, but he also modeled godliness before them, for Job was a man of integrity who feared God and shunned evil. His children seemed closely knit and enjoyed holidays together; but Job feared they partied too much, and he habitually prayed for them, offering sacrifices on their behalf.

If there's a more powerful force in the world than a praying dad, I don't know what it is.

Recently, a woman in West Virginia told me her father had a special room near the staircase where he went every morning to pray for his children. They could hear his muffled voice, pleading on their behalf. Though she herself is now aged, that precious memory is enshrined in the museum of her mind.

If you know what it is to worry about your children, follow Job's example and discover the power of earnest prayer.

The prayer of a righteous man is powerful and effective.

James 5:16 (NIV)

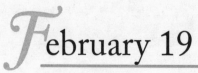

February 19

*Every one of you who does not say good-bye
to **all** his possessions cannot be My disciple.*

Luke 14:33

Jesus had little interest in halfway saints or part-time Christians, and He made no bones about demanding full surrender and steadfast devotion. He'd rather have one person 100 percent devoted to Him than one hundred people who are 90 percent yielded.

Here in Luke 14, He said we should hate our families, our lives, and our possessions; otherwise we're not worthy of Him and cannot be His disciples. When it comes to difficult passages, it's good to compare Scripture with Scripture, and Matthew's version clarifies Luke's meaning. Jesus was warning us against loving others more than we love Him (Matt. 10:37–39); but His words shouldn't be watered down so as to miss the point.

Our love for Him must eclipse all other loves. All we are and have is His. That doesn't mean we liquidate our assets, sell our possessions, give away all our money, and become homeless hermits. It does mean my car belongs to Him. He owns the clothes on my back, the money in my accounts, the air in my lungs, the family around my table, and the goals in my heart.

Frances Havergal put it this way:

In full and glad surrender we give ourselves to Thee,
Thine utterly, and only, and evermore to be!
O Son of God, who lov'st us, we will be Thine alone,
Our being and possessions, shall henceforth be Thine own!

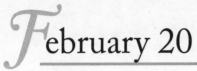

February 20

*Casting **all** your care upon Him,*
because He cares about you.

1 Peter 5:7

Rev. Frank Graeff was called the "Sunshine Minister" because of his sunny disposition as he labored among the Methodists in Philadelphia. His work in children's ministry was legendary. But on one occasion Graeff lost his sunshine and tumbled into despondency during misfortune. That's when he rediscovered 1 Peter 5:7 and wrote the words of a well-known hymn:

> Does Jesus care when my heart is pained
> Too deeply for mirth and song;
> As the burdens press, and the cares distress,
> And the way grows weary and long?
>
> Oh yes, He cares—I know He cares!
> His heart is touched with my grief;
> When the days are weary, the long nights dreary,
> I know my Savior cares.

King David once sighed, "No one cares about me" (Ps. 142:4), but Deuteronomy 11:12 says, "The LORD your God cares." Nahum 1:7 says, "He cares for those who take refuge in Him." Ephesians 5:29 tells us that Christ provides and cares for His children.

When Peter told us to cast all our cares on Him, he was simply restating a great Old Testament promise found in Psalm 55:22: "Cast your burden on the Lord, and He will support you; He will never allow the righteous to be shaken."

Don't give Him some of your cares. Cast all your cares and burdens on Him, for we know our Savior cares.

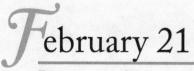# February 21

*"Come near and bring sacrifices and thank offerings to the LORD's temple." So the congregation brought sacrifices and thanks offerings, and **all** those with willing hearts brought burnt offerings.*

2 Chronicles 29:31

Sometime ago, I awoke in a dismal mood, worried about finances, health concerns, and family issues. But my morning Bible reading included a verse about thanksgiving, and I realized God expected me to change my attitude and to offer Him the sacrifice of praise. In my notebook, I listed eight things for which I could be thankful that day, and the effect on my disposition was immediate. Later I looked up every reference to thanksgiving in the Bible and was amazed at how many there are. Here's a sampling:

> Be thankful. . . . Coarse and foolish talking are not suitable, but rather giving thanks. . . . Whatever you do, in word or in deed, do everything in the name of the Lord Jesus, giving thanks to God the Father through Him. . . . Give thanks to the Lord, for He is good. . . . Give thanks to the Lord of lords. His love is eternal. . . . Give thanks to the Lord for His faithful love and His wonderful works for the human race.
>
> Enter His gates with thanksgiving and His courts with praise. Give thanks to Him and praise His name.
>
> As you have received Christ Jesus the Lord, walk in Him . . . overflowing with thankfulness. Never stop giving thanks.
>
> Thanks be to God, who gives us the victory through our Lord Jesus Christ! Thanks be to God for His indescribable gift![21]

February 22

In Him we have redemption through His blood,
the forgiveness of our trespasses, according to the riches of His grace
*that He lavished on us with **all** wisdom and understanding.*
Ephesians 1:7–8

Forbes magazine recently listed the twenty richest women in entertainment. The poorest of them is worth $45 million, and the richest—Oprah—is worth $1.5 billion. People like that live differently from you and I. They think differently, dress differently, travel differently, and act differently.

That's why Christians are different from everyone else. We're the richest souls around. Notice how in Ephesians Paul uses wealth-based imagery to describe our position in Christ:

- "the *riches* of His grace that He lavished on us" (1:7–8)
- "In Him we were also made His *inheritance*" (1:11)
- "He [the Holy Spirit] is the *down payment* of our *inheritance*" (1:14)
- "the glorious *riches* of His *inheritance* among the saints" (1:18)
- "God, who is *rich* in mercy" (2:4 NIV)
- "the *immeasurable riches* of His grace in His kindness to us in Christ" (2:7)
- "the *incalculable riches* of the Messiah" (3:8)
- "the *riches* of His glory" (3:16)

The Bible doesn't use such terminology haphazardly. The Lord wants His children to think of ourselves as being in the Upper Income Bracket, spiritually speaking. Our names may never be on a *Forbes's* list of wealthiest people, but we have assets that those people can't even imagine! That should impact our self-image and increase our thankfulness every single day.

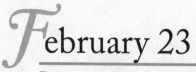

February 23

*God's wrath is revealed from heaven against **all**
godlessness and unrighteousness of people
who by their unrighteousness suppress the truth.*

Romans 1:18

Have you ever praised God for His wrath? The biblical writers had no inhibitions in discussing wrath as an essential attribute of the Almighty. Dr. A. W. Pink in his book on the attributes of God says there are more references in Scripture to the anger, fury, and wrath of God than to His love and tenderness. Nor did earlier generations of preachers and hymnists shy away from this subject. Jonathan Edwards's sermon "Sinners in the Hands of an Angry God" led to the Great Awakening. And here's the opening stanza of an Isaac Watts hymn:

> Adore and tremble, for our God
> Is a consuming fire!
> His jealous eyes His wrath inflame,
> And raise His vengeance higher.

We mustn't picture God as temper-prone or hot under the collar. His wrath isn't an emotional outburst; it's the judicial response of a holy God to the presence of evil in the universe. If He had no response to sin-induced suffering in this world, He'd be less than perfect. What kind of Moral Being would be unaffected by torture chambers, death camps, and sadistic cruelty?

The problem, of course, is that the wrath of God is revealed from heaven against *all* godlessness and unrighteousness—including mine. But God's wrath is balanced by His mercy, ingeniously displayed on the cross of Jesus Christ, who bore the wrath of God in our stead.

And that's why we praise Him.

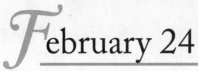

February 24

All the nations of the earth
will be blessed by your offspring.

Genesis 22:18

Genesis 22 is one of the most messianic chapters of the Old Testament, packed with pictures of the coming Messiah. Everything about Isaac in this chapter points to his being a type of Christ.

1. Both Isaac and Jesus were sons of promise. Angels announced their births in advance, even specifying their names before conception.
2. Both Isaac and Jesus were born miraculously, Isaac to an aged couple well past childbearing years, and Jesus to a virgin.
3. Both Isaac and Jesus were called the only begotten sons of their fathers (John 3:16, Heb. 11:17 NKJV).
4. Both Isaac and Jesus had fathers willing to sacrifice their only begotten sons on a hill far away, in Jerusalem.[22]
5. Both Isaac and Jesus carried on their backs the wood on which they would be sacrificed.
6. Both were to be offered as an offering for sin.
7. Both were placed on the wood they had carried to the top of the mountain and became obedient unto death.
8. Both Isaac and Jesus were dead for three days. In Jesus' case, it was a literal death. In Isaac's case, it was figurative. Genesis 22:4 says, "On the third day . . . ." And Hebrews 11:19 says, "Abraham reasoned that God could raise the dead, and figuratively speaking, he did receive Isaac back from death" (NIV).

Isaac prefigured Jesus to a *t*, and in Him—our Lord Jesus—is all the world blessed.

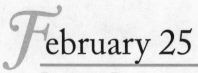

February 25

*For **all** have sinned and fall short of the glory of God.*
They are justified freely by His grace
through the redemption that is in Christ Jesus.

Romans 3:23–24

My friend Joy Christofferson told me how her family came to Christ. Years ago when they were attending a liberal church, Joy's sister told the pastor, "I've done things that have made me feel guilty and ashamed. I need to be forgiven of my sins. What should I do?"

The pastor patted her on the back and said, "Oh, Jean, you're such a good girl. You're one of the finest girls I know. Don't worry about it. You don't need to be forgiven."

But she did worry about it, and she did need forgiveness.

Later while attending school in Chicago, Jean heard the gospel and found Christ as her Savior. She wrote home about it. When her family received the letter, they thought Jean had fallen off her rocker, but gradually they all came to recognize their need for a Savior too. Jean's testimony became the means for the entire family coming to Christ.

Romans 3:23–25 is the spinning core of the Bible. We have all sinned and fallen short of God's holiness. Yet by trusting Christ and His atoning sacrifice, we can receive a life forgiven and a life forever.

Have you done that?

> Come, ye sinners, poor and needy
> Weak and wounded, sick and sore;
> Jesus ready stands to save you,
> Full of pity, love, and power.
>
> *—Joseph Hart, 1835*

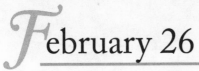

February 26

*The whole assembly fell silent
and listened to Barnabas and Paul describing **all**
the signs and wonders God had done through them.*

Acts 15:12

After World War I, Lawrence of Arabia visited Paris, accompanied by friends who had never been outside the desert. Lawrence showed them the City of Lights, but he was amused to find them most fascinated by the faucets in their rooms. They constantly turned them on and off, marveling at the instant supply of water. While packing to leave, Lawrence found them in the bathroom trying to detach the faucets. "It's very dry in Arabia," they explained. "What we need are faucets."

They didn't realize they also needed the plumbing that went with them.

When we labor for Christ, it's encouraging to see ourselves as faucets. It's not what we do for Jesus, but what He Himself does through us by His Spirit.

Jesus said, "If anyone is thirsty, he should come to Me and drink! The one who believes in Me, as the Scripture has said, will have streams of living water flow from deep within him" (John 7:37–38). Notice that we drink from Jesus ("come to Me and drink"), but from the drink comes a stream ("streams of living water flow from deep within him"). In response to simple faith, the Lord does far more through us than we can imagine.

It doesn't depend on our personalities, gifts, skills, or looks. Any old faucet will convey water so long as it's connected with the source. Don't think about what you can do for Christ, but never underestimate what He can do through you.

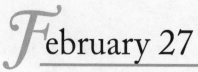# February 27

*My mouth is full of praise and honor to You **all** day long.*

Psalm 71:8

Last week I read about a man who trained himself, upon waking each day, to exclaim, "This is the day that the Lord has made! I will rejoice and be glad in it." Going to the breakfast table each day, he would say to his wife, "We're going to have a great day today!"

Thus he started each morning.

Thus can you too. Our attitudes are more important than our circumstances. We can't always control our circumstances, but our attitudes are our own prerogative. Remember the discovery made by Holocaust survivor Viktor Frankl? His family perished, his possessions were confiscated, his clothing was torn away along with all the comforts of life, and he endured the horrors of a death camp. But he discovered the one thing that cannot be taken from us—our right to choose our attitudes in any given set of circumstances.

How wonderful to choose praise! How much better to say, "My mouth will honor You all day long." There's not a moment during the day when we should allow anything to interrupt the electrical current of praise that lights up our lives and makes us high-voltage people. A breakdown there should be as rare and noticeable as a blackout in a major city.

Blind old Fanny Crosby put it this way:

> O glorious song that all day long
> With tuneful note is ringing,
> I'm saved by grace, amazing grace,
> And that is why I'm singing!

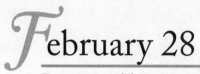

February 28

*You became imitators of us and of the Lord
when, in spite of severe persecution, you welcomed
the message with the joy from the Holy Spirit.
As a result, you became an example
to **all** the believers in Macedonia and Achaia.*

1 Thessalonians 1:6–7

If a package on the grocery shelf has the word *imitation* on it, I pass it up. The other day, I bought a blueberry muffin mix only to get home and discover the ingredients included little purple pellets called "imitation blueberries." I threw the package in the trash.

There's one time, however, when imitation is good—when we're imitating Christ. Paul told the Thessalonians, "You became imitators of us and of the Lord . . . . As a result, you became an example to all the believers in Macedonia and Achaia."

The Greek word used in the New Testament for *imitate* is *mimetes,* from which we get our English words *mime* and *mimic.* As we become more Christlike, others will be influenced through us to do the same.

I once read of a skid row bum named Joe who found Christ in a downtown rescue mission. He greatly admired an older Christian named Mike, and he would often pray, "Lord, make me like Mike, make me like Mike."

Someone asked him, "Why don't you pray, 'Lord, make me like Jesus?'"—to which Joe responded in childlike sincerity, "Is Jesus like Mike?"

March 1

Help me understand Your instruction,
*and I will obey it and follow it with **all** my heart.*

Psalm 119:34

When I was a sophomore in college, I found a phrase in a book that has helped me ever since in the area of full surrender: "Lord, I am not willing; but I am willing *to be* willing."

I was confused about life at the time, uncertain of my plans or future, yet I felt I should give myself wholly to the Lord. I needed His direction, and I knew that every area of my life—even the most cherished and personal—should come under His control.

There were some things I didn't want to yield. What if He wanted me to leave hearth and home to bury myself overseas in a primitive setting? What if He wanted me to remain single? What if His plan included pain or hardship or suffering?

Psalm 119:34 was exactly what God wanted me to say, and I eventually came to that point: "Help me understand Your instruction, and I will obey it and follow it with all my heart." But on the front end with some issues, I just said, "Lord, I'm willing to be willing"—and I found that those words allowed God to bring me to a point of yieldedness.

I recommend them to you: "Lord, I'm not sure I'm willing to go or do or be this or that, but I am willing *to be* willing."

The Lord Jesus will take it from there.

Draw me, Redeemer, I would seek Thee solely,
Help me to cherish, love, obey Thee wholly,
Fully surrendered, live a life that's holy.

—*Joel Blomqvist*

March 2

*When Job's three friends . . . heard about **all** the troubles*
that had come upon him, they set out from their homes . . .
to go and sympathize with him and comfort him.

Job 2:11 (NIV)

Job's problems brought his friends running, and their dialogue became the basis of one of the greatest works of literature in history. No other book in the Bible combines so many literary types or techniques. For example, Job opens and closes with *narrative* and *history*, but the middle of the book is *poetry*.

Some sections of Job resemble Jeremiah's lamentations and what scholars call complaint literature, in which sufferers detail their problems. But this book also contains prayers to God. Also included are hymns and psalms, such as Elihu's song about the wonders of God's creation in chapters 36–37.

Interwoven into Job, we find testimony, instruction, and predictive prophecy, such as Job's declaration that his Redeemer lives and will stand on the earth at the last day (Job 19:25–27). This book contains visions, and God's appearance in the whirlwind in chapter 38 reminds us of the vision in Ezekiel 1. Sprinkled throughout are proverbs, wisdom essays, and enriching dialogues.

Job also packs metaphors and similes into his book like jelly beans in a jar.

As you read Job, notice how many literary genres the writer employs. This book is unique in Scriptures for the variety of its forms because it's designed to meet a unique spot in our hearts. In the book of Job, the Lord pulls out every device from the writer's toolbox to drive home His message that we can fully trust Him with *all* our troubles.

I dare not trust the sweetest frame
But wholly rest on Jesus' name.

—Edward Mote

March 3

READING: ECCLESIASTES 1:12–18

*I have seen **all** the things that are done under the sun
and have found everything to be futile, a pursuit of the wind.*

Ecclesiastes 1:14

The land of China is named for its first emperor, Ying Cheng, who became a warlord at age thirteen and eventually amassed an army of a million troops. Dreaming of a dynasty that would last ten thousand years, Ying Cheng proclaimed himself a god and lived like one. The dimensions of his palace ran a mile and a half in all directions, with thousands of rooms and an audience hall seating ten thousand.

In the end, however, it was futile. At the height of his power, Ying Cheng was assassinated. The usurpers wanted to conceal his body as long as possible, and when it began rotting, they pulled a cart of salted fish into the area to obscure the odor.

King Solomon, another great monarch of antiquity, mused about the brevity and futility of life "under the sun." Those words—*under the sun*—are found twenty-seven times in Ecclesiastes, and they refer to the fact that without the transcendent and eternal God, there's nothing lasting or meaningful in life: "When I considered all that I had accomplished and what I had labored to achieve, I found everything to be futile and a pursuit of the wind. There was nothing to be gained under the sun."

Our lives have meaning "under the sun" only because of Him who dwells above the sun and beyond the stars—our transcendent Lord Jesus who alone gives us eternal significance.

> Shine forth, O Sun of boundless love,
> The night within our souls remove;
> Be Thou our Light; be Thou our Guide,
> O'er ev'ry thought and step preside.
>
> —*Simon Browne*

March 4

This stone that I have set up as a marker will be God's house,
*and I will give to You a tenth of **all** that You give me.*

Genesis 28:22

Long before the law was given, far in advance of Moses and Mount Sinai, Jacob vowed to give to God a tenth of all God gave to Him. I grew up in a home with a similar commitment. Through the years I saw my parents drop their tithe into the offering plate every Sunday. To the best of my memory, my wife and I have always done the same.

In my files is a clipping, the source of which I long ago lost. Once there was a man to whom God gave ten apples. Two of them were for food and the third was for the future. Three of the other apples were to trade for shelter from the sun and rain, and three apples were to trade for clothing and other needs.

God gave him the last apple so he would have something to give back to show his gratitude for the other nine.

The man ate the first two apples and saved the third for later. He traded the next six for shelter, clothing, and other things. Then he looked at the tenth apple. It seemed bigger and juicer than all the rest. He reasoned that God had other apples in the world. So the man ate the tenth apple—and gave God the core.

The story of Jacob is in the Bible for a reason. God deserves more than the core.

Thine the gold and Thine the silver,
Thine the wealth of land and sea,
We but stewards of Thy bounty,
Held in solemn trust for Thee.

—*Somerset Lowry, 1893*

arch 5

READING: HEBREWS 10:19–25

Not staying away from our meetings,
as some habitually do, but encouraging each other,
*and **all** the more as you see the day drawing near.*

Hebrews 10:25

I once saw a brochure that said, "Why I Never Take a Bath." Someone had listed a dozen reasons for avoiding bathtubs and showers, and I can recall some of the arguments.

1. I was forced to bathe as a child.
2. People who bathe are hypocrites; they think they're cleaner than others.
3. There are so many different kinds of soap, I can't decide which is best.
4. It's boring.
5. I wash only on special occasions, like Christmas and Easter.
6. The soap makers are only after your money.
7. The last time I bathed, someone was rude to me.
8. I'm too dirty to get clean; I'd clog up the drain.
9. I'll bathe only when I find a bathroom exactly right for me.
10. I can watch other people bathing on television.
11. I can bathe at the golf course.
12. The bathroom is never the right temperature, and I don't like the sound of the plumbing.

The Lord Jesus established His church to carry on His work till He comes again. There's never been an organization like it and never will be again. It has a limited engagement on earth; it began on Pentecost and will end at the Rapture. It's not perfect, but it has changed the world.

Don't stay away, but encourage others by your involvement—and all the more as you see the day approaching.

arch 6

Since the children have flesh and blood . . . ,
He also shared in these, so that through His death He might
destroy the one holding the power of death—that is, the Devil—
*and free those who were held in slavery **all** their lives*
by the fear of death.

Hebrews 2:14–15

This passage is one of the Bible's greatest answers to the problem of dying. Since we are flesh-and-blood humans, God Himself became flesh and blood. Through His death, He destroyed the one holding death's power, freeing us from slavery to the fear of death.

This truth is previewed in the story of David and Goliath. Having struck the giant with a rock from his slingshot, David ran over, grabbed Goliath's own sword, and sliced off his head, destroying him with his own weapon—just as Jesus did when He used death to destroy him who held the power of death—Satan.

Several years ago, I was in Poteau, Oklahoma, when my sister called from our mother's bedside. Mom wasn't feeling well, and Ann had called an ambulance. While waiting for the paramedics, our mother gave a little gasp and went right to heaven. I was stunned at the news, but I'll never forget how a verse of Scripture came forcibly to mind and strengthened me. Psalm 116:15: "Precious in the sight of the LORD is the death of His saints" (NKJV).

If I had strength enough to hold a pen,
I would write how easy and pleasant a thing it is to die.

—*Dr. William Hunter, on his deathbed*

READING: ACTS 6:8–15

*When Aaron and **all** the Israelites saw Moses,*
the skin of his face shone!

Exodus 34:30

***All** who were sitting in the Sanhedrin looked intently at him*
and saw that his face was like the face of an angel.

Acts 6:15

Our English word *countenance* comes from the Middle English *contenaunce*, which descends through Old French from the Latin word *continentia*, meaning, literally, "the way one contains oneself." The way we compose ourselves—the way we think in our hearts—shows up on our faces.

The Bible has a remarkable number of verses on this subject, and it provides both good and bad examples. When Cain grew jealous of his brother Abel, the Bible says his face fell; and when the rich young ruler heard the stipulations of Christ, his countenance, too, fell. But in Psalm 43:5, the psalmist wrote, "Why are you cast down, O my soul? And why are you disquieted within me? Hope in God; for I shall yet praise Him, the help of my countenance and my God" (NKJV).

Proverbs 15:13 says, "A joyful heart makes a face cheerful." And Ecclesiastes 8:1 says, "A man's wisdom brightens his face, and the sternness of his face is changed."

Americans spend billions of dollars every year on cosmetics and on cosmetic surgery, yet the greatest beauty secret of all time is the simplest—what's down in the heart shows up on the face.

A person's face is the signature of his soul.

—*William L. Stidger*

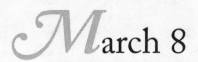# March 8

READING: JONAH 1:1–17

All Your breakers and Your billows swept over me.
Jonah 2:3

The book of Jonah is given to show us that even the greatest saints have emotional struggles, and God knows how to counsel us through them.

Jonah, the "Billy Graham" of his day, is introduced in 2 Kings 14:25, where he's pictured as a powerful preacher of God's truth.

The book of Jonah, however, is the prophet's memoir of two personal problems he encountered in ministry. The first, in Jonah 1–2, is a rebellious spirit, and the Lord used a great fish to bring Jonah to his senses.

The prophet's second problem, in Jonah 3–4, was lack of compassion; and the Lord used a tiny worm to teach Jonah a lesson about that. When the worm destroyed Jonah's shady vine, the prophet was more upset than he'd been about the lost souls of Nineveh. The Lord said, in effect, "You're more disturbed about your comfort than you are about the people of this great city. Something's wrong with your compassion and priorities."

The fact that Jonah wrote his book is proof that he learned God's lessons and wanted to pass them on to us.

I find great comfort in the book of Jonah at just this point. Sometimes I, too, have emotional and spiritual struggles in ministry. My faith goes wobbly. I become upset and angry with people. Sometimes I just want to quit. But our Lord knows how to help us, even if He has to send whales or worms to do it.

# March 9

READING: 1 SAMUEL 9:19–27

*Saul responded, "Am I not a Benjaminite
from the smallest of Israel's tribes and isn't my clan
the least important of **all** the clans?"*
1 Samuel 9:21

The story of King Saul is the Bible's great warning about drifting, disobedience, and disaster. Saul began in humility ("Isn't my clan the least important of all the clans?"), but ended in humiliation. It's a tragedy in five acts:

1. *His charisma was obvious.* According to 1 Samuel 9, Saul's physical presence was stunning—he was tall, athletic, and handsome. "There was no one more impressive among the Israelites than he" (v. 2).
2. *His calling was noble.* He was chosen as Israel's first king. In 1 Samuel 10, Samuel poured oil over his head, signifying the anointing of the Holy Spirit for his role.
3. *His career was promising.* Saul began his reign by uniting the straggling Israelites in a stunning victory over the Ammonites.
4. *His character was flawed.* In simplest terms, Saul failed to trust and obey God as he let himself lapse into a long, slow, painful, shameful slide.
5. *His crown was lost.* Saul disobeyed ever more deeply until his confidence was gone. On the last day of his life, he was despairing and despondent. He had lost his relationship with the Lord; his mentor was dead; his enemies were encircling him. In anguish, he turned to the occult and died in battle.

The Lord has a noble calling and a promising work for each of us. Beware lest inner corruption, outward compromise, and spiritual carelessness drain away our confidence and steal away our crown.

March 10

*Many of the Samaritans of that city believed in Him
because of the word of the woman who testified,
"He told me **all** that I ever did."*

John 4:39 (NKJV)

Most Holy Land tours bypass Samaria. Busses have been stoned there, and the roads are steep and narrow. But on one occasion I visited Sychar and we stood by Jacob's well (now enclosed within an old church) and read the story of the Samaritan woman in John 4. This is the account of:

- *A woman who is no longer thirsty.* As Jesus rested by the well, a woman came to draw water. He spoke to her, telling her all she had ever done. He knew her checkered past, yet He loved her and offered her the water of life. Her thirsty soul was drawn to His words.
- *A Savior who is no longer hungry.* As the woman left, the disciples returned with lunch, but Jesus no longer felt hungry. He explained, "My food is to do the will of Him who sent me and to finish His work" (v. 34). Soul-winning is nourishing work.
- *Fields that are no longer barren.* "Listen to what I'm telling you," Jesus said. "Open your eyes and look at the fields, for they are ready for harvest" (v. 35). Perhaps while speaking He looked up and saw the white-robed Samaritans coming toward Him in droves.

God has placed us in the middle of a harvest field. We have the water of life, and our food is to do the will of Him who sent us. Don't bypass Samaria.

March 11

I wrote the first narrative, Theophilus,
about all that Jesus began to do and teach
until the day He was taken up.

Acts 1:1–2

When I began pastoring the Donelson Fellowship in 1980, one of my first sermons was from this text, and it still represents my philosophy of ministry. Luke wrote the book of Acts to a man named Theophilus (God-lover); and in the opening verse, Luke summarized the twenty-four chapters of his prior work, the Gospel, as an account of all that Jesus began to do and to teach until the day He ascended to heaven.

Luke's Gospel was not the account of all that Jesus did and taught, but the account of all Jesus *began* to do and to teach.

Luke was not only summarizing his first book but previewing his second. He was saying, in effect: "My first book, the Gospel of Luke, is the story of all Jesus *began* to do and to teach while on earth in the flesh. My second book, the Acts of the Apostles, is the account of all that Jesus *continued* to do and to teach by His Spirit through His church."

That statement applies to subsequent Christian history and to us today. It's not our work, nor is it a matter of working for Him. It's His work, and it's a matter of His working through us. Jesus is continuing to do His work and teach His truths just as surely as He did in the Gospels. It's by His Spirit and through His people like you and me.

Channels only, blessed Master,
But with all Thy wondrous power
Flowing through us, Thou canst use us
Every day and every hour.

—*Mary Maxwell*

March 12

*You are **all** worthless doctors. . . .*
*You are **all** miserable comforters.*

Job 13:4, 16:2

Dr. Calvin Miller tells of a friend with whom he once attended seminary. This man later abandoned his faith and became an atheistic professor of philosophy in a city where Miller pastored. One day after visiting a dying woman in the hospital, Miller met his friend for tea. As the men talked, Miller asked his friend how he, as an atheist, would have spoken to this needy, dying woman. The professor said he would probably have told her she must count on the love of Jesus and look to Him for hope.

"But," Calvin Miller protested, "you don't believe that."

"No," he said, "but what I believe would be of no help to her in her time of need."[23]

There's something wrong with a philosophy that fails at life's most critical moments. Job's friends certainly believed in God, but their theology was inadequate and their understanding of God was faulty. As a result, their counsel was of little help in Job's time of need.

If you want to help others, internalize the Bible and ask God to convert it into the hidden wisdom of the heart. Memorize helpful Bible verses, not to shoot at people like darts, but as a reservoir of wisdom from which to dispense cupfuls of grace. Never be afraid to gently quote a passage from God's Word as the Spirit prompts you. Be alert for such opportunities, and you'll be a worthwhile physician and a counselor of encouragement.

March 13

The Lord said to Moses,
"How long will these people despise Me?
How long will they not trust in Me
*despite **all** the signs I have performed among them?"*

Numbers 14:11

Years ago, a young man had a falling out with his father, a world-class musician. The fellow would come home in the wee hours, and just to torment his dad, he'd pause by the grand piano in the parlor and play the notes up the scale—"do, re, mi . . . ." But he would never play the last note. He'd leave the scale unresolved, knowing that his father couldn't stand it. And every night the dad would stagger down the stairs in his pajamas and strike the last note of the scale before he could go back to sleep.

Most of us are like that dad. We want everything nicely resolved. We don't like messy situations or outstanding issues. It bothers us when we encounter problems we cannot solve and knots we cannot untangle.

Remember that the Lord has given you many signs through the years of His faithfulness. He has recorded hundreds of promises in His Book. The tokens of His love and grace are beyond number. He has never failed us yet. We can trust Him with loose ends, unsolved problems, and unresolved chords. He expects us to depend on Him with life's outstanding issues.

God was angry with the Israelites because they still didn't trust Him despite all the signs He had performed among them; and we, too, have reason to trust Him.

What's the unresolved scale in your life? It's an opportunity to lean wholly on Him.

March 14

Yet I have reserved seven thousand in Israel,
***all** whose knees have not bowed to Baal,*
and every mouth that has not kissed him.

1 Kings 19:18 (NKJV)

The rugged Elijah, man of prayer and passion, collapsed under the strain of work and asked the Lord to take his life. "I have been very zealous for the LORD God of Hosts," he prayed, "but the Israelites have . . . killed Your prophets with the sword. I alone am left, and they're looking for me to take my life" (1 Kings 19:14). In his dejection and self-pity, Elijah thought he was the last man standing, the final prophet in Israel.

Patiently the Lord gave Elijah a new set of instructions, speaking to him in still, small tones. He told Elijah to return by the way he came and to resume his work with renewed power. He also gave him a human friend, a young man named Elisha.

"Oh, yes, by the way," the Lord added (my paraphrase). "This business about your being the last prophet standing? Well, for your information I have seven thousand in Israel, all whose knees have not bowed to Baal and whose mouths have not kissed him."

Elijah was seven thousand times more pessimistic than he should have been, and the Lord was seven thousand times more powerful than Elijah thought.

The lesson for us: Sometimes things seem to be going badly, and sometimes we collapse in discouragement and exhaustion. But remember—where God is concerned, things are never as bad as they seem. He has resources of which we know nothing.

March 15

You are near, LORD,
*and **all** Your commands are true.*

Psalm 119:151

Nestled in the Tennessee mountains is a little stone church that was my first pastorate. One of the most energetic members was Miss Alice Woolsey, who, as we say, was a character. One Sunday, she took the whole Sunday school hour to talk about how children could memorize large chunks of Scripture; and to prove it she proceeded to quote all of Psalm 119, which she'd memorized in childhood and retained to old age.

Psalm 119 is the longest chapter in the Bible, with 176 verses. It's an acrostic psalm divided into twenty-two segments corresponding to the twenty-two letters of the Hebrew alphabet. The writer, intending for Psalm 119 to be memorized, built a memory technique into the very structure of the psalm. In Hebrew, the first eight verses begin with the equivalent of *a*, the next eight with *b*, etc.

I confess I've not memorized Psalm 119—Miss Woolsey is the only person I know who has—but I do know portions of it by heart. The topic that ribbons through all 176 verses is the wonder of God's Word, and verse 151 summarizes the entire chapter: "You are near, LORD, and all Your commands are true."

We don't experience God's presence by working ourselves into a spiritual trance, but by diving into the Scriptures. Unsolvable problems and unpleasant people may stalk us, but God is closer than any danger, and all His commands are true. When we draw near to His Word in full assurance of faith, we are drawing near to Him.

March 16

READING: HAGGAI 2:1–7

*And I will shake **all** nations,*
*and the desire of **all** nations shall come:*
and I will fill this house with glory.

Haggai 2:7 (KJV)

Many nations feel, somehow or other, that political affairs do not go as one could wish. This world is altogether out of joint; it is a crazy old concern.

The fact is, it needs the Maker, who made it, to come in and put it to rights. It needs the Hercules that is to turn the stream right through the Aegean stable; it needs the Christ of God to turn the stream of His atoning sacrifice right through the whole earth, to sweep away the whole filth of ages, and it never will be done unless He does it.

He is the one, the true Reformer, the true rectifier of all wrong, and in this respect the Desire of all Nations. Oh! If the world could gather up all her right desire; if she could condense in one cry all her wild wishes; if all true lovers of mankind could condense their theories and extract the true wine of wisdom from them; it would just come to this, we want an Incarnate God, and you have got the Incarnate God!

Oh! Nations, but you know it not! You in the dark are groping after Him, and know not that He is there.

—*Charles H. Spurgeon*
in his sermon "The Desire of All Nations"
August 25, 1870[24]

March 17

How I love your teaching!
*It is my meditation **all** day long.*

Psalm 119:97

Recently in a Sunday sermon, I spoke of missionary Geoffrey Bull, who had been captured by Chinese Communists. They took away his Bible, and for three years he was subjected to extreme conditions. He kept sane by systematically going over the Scriptures in his mind. He started with Genesis 1:1 and worked his way mentally through the Bible. It took him about six months to go from Genesis to Revelation, then he started again. This practice, he later claimed, kept his mind from unraveling.

The week following my sermon, I received a letter from a woman in our church who is battling multiple infirmities. "I just got back home from having a PET scan," Wendy wrote. "They put radioactive sugar in my vein so that particles clinging to any cancer cells show up on the screen."

It was a horrendous, prolonged procedure, during which Wendy had to be perfectly still.

"So I decided to use the tool you mentioned Sunday and work my way through the Bible, starting with Genesis. I tried to be as detailed as I could, and at times I had to go retrace my steps (I forgot the whole Tower of Babel thing and had to go back and insert it). Anyway, concentrating on God's Word helped me stay calm and kept my mind focused on the Lord."

By the time the Israelites got to Mount Sinai, she was out of the tube and ready to go home!

[Meditation] is the sister of reading . . .
[and] the mother of prayer.

—*William Bridge, seventeenth-century Puritan*

# March 18

Be strong and courageous, and do the work.
Don't be afraid or discouraged,
for the LORD God, my God, is with you.
*He won't leave you or forsake you until **all** the work*
for the service of the LORD's house is finished.

1 Chronicles 28:20

King David, suffering the afflictions of age, turned over the kingdom to Solomon and told him to build a great temple for God. It would be a massive undertaking, the most daunting building program ever attempted; but David told his son to immunize himself against discouragement: "The Lord my God is with you. He won't leave you or forsake you until all your work for Him is finished."

This is a promise for us too.

We sometimes fear we'll outlive our usefulness to the Lord. But our days are numbered, and each has purpose. He'll not leave or forsake us until all our work for Him is done.

Someone wrote, "God's man, living in God's will, is immortal until God's plan for Him on earth is fulfilled." That goes for God's woman too. We never retire from His service. Oh, we might retire from our jobs, our professions, or our specific ministry roles. But retirement is God's way of releasing us for further service. And sometimes retirement is God's way of releasing us from doing "big" things so we can do "little" things, which are often more significant than the big things.

Whatever your phase of life, don't be afraid or discouraged. The Lord will bless us until all our work for Him is done.

arch 19

*His presence **all** our days.*
Luke 1:75

As missionary-explorer David Livingstone trekked down the Zambezi River, he was captivated by parades of elephants, buffalo, and other wildlife filling the landscape. He was also beset by a thousand dangers from snakes, bugs, fevers, and savages. Pressing further into the heart of unexplored Africa, he skirted hostile tribes, and his guides were panicky.

Livingstone constantly calmed himself by recalling God's presence with him all his days. He would often pull his Bible from his baggage and run his finger across his favorite passage, Matthew 28:20, and remind himself how Jesus had promised to be with him even to the end of the earth.

He once wrote in his journal: "Felt much turmoil of spirit . . . . But I read that Jesus said, 'Lo, I am with you always, even unto the end of the world.' It is the word of a gentleman of the most strict and sacred honor, so there's an end of it! I feel quite calm now, thank God!"

Later while furloughing in Great Britain, Livingstone attended a ceremony in his honor at Glasgow University. He told the crowd that he was determined to return to Africa. "But," he added, "I return without misgiving and with great gladness. For would you like me to tell you what supported me through all the years of exile among people whose language I could not understand, and whose attitude toward me was often hostile? It was this: 'Lo, I am with you always, even unto the end of the world.' On those words I staked everything, and they never failed."

March 20

And He said, "Abba, Father!
***All** things are possible for You.*
Take this cup away from Me.
Nevertheless, not what I will,
but what You will."

Mark 14:36

If you're perplexed by the mystery of unanswered prayer, you're in good company. Some earnest prayers in the Bible were left unanswered or were answered with a "No." Remember Abraham's plea that Ishmael become the son of promise (Gen. 17:18), Elijah's prayer for death (1 Kings 19:4), or Paul's thrice-offered plea for healing from a thorn in the flesh (2 Cor. 12:8).

The greatest "unanswered" prayer in Scripture is the one Jesus offered in Gethsemane. He began by acknowledging that the heavenly Father has the power to do whatever He wishes: "All things are possible for You." Then came His poignant request: "Take this cup away from Me." But Jesus was willing for the Father to say no to His entreaty: "Nevertheless, not what I will, but what You will."

When the Lord answers our earnest request with a no, it's because He has a wiser plan, a broader perspective, and a higher aim for our good.

In one of her lesser-known hymns, Fanny Crosby wrote of this:

> God does not give me all I ask,
> Nor answer as I pray;
> But, O, my cup is brimming o'er
> With blessings day by day.
> How oft the joy I thought withheld
> Delights my longing eyes,
> And so I thank Him from my heart
> For what His love denies.

March 21

No, I tell you; but unless you repent,
*you will **all** perish as well.*

Luke 13:5

Years ago while working with the Billy Graham Crusades, I remember hearing Mr. Graham tell of a European performer who could juggle anything—pins, balls, flaming torches; and he never dropped anything. He astounded both royalty and commoners, and was the star of the circus and the life of any party.

Growing older, this man decided to move to America, and he hit upon a novel scheme of converting his wealth into portable form. He sold his home, cashed in his accounts, and purchased a beautiful jewel. It represented all he had. Materially speaking, his entire life was contained in that jewel.

One day aboard deck, he offered to amuse his fellow passengers. Taking the stone, he tossed it into the air and caught it. He tossed it again, this time a little higher. His audience gasped as it glittered and gleamed in the sunlight. With absolute confidence in his abilities, the juggler threw it higher into the air. It flew upward as straight as an arrow, glittering in the sunshine. Suddenly the ship lurched, and the jewel plunged into the water and sank to the bottom of the ocean. He had gambled with the totality of his life and lost.

It's possible to gain the whole world but lose our own souls, and that's why Jesus preached repentance. We must turn from our sins to Him. To do otherwise is to gamble with our eternal destiny.

> While we of every sin repent,
> Let our remaining years be spent
> In holiness and sweet content.
>
> —*Ancient Greek Hymn*

arch 22

*The gospel . . . has come to you . . . bearing fruit and growing **all** over
the world, just as it has among you since the day you heard it.*

Colossians 1:6

One day I was having lunch with a man when a woman stopped to chat with him. As she left, he told me, "That woman has been a Christian only one day less than me." I asked what he meant. "I was selling insurance out of a particular office, but I was pretty wild," he said. "But one night I was so miserable I searched out a pastor who helped me find Christ as my Savior. The next morning I excitedly told someone at the office what had happened, that I was a changed man. That lady you just met overheard me. She came over and listened as I spoke of Christ. 'That's what I need in my life,' she said. I took her then and there to see the pastor who had helped me the previous night, and she, too, was born again."

The gospel has come to us, and it keeps bearing fruit and growing all over the world.

I was there when it happened, and I ought to know;
His Spirit burning in me, set my heart aglow;
So I praise the Lord today, He has washed my sins away;
I was there when it happened, and I ought to know.

—Herbert Lacey, 1920

There is no joy in the world like the joy
of bringing one soul to Christ.

—William Barclay

To be a soul-winner is the happiest thing in this world.

—Charles H. Spurgeon

March 23

Be on guard for yourselves
*and for **all** the flock,*
among whom the Holy Spirit has appointed you as overseers,
to shepherd the church of God,
which He purchased with His own blood.

Acts 20:28

Several years ago at a conference in Edinburgh, I sat near a Scottish minister who worked in the Highlands. One day before the session started, I asked him about his church. He told me he had a circuit of three churches every Sunday. It was a sixty-five-mile loop in rural areas, up in the legendary Scottish High Country.

The first church had five members, but there were another five who sometimes attended, so on high-attendance days he might have ten or twelve. The second church had seven people, and the third one had an average group of six to eight. There was little growth, and the only time he preached to large crowds was at funerals when the whole town showed up.

I asked him, "Andrew, do you ever get discouraged? Do you have trouble keeping your morale up week-after-week, and year-after-year?"

"Yes, sometimes."

"Well, do you ever think of quitting?"

"Sometimes," he said in his rough Scottish brogue, adding, "but I've found that I cannot *not* preach."

God had called him to that ministry, and even though it seems small and meager by human standards, he cannot *not* do all that God has appointed him to do. God has called each of us to oversee a portion of His work; and if He calls us, we cannot *not* do what He has appointed for us.

March 24

READING: GENESIS 42:35–38

All these things are against me.
Genesis 42:36 (NKJV)

Yes, it certainly seemed so.

It was the old man Jacob who moaned these words. The blows of life had gotten to him. His beloved Joseph had been killed by a wild animal, or so he thought. His other sons had caused endless problems for him, and one of them, Simeon, was in an Egyptian prison. His wealth had suffered from prolonged famine. His youngest son, Benjamin, was in political danger. And Jacob himself, whose own past had been checkered with deceit and estrangement, collapsed in his spirit. "All these things are against me," he said. "Everything in my life is a disappointment. Everything turns into a tragedy for me."

What Jacob didn't know is that every single one of his "disappointments" was part of a mosaic that would eventually bring him indescribable joy. Shortly afterward, against all odds, he was reunited with Joseph, restored to Simeon, given the richest land of Egypt, introduced to the royal family of the Pharaohs, and provided for in a way he couldn't have imagined. His son was prime minister, and he himself spent his old age surrounded by his children, grandchildren, and great-grandchildren. His sojourn in Egypt became the means by which God turned his descendants into a great nation and prepared them to possess the Promised Land.

Every day we have to decide which verse we'll live by: Genesis 42:36 or Romans 8:28. Disappointments and disasters will come, but we have to choose our response—either all these things are against me, or all these things are working together for those who love God.

March 25

*Finally, **all** of you,*
live in harmony with one another;
be sympathetic.
1 Peter 3:8 (NIV)

Look at the word *harmony*. Our English word *arm* comes from the same Greek root. The letters *a-r-m* are right in the middle of *h-a-r-m-o-n-y*. The Greek *harmos* means "joint." Your adult body contains 206 bones, and it's our God-designed joints that enable them to function as a unified whole—at least until they get "out of joint."

Relationships can get out of joint too. A difference of opinion, a quick word, an angry exchange—they can destroy friendships, split churches, or spoil marriages.

Peter advised his readers to live in harmony, and he suggested a way to do that—by being sympathetic. Have compassion on others and understand their feelings, needs, and situations. Train yourself to under-react, to give a soft answer, and to overlook insults.

Rev. F. W. Boreham once lost patience with a difficult man named Crittingden. He wrote a flaming letter to him, but while on his way to mail it he learned Crittingden had died. A mutual friend told him of Crittingden's misfortunes. His wife had died, his son had been killed, and his daughter had lost her mind and was in an asylum. "Poor old Crittingden never got over it," said the friend. "It soured him." Returning home, Boreham burned the letter in the fire.

The person who aggravates us is probably the one most needing our sympathy; and that's important to remember, for all of us are commanded to live in harmony with one another.

arch 26

In Him also we have obtained an inheritance,
being predestined according to the purpose of Him
*who works **all** things according to the counsel of His will.*

Ephesians 1:11 (NKJV)

Romans 8:28 says that God works all things together for good, and Ephesians 1:11 says that He works all things according to the counsel of His will. These are the two sides of the coin of sovereignty. He is a God who does as He pleases, and His good pleasure always works for our benefit.

Think of it this way.

Have you ever boarded a flight on an overcast day? From the ground, the clouds look dark and troubling; but a half hour after takeoff, how do they look? They're so blindingly glorious that sometimes we have to pull down the window shade. An airy carpet of burning clouds extends to the horizon, reflecting the brilliance of the sun and billowing into majestic shapes and sizes. Sometimes we gaze down on mountains, chasms, and canyons of dazzling vaporous forms, breathtaking in their beauty.

Romans 8:28 is a picture of how the promise of God looks below the clouds; Ephesians 1:11 is the same truth from a higher perspective. Romans 8:28 is the view from the ground, as it were; and Ephesians 1:11 is how it's seen from heaven.

Here on earth we see that everything works together for our good, but from a loftier perspective we see that everything works together for our good because all things work out in conformity with the purpose of His immutable will.

And we say, "Hallelujah!"[25]

March 27

*We **all** stumble in many ways.*
If anyone does not stumble in what he says,
he is a mature man
who is also able to control his own body.

James 3:2

The barometer of maturity is our ability to control our tongues and our tempers, especially in relationships. After thirty years in the pastorate, I'm still amazed at how often church people become angry with church workers—and sometimes vice versa.

There are three ways of handling provocation. Some people *clam up.* In a marriage, we call this the "silent treatment." A classic biblical example is King Ahab after his confrontation with Naboth. The king lay on his bed sulking, refusing to eat, and moping around with stifled, simmering anger (1 Kings 21:4). This pattern internalizes anger and lets resentments build up until our own hearts are damaged with bitterness.

The second way of dealing with conflict is to *blow up.* Marriage counselors speak of *escalation,* which occurs when a person says something negative and his or her spouse responds with an even harsher statement. The conversation spirals downward and can destroy years of love.

The best way of processing anger is to *wise up,* which is what the Lord commands. James 3 is all about managing our tongues and tempers wisely, with the wisdom from above (v. 17). The book of Proverbs says, "Losing your temper causes a lot of trouble, but staying calm settles arguments" (Prov. 15:18 CEV).

We shouldn't *slug it out,* and sometimes we can't *shrug it off,* but we can often *talk it through* if we'll just wise up.

March 28

READING: 1 CORINTHIANS 10:31–11:1

So whether you eat or drink
or whatever you do,
*do it **all** for the glory of God.*

1 Corinthians 10:31 (NIV)

A ll of life is doxology.
Upon awakening in the morning, we praise God from whom all blessings flow. We bathe and dress that we might be presentable in our service for the Lord. We eat and drink, asking God to bless the food for our bodies and our bodies for His service. As we go about our housework or labor at office, factory, or school, it's as His ambassadors. Our exercise and entertainment is purposeful—that we might remain healthy and happy in our service for Him. Crawling into bed at night, it's another day finished for Jesus and another day closer to heaven.

Worship is a lifestyle, and our every moment and movement is for Him. This is, in Charles Spurgeon's phrase, the art of holy and happy living.

Teach me, my God and King,
In all things Thee to see,
And what I do in anything
To do it as for Thee.

—*George Herbert*

And whatever you do, whether in word or deed,
*do it **all** in the name of the Lord Jesus,*
giving thanks to God the Father through Him.

Colossians 3:17 (NIV)

March 29

*Let it be known to **all** of you . . .*
that by the name of Jesus Christ the Nazarene—
whom you crucified and whom God raised from the dead.

Acts 4:10

Thousands crammed into St. Paul's Cathedral Sunday after Sunday to hear Henry Parry Liddon (1829–90) preach on his great theme—the risen Savior. Had we been among the crowds, here's what we'd have heard:

> The Resurrection is proof that the Christian faith is true. It is the certificate of our Lord's mission from heaven. He laid this stress on His coming Resurrection on two occasions especially: in His saying about the destruction and rebuilding of the temple, and in His saying about the sign of the Prophet Jonah.
>
> His words came in effect to this: "You doubt whether I have any right to teach you, and to proclaim Myself as I do. Very well; wait a short while, and an event will take place which will prove that your misgivings or doubts are unwarranted. I shall be put to death, and then I shall rise from the dead on the third day. This will be a countersign of My mission from heaven: if it does not take place, reject; if it does, believe Me."
>
> The first preachers of Christianity understood this. The Resurrection was the proof to which they constantly pointed. "Jesus and the Resurrection" was the popular name for the Gospel as taught by St. Paul. The Resurrection was the truth which filled the early Church with its first converts. The Resurrection was the decisive proof that Christianity was from God.[26]

# March 30

Know well the condition of your flock,
and pay attention to your herds, for wealth is not forever;
*not even a crown lasts for **all** time.*
Proverbs 27:23–24

The book of Proverbs is wisdom in portable form. There are thirty-one chapters packed with advice about working hard, eating and drinking wisely, speaking well, avoiding immorality, and making good decisions in matters great and small.

Proverbs 27:23 tells us to watch over our material possessions with diligence, and it's only one of many verses in the book on the subject of our worldly goods. Here's a summary of what Proverbs tells us about financial management:

1. *Live simply:* "Give me neither poverty nor wealth; feed me with the food I need. Otherwise, I might have too much and deny You, . . . or I might have nothing and steal" (Prov. 30:8–9).
2. *Work hard:* "Go to the ant, you slacker! Observe its ways and become wise" (Prov. 6:6).
3. *Don't work too hard:* "Don't wear yourself out to get rich" (Prov. 23:4).
4. *Have a saving plan, even if it's small:* "Dishonest money dwindles away, but he who gathers money little by little makes it grow" (Prov. 13:11 NIV).
5. *Use debt sparingly:* "The borrower is a slave to the lender" (Prov. 22:7).
6. *Avoid co-signing for another's loan:* "One without sense . . . puts up security for his friend" (Prov. 17:18).
7. *Leave an inheritance for your children and grandchildren:* "A good man leaves an inheritance to his grandchildren" (Prov. 13:22).
8. *Tithe:* "Honor the LORD with your possessions and with the first produce of your entire harvest" (Prov. 3:9).

March 31

Does He not see my ways
*and number **all** my steps?*

Job 31:4

The book of Job records the conversations Job had with friends who visited him during his troubles. Though wanting to help, they added insult to injury by accusing Job of wrongdoing.

In chapters 26–31, Job defended himself. Without claiming to be sinless, he told them he had lived an upright life. In chapter 31, he spoke of his personal commitment to purity and to divert his eyes continually from any provocative scene: "I have made a covenant with my eyes. How then could I look at a young woman?" In other words, Job had made a commitment to himself and to God that he wouldn't let his eyes linger on sensuality. Additionally, in verses 9–12, he told them of his decision to remain faithful to his wife.

The reason for this commitment to purity is given in Job 31:4: "Does He not see my ways and number all my steps?"

A constant awareness of God's perpetual presence and of His oversight is a great deterrent to sin. The same Lord who counts every hair on your head each morning also counts every step you take during the day. He knows all your ways, so be holy in all you do.

He sees all our steps (Job 31:4).
He counts all the hairs on our heads (Matt. 10:30).
He reads all our thoughts (Ps. 139:2).
He knows all our ways (Ps. 139:3).
He hears all our words (Ps. 139:4).
Nothing in all creation is hidden from God's sight
    (Heb. 4:13 NIV).

# April 1

All these were approved through their faith,
but they did not receive what was promised,
since God had provided something better.
Hebrews 11:39–40

Lord, give me faith!—to live from day to day,
With tranquil heart to do my simple part,
And, with my hand in Thine, just go Thy way.

Lord, give me faith!—to trust, if not to know;
With quiet mind in all things Thee to find,
And, child-like, go where Thou wouldst have me go.

Lord, give me faith!—to leave it all with Thee.
The future is Thy gift; I would not lift
The veil Thy Love has hung 'twixt it and me.

—*John Oxenham*

O, for a faith that will not shrink,
Though pressed by every foe,
That will not tremble on the brink
Of any earthly woe!

A faith that shines more bright and clear
When tempests rage without;
That when in danger knows no fear,
In darkness feels no doubt.

Lord, give me such a faith as this,
And then, whate'er may come,
I'll taste, e'en here, the hallowed bliss
Of an eternal home.

—*William Hiley Bathurst*

April 2

*They **all** became encouraged.*
Acts 27:36

Paul's voyage and shipwreck in Acts 27 is one of the Bible's most fascinating stories, both for its vivid drama and for its life-lessons. In the final analysis, it was Paul's faith that encouraged the sailors and passengers. He knew how to stay encouraged and how to encourage others in hard times.

Several years ago, I met a man in Chicago—I'll call him Ralph—who told me, "I thought I had a good relationship with my daughter, Dawn. But when she was diagnosed with leukemia, I went to the hospital, and she told me she'd been afraid of me all her life. I was shocked.

"I said, 'Dawn, what are you talking about? We've never had words.' She said, 'That's just it, Dad. We've never talked, and I've been afraid of you because you've been a negative person.'

"'A negative person?' said Ralph.

"'Yes, I've been negative all my life, and I got it from you. We see things negatively. I remember when I was a little girl, I wanted to get my hair cut, but I didn't because I was afraid you'd be negative. And it's always been that way.'

"Dawn said, 'Dad, I think this helped bring on my leukemia. To have physical healing, I need emotional healing. And you have to help me.'"

The two started talking to each other honestly yet positively. Ralph told me, "It changed both our lives around. Now we can sit and talk for hours."

And the last I heard, Dawn's leukemia was in remission.

Correction does much, but encouragement does more.

—*Johann Wolfgang Goethe*

April 3

*The brilliant light **all** around*
was like that of a rainbow
in a cloud on a rainy day.
This was the appearance
of the form of the LORD's glory.
When I saw it, I fell facedown
and heard a voice speaking.

Ezekiel 1:28

The book of Ezekiel opens with a riddle: "In the thirtieth year, in the fourth month, on the fifth day of the month, while I was among the exiles by the Chebar Canal, the heavens opened and I saw visions of God."

What did Ezekiel mean by: "In the thirtieth year"? Scholars have puzzled over that, but I believe he's referring to his thirtieth year of life. He was thirty years old, plus four months and five days. Ezekiel was by lineage a priest, and according to Numbers 4, priests began their priestly service at age thirty. All his life he'd been trained for the moment when he'd join the regal pageantry of temple worship and be a spiritual leader in Jerusalem. But instead he was seized by Babylonian soldiers, dragged nine hundred miles away, and interred in a refugee camp.

Ezekiel must have felt desolate. His training seemed wasted, his life's purpose gone.

That's when the glory of the Lord appeared to him, glowing with brilliance all around; and Ezekiel realized that the glory of God wasn't just in Jerusalem, it was there in Babylon, too, by the Chebar Canal, and that's where God wanted to use him.

We're not always where we want to be in life. But wherever we are, the glory of God is present to use us for His purpose.

April 4

*And they **all** condemned Him*
to be deserving of death.

Mark 14:64

Holocaust survivor Elie Wiesel tells of being singled out for punishment one day in the Nazi death camp. He was a teenager at the time, and he'd inadvertently stumbled onto an officer taking advantage of a woman in a back room of a warehouse. Shortly thereafter, the officer, enraged at being caught, assembled the prisoners, including Wiesel and his father, and a wave of dread swept over the group.

Wiesel felt sweat running down his back as his number was called. As he stepped forward, a crate was pulled into place and the boy was ordered to lie across it to be whipped. The pain was indescribable, and the beating left him barely conscious. But Wiesel later said that one person suffered more than he did—his father, standing among the prisoners, helplessly watching, unable to do anything to save or spare his son.[27]

It amazes us that all the leaders of Israel condemned their Messiah to death, but there's a greater mystery to Calvary: the silence of the Father Himself, who willingly stood aside and watched His Son being scourged and crucified, even as Jesus cried out, "My God, My God, why have You forsaken Me?" (Matt. 27:46).

Not even in heaven will we fully understand the wonder of the cross, but this we know assuredly: it's by His blood that we are saved and by His stripes that we are healed.

Lord, by the stripes which wounded Thee,
From death's dread sting Thy servants free,
That we may live, and sing to Thee: Alleluia!

—Twelfth-century hymn

April 5

Go about your business without fretting or worrying.
*Relax. When it's **all** over, you will be on your feet*
to receive your reward.

Daniel 12:13 (MSG)

We need to "relax for easy power." There's something about growing tense and worried that shuts off the pipelines of vitality to our minds and bodies. I was thinking about it today while riding my bicycle. Coming to a rough patch, I tensed up; then I remembered that when I relax and take the bumps as they come, I'm less likely to have a spill. I relaxed the muscles in my arms and legs, resumed breathing, and rolled along without mishap.

Years ago, I heard Methodist preacher Charles Allen tell of his early experiences in the pulpit. As a young man, preaching put a strain on his vocal cords, and he was hoarse after every sermon. One day a speech teacher in his congregation approached him saying, "You're going to ruin your voice. Your vocal cords are too tense when you preach."

"Yes, I know," said Allen, "but what can I do about it?"

"Relax your hands," said the teacher. "Your vocal cords will relax if your body relaxes, and your body cannot be tense if your hands are relaxed." Dr. Allen took the man's advice, and his problem cleared up. "I may not be much of a speaker," Dr. Allen said dryly, "but I've got the most relaxed hands of any preacher you've ever met!"

Go about your business without fretting or worrying.
*Relax. When it's **all** over, you will be on your feet*
to receive your reward.

April 6

READING: LUKE 9:23–27

*He said to them **all**,*
"If anyone wants to come with Me,
he must deny himself,
take up his cross daily, and follow Me."
Luke 9:23

You know about the dropping of the atomic bomb on Nagasaki in 1945. But do you know the other catastrophic event in Nagasaki's history?

When missionary Francis Xavier entered Japan in the sixteenth century, he found some Christians already there, descendants of believers who had immigrated from China and Korea. As Xavier preached, these people returned to the Lord with all their hearts, sparking a revival in which multitudes of Japanese came to the Lord.

In response, the government launched a series of persecutions lasting 250 years. No one knows how many believers died, but estimates range upward to a million.

The purge began on February 5, 1597, atop a hill in Nagasaki where twenty-six Christians were nailed to twenty-six crude crosses. The oldest martyr was sixty-four. The youngest was a twelve-year-old boy named Ibaragi Kun. As the torture began, a government official begged the boy to recant his faith. The youth reportedly replied, "Sir, it would be better if you yourself became a Christian and could go to heaven where I am going."

Then he asked, "Sir, which is my cross?"

The stunned official pointed to the smallest cross on the hill, and the boy knelt in front of it. On those crosses, the "Twenty-Six Martyrs of Nagasaki" died for their faith.

We may never be nailed to a literal cross, but to bear our testimony in a hostile world is our daily job and joy.

April 7

The news about Him spread throughout Syria.
*So they brought to Him **all** those who were afflicted,*
those suffering from various diseases and intense pains, the demon-
possessed, the epileptics, and the paralytics. And He healed them.

Matthew 4:24

Welcome to the Great Physician's
Office hours are as you come,
He's a specialist in all problems
And His day is never done.

He can heal a heart that's broken
He can mend the spirit too,
No matter what your ailment
He does have the cure for you.

There's no fee for services rendered
All He asks is we believe
That He bled and died to save us
And all His blessings we'll receive.

Do you have a special problem
That is troubling you this hour?
Then just simply leave it with Him
You can find no greater power.

—*Author unknown*

The Great Physician now is near,
the sympathizing Jesus;
He speaks the drooping heart to cheer,
Oh! hear the voice of Jesus.

—*William Hunter*

# April 8

*He repeatedly turns His hand against me **all** day long.*
Lamentations 3:3

Lamentations is the saddest book in the Bible, a collection of funeral dirges written by Jeremiah in his anguish over the destruction of his people. Chapter 3 begins with these bitter words: "I am the man who has seen affliction. . . . [God] has driven me away and forced me to walk in darkness . . . . He repeatedly turns His hand against me all day long. He has worn away my flesh and skin; He has shattered my bones. He has laid siege against me."

In verse 7, he continued: "He has walled me in so I cannot escape. He has weighed me down with chains." Jeremiah described God as a bear that had torn him to pieces. In verses 12–13, he accused God of shooting him with an arrow in his kidneys. "I have forgotten what happiness is. . . . My future is lost, as well as my hope from the Lord" (vv. 17–18).

Some moments in life are so horrendous that our faith is shaken and we lose all sense of God's goodness.

But not quite . . . .

Though we sometimes lose our grip on God, He never loses His grip on us. In verse 21, Jeremiah emerges from "the dark night of the soul" to give us one of Scripture's sweetest passages and words that inspired the hymn "Great Is Thy Faithfulness."

> Yet I call this to mind, and therefore I have hope:
> Because of the LORD's faithful love we do not perish,
> for His mercies never end.
> They are new every morning;
> great is Your faithfulness!

All I have needed Thy hand hath provided.

pril 9

*This is so that **all** the people of the earth*
may know that the LORD's hand is mighty,
and so that you may always fear the LORD your God.

Joshua 4:24

I grew up beside a river in Tennessee that's about the size of the Jordan in Israel. I fished in it, swam in it, and in dry seasons waded across it. But when the Doe flooded, it was a sight to see, overspilling its banks, washing away bridges, and driving residents to higher ground.

When Moses led the Israelites out of Egypt, the Red Sea rose up in towering walls of water, providing a way of escape. Forty years later, the same thing happened when Joshua led the Israelites into the Promised Land. The Jordan was at flood stage, but the waters parted, allowing the Israelites to enter dryshod.

God could have brought the Israelites to the Jordan during dry season when they could have waded across. But in His providence, they arrived at flood stage. Why? To remind them of His prior miracle.

The Israelites both entered and exited the wilderness through parted waters. Joshua 4:23–24 says, "The LORD your God dried up the waters of the Jordan . . . just as the LORD your God did to the Red Sea . . . so that all the people of the earth may know that the LORD's hand is mighty."

God wants us to remember what He's done for us in the past. His past blessings are encouragements in present trials. His faithfulness in earlier days is a harbinger of His care now and in the future. Our help in ages past is our hope in years to come.

April 10

*Why **all** this commotion and wailing?*
The child is not dead but asleep.

Mark 5:39 (NIV)

I recently conducted the funeral of a little girl. During the service, the guests had trouble hearing because of the mother's wailing: "I don't want her to die. . . . Just let me hold her! . . . I miss her so much. . . ." Asking the Lord for guidance, I rose and said, "Jesus once attended the funeral of a little girl, and He spoke the most astounding words. He said, "What is all this commotion and wailing?"

I had everyone's attention, for my words had such direct bearing. Even the mother stopped her sobbing long enough to look up. I continued, "The Bible says that while it's all right to sorrow, Christians ought not to grieve like others who have no hope."

I went on to speak from 2 Kings 4:26 about the death of the Shunammite's son, and of the mother's words in that passage, "It is well with the child." I discussed God's mercy, the healing and hope the little girl instantly experienced in heaven, how happy she was, and I talked about the coming resurrection and reunion.

After the service, the mother approached the open coffin for the last time, but there was a glow on her face. "Thank you for what you said," she whispered. "I see things so differently now."

Too much weeping and wailing can betray a lack of trust in our Lord. His presence and promises compose our hearts and bring morning out of mourning.

When I can read my title clear to mansions in the skies,
I bid farewell to every fear, and wipe my weeping eyes.

—*Isaac Watts*

April 11

*Ahab told Jezebel everything that Elijah had done
and how he had killed **all** the prophets with the sword.*

1 Kings 19:1

A comedian once quipped, "Sometimes I get the feeling the whole world is against me, but deep down I know that's not true. Some of the smaller countries are neutral."

In 1 Kings 19, Elijah got the feeling the whole world was against him, and this chapter records the poignant story of his breakdown. It's the Lord's way of showing us how to recover from similar breakdowns. Read this story, noticing the tools He uses to restore Elijah's morale.

- *Rest and nutrition (vv. 5–8).* Part of Elijah's problem was exhaustion. When we're hungry and tired, we have less control over our moods and emotions.
- *Angelic intervention (vv. 5–7).* Angels are unseen spirits sent to serve believers (Heb. 1:14).
- *Questions (vv. 9–10, 13–14).* Notice how the Lord encouraged Elijah to open up and identify his feelings.
- *God's still, small voice (vv. 12–13).* God's Word speaks to us quietly as we find verses that meet our needs.
- *Remember that where God is concerned, things are never as bad as they seem (v. 18).*[28]
- *Determine to complete God's will for your life (vv. 15–18).* Elijah's best days of ministry were still ahead.
- *Find a friend with whom to share your burdens and blessings (vv. 19–21).*

This was God's personalized treatment program for His defeated prophet. If it worked with Elijah, it can work for us.

April 12

During those days
He went out to the mountain to pray
*and spent **all** night in prayer to God.*
Luke 6:12

On two occasions, I've prayed straight through the night, once for church needs and once for family problems. More frequently, however, I've spent a *day* in prayer, spurred on by a little booklet by Lorne Sanny titled *How to Spend a Day in Prayer*.

Sanny observed that Jesus spent whole nights praying, and Nehemiah prayed "certain days" about the plight of Jerusalem. Moses spent forty days with God on Mount Sinai, and Christ did the same in the Judean hills.

Sometimes we need extended times in the Lord's presence.

Don't think of a Prayer Day as kneeling by your bedside for twelve straight hours, but as a sort of vacation for the soul. Set aside a day; pack a lunch; take your Bible, a hymnbook, your prayer lists, a devotional book or your journal; and get away from your normal schedule. Go to the woods, to a retreat center, or to a secluded spot.

When I set aside a Prayer Day, I jot down a schedule for the day, interspersing prayer with Bible study, thanksgiving, journaling, walking, interceding, memorizing, singing, listening to tapes, and reading. The important thing is to think of it as a day just for you and the Lord to enjoy being together.

When we're too busy, our thoughts become scattered and our prayers grow shallow. Sometime soon, set aside a day or a night for unhurried fellowship with the Father.

Hurry is the death of prayer.
—*Samuel Chadwick*

April 13

You will keep in perfect peace
the mind that is dependent on You,
for it is trusting in You. . . .
LORD, you will establish peace for us,
*for You have also done **all** our work for us.*

Isaiah 26:3, 12

The result of righteousness will be peace; the effect of righteousness will be quiet confidence forever. Then my people will dwell in a peaceful place . . . . Peace I leave with you. My peace I give to you. I do not give to you as the world gives. Your heart must not be troubled or fearful. . . . I will give peace to the land, and you will lie down with nothing to frighten you. . . . I will make peace flow . . . like a river.

I will both lie down and sleep in peace, for You alone, LORD, make me live in safety.

The mind-set of the Spirit is life and peace. . . . The fruit of the Spirit is . . . peace . . . . The LORD gives His people strength; the LORD blesses His people with peace. . . . Abundant peace belongs to those who love Your instruction . . . .

He will be named . . . Prince of Peace. . . . He was pierced because of our transgressions, crushed because of our iniquities; punishment for our peace was on Him, and we are healed by His wounds. . . .

And as they were saying these things, He Himself stood among them. He said to them, "Peace to you!" But they were startled and terrified and thought they were seeing a ghost. "Why are you troubled?" He asked them. "And why do doubts arise in your hearts? Look at My hands and My feet, that it is I Myself!" . . .

He is our peace.[29]

# April 14

READING: PSALM 16

> *The LORD said to Aaron, "You will not receive any property that can be inherited, and no part of the land of Israel will be assigned to you. I, the LORD, am **all** you need."*
>
> **Numbers 18:20 (TEV)**

He was all Aaron needed, and He's all we need. The psalmist put it this way: "You, Lord, are all I have, and you give me *all I need*; my future is in your hands. How wonderful are your gifts to me; how good they are!" (Ps. 16:5 TEV).

When the writer of Psalm 73 was bewildered by life, he went to the temple of God and declared, "But as for me, God's presence is *all I need*. I have made the sovereign Lord my shelter, as I declare all the things you have done" (Ps. 73:28 NET).

In 2 Corinthians 9:8, encouraging his readers to be good stewards, Paul promised, "And God will generously provide *all you need*" (NLT).

The Lord told Paul in his illness: "My gracious favor is *all you need*" (2 Cor. 12:9 NLT).

He is our portion. He Himself is all we need.

He is *all I need.*
Jesus is the living water to quench my thirst,
the heavenly bread to satisfy my hunger,
the snow-white robe to cover me, the sure refuge,
the happy home of my soul, my meat and my medicine,
my solace and my song, my light and my delight.
He is all I desire.

—*Charles H. Spurgeon*

All I need, in Thee I see;
Thou art all in all to me.

—*Thomas Hastings, 1858*

April 15

Come to Me,
all *of you who are weary and burdened,*
and I will give you rest.
All *of you, take up My yoke and learn from Me,*
because I am gentle and humble in heart,
and you will find rest.

Matthew 11:28–29

This passage comes at the end of a long day. As Jesus threaded through the towns of Galilee, preaching without observable success, He met messengers from John the Baptist who asked: "Are you the One who is to come, or should we expect someone else?" It seemed to be going quite badly. So Jesus stopped and offered a word of praise in verse 25: "I praise You, Father, Lord of heaven and earth." Then, looking at His downcast little flock, He said tenderly: "Come to Me, all of you who are weary and burdened . . . . All of you, take up My yoke."

The word *weary* comes from the Greek verb *kopto,* which, in its original sense, means "to strike or to hit." It refers to someone beaten down by life. The word *burdened* literally means "loaded down." In Middle Eastern society certain people were burden-bearers who sold themselves out to carry great loads on their backs.

If you are a burden-bearer today, carrying a great load, imagine Jesus speaking these words to you: "Come to Me, . . . I will give you rest. . . . You will find rest for yourselves. . . . My yoke is easy and My burden is light."

I came to Jesus as I was, weary, and worn and sad;
I found in Him a resting place, and He has made me glad.

—Horatius Bonar

April 16

> *Rejoice! Let your gentleness be evident to **all**....*
> *And the peace of God, which transcends **all** understanding,*
> *will guard your hearts and your minds in Christ Jesus.*
> **Philippians 4:4–5, 7 (NIV)**

Recently I received a brochure of a seminar that could teach me five ways to manage my time, eight techniques to handle co-workers, and seven ways to close a deal. I was reminded that we like our information in concise, numerical steps.

In Philippians 4:4–9, the apostle Paul gives us five steps to transcendent peace:

1. *Learn to rejoice in the Lord (v. 4).* We can't always rejoice in our situation, but we can deliberately direct our thoughts to Him and rejoice in His presence, His promises, His power, and His providential control of all that touches us.
2. *Be gentle (v. 5).* Much of our anxiety comes from tension with others. We may not be able to put out all the fires, but we can usually lower the temperature by being gentle with one another.
3. *Remember the nearness of the Lord (v. 5b).* The Lord is at hand, with us, near us, all around us.
4. *Pray with thanksgiving (v. 6).* Don't worry about anything, but pray about everything—with thanksgiving.
5. *Meditate on Scripture (vv. 8–9).* Let your mind think about what is true, noble, right, pure, lovely, and admirable.

This five-step formula is backed by the full authority of God, and it concludes with a double promise: The peace of God will guard our hearts and minds (v. 7), and the God of peace will be with us (v. 9).

# April 17

All the angels stood around the throne,
the elders, and the four living creatures,
and they fell on their faces
before the throne and worshiped God.

Revelation 7:11

The last chapters of the Bible describe the city of New Jerusalem, our eternal home. At its center is the throne of God, from which runs a broad street, a fabulous park, and a crystal river (Rev. 22:1–2). The throne itself isn't described here because John had already given a description of it in Revelation 5, 6, and 7. These accounts correspond to what Ezekiel saw in chapter 1 of his book.

Ezekiel said, "The shape of a throne with the appearance of sapphire stone was above the expanse. There was a form with the appearance of a human on the throne high above. . . . The appearance of the brilliant light all around was like that of a rainbow in a cloud on a rainy day" (vv. 26, 28).

John said, "There in heaven a throne was set. One was seated on the throne, and the One seated looked like jasper and carnelian stone. A rainbow that looked like an emerald surrounded the throne. . . . From the throne came flashes of lightning, rumblings, and thunder" (Rev. 4:2–3, 5).

Whenever we see the throne of God of Scripture, the angels are surrounding it and worshipping Him seated upon it. I believe one day we, too, will literally worship God before His rainbow-canopied throne in New Jerusalem.

Perhaps we should start learning one of the hymns sung there: "Amen! Blessing and glory and wisdom and thanksgiving and honor and power and strength, be to our God forever and ever. Amen" (Rev. 7:12).

April 18

*They entered into a covenant to seek the LORD God of their ancestors
with **all** their mind and **all** their heart.*

2 Chronicles 15:12

When George Washington assumed the presidency in 1789, the spiritual life of America was at low ebb. The writings of the French skeptics had swept the land, and the nation was on the verge of being totally secular and irreligious. The influence of the Great Awakening had waned, and the presence of Christians on college campuses was virtually nonexistent.

At Hampden-Sydney College, however, one student found Christ—Cary Allen. Then another student, William Hill, acquired an evangelistic book that he hid in his trunk and read secretly.

One Saturday Hill locked himself in his room to read the book when someone knocked on the door. It was another student, James Blythe, who, entering the room and seeing the book, started sobbing, saying he had locked his Bible in his trunk and had turned his back on God.

Hill and Blythe gave their lives to Christ, and, together with Cary Allen, they began secret prayer meetings. When word leaked out, a mob of students harassed them. But a revival broke out on that campus, resulting in half the students coming to Christ. Spreading to other schools and churches, it paved the way for the Great Revival of 1800 that, in many ways, laid the spiritual foundation for America.

There's no telling what will happen when a small band of committed souls enter a covenant to seek the Lord God of their ancestors with all their mind and all their heart.

We cannot organize revival,
but we can set our sails to catch the wind from heaven
when God chooses to blow upon His people once again.

—*G. Campbell Morgan*

April 19

*Let the peoples praise you, God; let **all** the peoples praise You.*
Psalm 67:3

English poet and hymnist Adelaide A. Procter (1825–64) wrote of a woman who sat at the organ one autumn's day at twilight. She struck a chord that swelled with soft majesty. It flowed through the room and filled the house with melody and peace.

> It quieted pain and sorrow, like love
>   overcoming strife;
> It seemed the harmonious echo for our
>   discordant life.
> It linked all perplexéd meanings into one
>   perfect peace,
> And trembled away into silence as if it were loath
>   to cease.

Something broke the spell, and when the woman tried again, she couldn't find that beautiful chord. She couldn't recall the notes. It was a lost chord.

For many people, worship is the missing chord. It's the one thing that quiets pain and sorrow like love overcoming strife. It makes harmonious echoes from our discordant strife. But for many, it's a lost experience.

God wants all the peoples to praise Him. He deserves total worship, of course, for He alone is God. But He desires it for our sakes too. When we worship and praise Him as we should, the internal gyroscopes of our souls are aligned correctly, and we're happier, holier, and healthier in mind, soul, and spirit.

> *Let the peoples praise You, God;*
> *let all the peoples praise You.*
> *Let the nations rejoice and shout for joy, . . .*
> *God will bless us,*
> *and all the ends of the earth will fear Him.*

April 20

That power is like the working of his mighty strength,
which he exerted in Christ when he raised him from the dead
and seated him at his right hand in the heavenly realms,
*far above **all** rule and authority, power and dominion,*
and every title that can be given, not only in the present age
*but also in the one to come. And God placed **all** things*
under his feet and appointed him to be head over everything.

Ephesians 1:19–22 (NIV)

Oh, if only we comprehended the power of Jesus Christ on our behalf!

- *It is Resurrection power:* "That power is like the working of his mighty strength, which he exerted in Christ when he raised him from the dead . . ."
- *It is Exaltation power:* ". . . and seated him at his right hand in the heavenly realms, . . ."
- *It is Lordship power:* ". . . far above all rule and authority, power and dominion, and every title that can be given, not only in the present age but also in the one to come. . . ."
- *It is Headship power:* "And God placed all things under his feet and appointed him to be head over everything for the church."

Are we living in the supernatural power of Christ today? The power of His resurrection, His exaltation, His lordship, and His headship is available to change our lives, to answer our prayers, to resolve our difficulties, to strengthen our souls, and to give us everlasting life.

May He strengthen us with all power in our inner beings (Eph. 3:16).

April 21

We must not get tired of doing good,
for we will reap at the proper time
if we don't give up.
Therefore, as we have opportunity,
we must work for the good of all.
Galatians 6:9–10

Fatigue is one of our greatest enemies. I know all about it, and I don't want to live in the Land of Nod any longer. For many years I worked too many nights, burned too much midnight oil, rose too early, and skipped too many days off. It finally caught up with me when I realized I had become short-tempered and irritable—qualities that just won't do in a pastorate!

But it's not just Christian workers. Our 24/7 society gives us electricity at all hours. We no longer go to bed when the sun goes down. We work into the night, or we entertain ourselves by watching late-night comics elicit halfhearted laughs with crude humor and off-color jokes. We do our grocery shopping at midnight, check our e-mail at 3:00 a.m., and drag ourselves out of bed when our cell phone alarm clocks render a tech-sounding version of our favorite pop song.

In Galatians 6, Paul was concerned about another kind of fatigue. The devil's greatest weapon is discouragement; and if he can steal away our enthusiasm, he has countermanded our effectiveness for Christ.

The combination of physical fatigue with internal discouragement has trounced some of the mightiest saints, but the remedy is simple—Galatians 6:9–10. Take time to rest in body and soul, and remember that God has assuredly promised that our work for Him is never in vain.

Work hard, but don't wear yourself out. Do not grow weary of doing good.

# April 22

The revelation of Jesus Christ that God gave...
to His slave John, who testified to God's word
*and to the testimony about Jesus Christ, in **all** he saw.*
Revelation 1:1–2

I flew into New Orleans several years ago for a speaking engagement, and the man who met me at the airport was a geophysicist for an oil company. He told me that oil deposits are formed when living things like forests and foliage are covered, buried, and decompose. Oil and petroleum are found all over the world, he said, even under the ice of the Arctic and Antarctic. That means forests and foliage once covered the globe until destroyed in a vast, global cataclysm (like a worldwide flood). Earth's richest oil deposits, he said, are found under the sands of countries just east of Israel in the place described in the Bible as the location of the Garden of Eden, and he suggested that the gasoline I pump into my car might be the ruined remnants of Eden.

I was amazed, and I've often thought of what he said. In these Last Days, when so much of history is converging in the Middle East as prophesied in Scripture, these oil deposits are triggering the largest transfer of wealth in human history. Billions of dollars are flowing from the West to the Arab oil producers and setting the stage for who-knows-what, with Israel right in the middle of it.

Over the years, I've studied through the book of Revelation several times, and each time I've understood it better and appreciated it more. We don't have to understand every verse of Revelation to get the main point: Jesus is coming soon!

∞

Jesus is coming! The dead shall arise,
Loved ones shall meet in a joyful surprise.
Caught up together to Him in the skies!
Jesus is coming again!

—*Daniel Whittle, 1894*

# April 23

All Israel from Dan to Beer-sheba knew
that Samuel was a confirmed prophet of the LORD.
1 Samuel 3:20

Samuel became the spiritual leader of Israel at a young age, and many of his qualities were apparent in childhood. His chief qualifications were *availability* and *dependability*, both of which are summed up in a phrase he used five times in this one chapter.

1. "Then the LORD called Samuel, and he answered, '*Here I am*'" (v. 4).
2. "He ran to Eli and said, '*Here I am;* you called me'" (v. 5).
3. "Samuel got up, went to Eli, and said, '*Here I am;* you called me'" (v. 6).
4. "For the third time, the LORD called Samuel. He got up, went to Eli, and said, '*Here I am;* you called me'" (v. 8).
5. "Eli called him and said, 'Samuel, my son.' '*Here I am,*' answered Samuel" (v. 16).

When we say to the Lord, "Here I am," He returns the favor, saying to us, "Here I am too! I'm here for you."

When you call, the Lord will answer;
when you cry out, He will say: Here I am. . . .
Therefore they will know on that day
that I am He who says:
Here I am.
Isaiah 58:9, 52:6

Here I am. Send me.
Isaiah 6:8

# April 24

Even when I am old and gray,
God, do not abandon me.
Then I will proclaim Your power
to another generation,
*Your strength to **all** who are to come.*

Psalm 71:18

I've read that when the French farmers were nearly starving during a famine of the 1800s, they were kept alive by what is called "The One-Hundred-Year-Old Soup." The farmers' wives would keep a pot simmering on the back of the woodstove. Every day they'd throw in whatever was available, along with some more water. It might be a carrot, some meat, a potato, or even a handful of dandelions.

When children left home, they'd take a pot of the soup with them, and when immigrants came to America some of them brought little pots of the one-hundred-year-old soup. It's claimed that some of the soup eaten today in South Carolina derives from this source.

The church of Jesus Christ has been boiling a pot of nourishment for two thousand years. Many ingredients have been added and many people have been fed. It's ever old, yet ever new. It's a constant, life-giving gift from generations that have preceded us, but it needs constant replenishing that those who follow may also be fed.

Psalm 71:18 is a prayer. When we have served our generation, we should ask God for strength and opportunities to serve the next. We have grandchildren to influence, children's ministries in which to volunteer, and neighborhood youngsters to invite to church.

Perhaps we feel we can't do much, but don't you have a handful of dandelions you can throw in the soup?

April 25

*I hear of your love and faith
toward the Lord Jesus
and for **all** the saints.*

Philemon 5

Last Sunday in my morning sermon, I mentioned that the Lord sometimes speaks to us through a mere phrase of Scripture. Later I received this letter:

> I've been meaning to send you a note since Sunday, as I wanted to tell you of finding strength in a simple phrase I saw on the way from New York last week. We'd gone to visit my mother. I'm concerned for her, as she's alone in the old farmhouse I grew up in. We don't know when she'll decide to move out, but it's obvious she'll soon need some sort of regular care.
>
> In addition, I'm pregnant, and I have a broken foot and several other concerns. I was fretting about it, but as we rolled down the highway, I saw a phrase someone had written in the dirt on the back of a truck. It simply said: "Trust Jesus."
>
> I couldn't get it off my mind. I recalled years ago singing a little song that said, "Why Worry, When You Can Pray?" I remembered the entire tune. I've found great comfort in that, and have ever since we returned, even though I'm 825 miles from my mom.

It reminded me of the time Jesus stooped down and wrote in the dirt in John 8.

We bolster the sinking spirits of all the saints whenever our love and faith writes a graffiti of grace in the grime of this world.

April 26

The commandments:
Do not commit adultery, do not murder,
do not steal, do not covet,
and if there is any other commandment—
***all** are summed up by this:*
Love your neighbor as yourself.

Romans 13:9

The Autobiography of Peter Cartwright is a classic in American history, every page telling a gripping story. Cartwright was an eccentric circuit-riding preacher who brought the gospel to the frontier. One of his stories involves two young men who were bitter enemies sworn to kill each other. Both of them showed up, armed with pistols, to hear Cartwright preach.

In his sermon, Cartwright warned the audience to flee from the coming wrath, to flee to Christ. When he gave the invitation, he noticed one of the young men responding and kneeling at one side of the altar. The other young man was kneeling at the other side. Cartwright went to the first one, prayed with him, and asked for his pistol. Then he prayed with the other and took his sidearm as well.

Rising from the altar, the young men suddenly saw each other and instantly started toward one another. For a second, the audience held its breath, but the young men embraced and from that day they were brothers in Christ.

Most of our problems with others would be resolved if we'd get our own hearts right with the Lord. We're proud and stubborn by nature, but at the foot of the cross we find the love of Jesus and the capacity to love our neighbor as ourselves and thus to fulfill all the law of God.

pril 27

*Are you unaware that **all** of us*
who were baptized into Christ Jesus
were baptized into His death?

Romans 6:3

When we give ourselves to Jesus, we meet ourselves coming and going in the cemetery. There's a sense in which we pass from death to life (Eph. 2), but we also pass from life to death (Rom. 6). We're crucified with Christ, and we die to sin. Many Christians focus on the joys of the New Life and forget about the obligations of the New Death.

When James Calvert sailed as a missionary to the cannibals of Fiji, the captain tried to dissuade him, warning he would lose his life. Calvert replied, "We died before we came here."

George Müller, when asked the secret of his work, replied, "There came a day when George Müller died, utterly died! No longer did his own desires, preferences, and tastes come first. He knew that from then on Christ had to be all in all."

I once asked a prominent minister how he remained so visionary and passionate. "I execute myself every day with 220 volts," he said. "Galatians 2:20—I'm crucified with Christ."

Dietrich Bonhoeffer, the German Christian killed by Nazis, wrote, "When God calls a man, he bids him come and die."

Set your minds on what is above ....
For you have died, and your life is hidden with the Messiah in God.

Colossians 3:2–3

We dye to live, we live to dye;
The more we dye, the more we live;
The more we live, the more we dye.

—Sign in a dry-cleaning and dyeing shop

pril 28

> *On that day*
> *a severe persecution broke out*
> *against the church in Jerusalem,*
> *and **all** except the apostles were scattered*
> *throughout the land of Judea and Samaria.*
>
> **Acts 8:1**

Somewhere I remember reading a story of the great Chinese Christian, Watchman Nee, when he spoke to a group of ministers during a time of persecution. Spies had infiltrated the meeting to trap Nee in his words, and he knew that as soon as he opened his mouth he'd be arrested. His solution was to act out his sermon.

Looking over the audience, he picked up a glass of water and hurled it to the floor, smashing it. His face assumed smug arrogance, and for five minutes he walked around the platform crunching glass under his feet.

Suddenly his expression changed to alarm. He tried to pick up the pieces and reassemble them, but it couldn't be done. Finally, he threw the pieces in the air, and they fell to the platform like a chorus of raindrops. Then he walked away.

The spies never understood the parable, but the ministers did. Years later, a pastor in Shanghai gave the interpretation. The Communists would try to smash the church and grind it under their feet, and they would seem successful. But, in fact, they would fail. Instead of smashing it, it would be dispersed across China—which is exactly what happened.

Today Christianity is under attack as never before, and millions of believers are facing persecution. The devil should have learned his lesson in Acts 8. He can't win. Those who are persecuted still go everywhere, preaching the Word.

April 29

*Bring **all** the tithes into the storehouse,*
That there may be food in My house,
And try Me now in this,"
Says the LORD of hosts,
"If I will not open for you the windows of heaven
And pour out for you such blessing
That there will not be room enough to receive it."

Malachi 3:10 (NKJV)

When I was very young, the pastor of my church in Elizabeth-ton, Tennessee, was Harvey Hill. A few years ago, he wrote his life's story, and I found it very interesting because some of his recollections concerned people I knew and loved.

Near the beginning of his book, Harvey said that when he and his wife, Sylvia, were married, they didn't have a penny. It was the Great Depression, and few people had cars. They walked wherever they went and lived hand to mouth.

One day the pastor of their church bluntly asked Harvey and Sylvia if they were tithing, giving at least 10 percent of their income to the Lord.

"No," said Harvey, "we can't afford it."

The pastor said, "Just try it and see if God doesn't bless you."

Harvey and Sylvia took up the challenge, and from that day until their deaths within a few weeks of each other seventy years later, they never failed to bring God their tithes and offerings. And God never failed to bless them.

"Bring the tithe into the storehouse, that there may be food in My house," said the Lord. "Test Me in this way. See if I will not open the floodgates and pour out blessings on you without measure."

April 30

This grace was given to me . . .
*to shed light for **all** about the administration*
of the mystery hidden for ages in God
who created all things.

Ephesians 3:8–9

Surveys suggest a third of all church-attenders will be in a different congregation in five years. Many modern worshippers are consumer-driven, and when they grow disgruntled, don't like the music, have a conflict with someone, or find a church with better programming, they're off.

If only we understood Ephesians 3 and valued each congregation as God does! In this chapter, Paul announced something unknown in earlier eras. The Old Testament prophets had predicted a Messiah, but one bit of information was withheld from them: They didn't realize there was a *First* Coming and a *Second* Coming, with a gap between the two. They didn't know about the age of the church, the age of grace, and the era of global missions. It was God's secret. "The mystery was made known to me by revelation," said Paul in verse 3. "This was not made known to people in other generations as it is now revealed . . . the Gentiles are co-heirs, members of the same body, and partners of the promise" (vv. 5–6).

When the trumpet sounds and we meet the Lord in the air, the age of the church will be over and Israel will again take center stage on the prophetic calendar. Until then, the church is God's special assembly, made up of both Jews and Gentiles, indwelled by the Spirit, and commissioned with the evangelism of the world.

Every congregation is special in God's sight.

There are rare occasions when we need to change churches, but sometimes all we need to change is our attitudes.

May 1

Not one of all the LORD's good promises to the house of Israel failed.
Joshua 21:45 (NIV)

The LORD is faithful to all his promises.
Psalm 145:13 (NIV)

The *faithfulness* of God is that aspect of His character that results in His complete adherence to fulfilling His Word and keeping His *promises*. He is unalterably reliable to do exactly as He has said. Because He is trustworthy, we can trust and not worry.

God is not a man who lies, or a son of man who changes His mind.
*Does He speak and not act, or **promise** and not fulfill?*
Numbers 23:19

You know with all your heart and all your soul that none
*of the good **promises** the Lord your God made to you has failed.*
*Everything was fulfilled for you; not one **promise** has failed.*
Joshua 23:14

*Not one of all the good **promises***
He made through His servant Moses has failed.
1 Kings 8:56

*Lord, You have treated Your servant well, just as You **promised**. . . .*
*May Your faithful love comfort me, as You **promised** Your servant. . . .*
*Sustain me as You **promised**. . . . Defend my cause,*
*and redeem me; give me life, as You **promised**.*
Psalm 119:65, 76, 116, 154

Splendid to be so near the gates of heaven!
I am lost in amazement!
There has not failed one word of all His good *promises!*
—*Frances Ridley Havergal on her deathbed*

 # May 2

*First of **all**, you should know this:*
no prophecy of Scripture comes from one's own interpretation.
2 Peter 1:20

First of all—before all else!—we should know something about the promises of God.

God's promises are available (2 Pet. 1:1–11). Peter begins by saying God has given us exceedingly great and precious promises, enabling us to acquire a new nature and escape the corruption in the world caused by lust (v. 4). These promises protect us from anger, anxiety, apathy, and anguish. They chart the route of grace in our lives and provide a foundation for personal growth (vv. 5–11).

God's promises are forgettable (2 Pet. 1:12–15). It's possible to become so busy that we don't search out God's promises. We fail to locate, claim, appropriate, and believe them in times of need. Peter's job was to "remind you about these things, even though you know them, . . . to wake you up with a reminder" (vv. 12–14).

God's promises are infallible (2 Pet. 1:16–21). Though Peter was an eyewitness to the transfiguration of Jesus, he said, in effect, "I've something more certain than my experience. I have God's Word." No prophecy of Scripture came from private *interpretation*. The Greek word implies "unloosing," as in *origination*. No promise had its origin in mere human invention, but "moved by the Holy Spirit, men spoke from God." The promises are authoritative and unfailing.

Many times when I could have gone insane from worry,
I was at peace because my soul believed the truth
of God's promises. God's word, together with the whole
character of God . . . settles all questions.

—*George Müller*

May 3

*A friend loves at **all** times,*
and a brother is born for a difficult time.
Proverbs 17:17

The only way to *have* a friend is to *be* one," wrote Ralph Waldo Emerson.

Dale Carnegie observed that we can make more friends in two months by becoming interested in other people than in two years by trying to get others interested in us.

It helps when we put our own needs aside and do little things for others. It helps to be relaxed and easy-going, so that things don't ruffle you. It helps to practice liking others and being likable. Proverbs 18:24 says, "A man that hath friends must shew himself friendly" (KJV).

Queen Victoria once shared her impressions of her two prime ministers. She said when she was with William Gladstone, she felt she was with one of the most important people in the world. But when she was with Benjamin Disraeli, he made her feel that she was one of the most important people in the world.

My father was a schoolteacher who served under a number of school superintendents, two of whom he compared in this way: "When I went to Mr. Jones with a request, he could turn it down yet make me feel good. But when I went to Johnson, he could grant the request but make me feel bad in the process."

A warm smile, a relaxed way, genuine concern for others, and the ability to love at all times—that's what it takes to enjoy the blessings of friendship.

May 4

*Marriage must be respected by **all**,*
and the marriage bed kept undefiled,
because God will judge immoral people and adulterers.

Hebrews 13:4

The BBC recently told of a couple in England who were married during the London Marathon. The bride's knee-length dress and the groom's top hat and tails were made from lightweight materials, suitable for running. The couple started the race, paused along the way for the brief ceremony, then rejoined the race for the remaining miles. The idea sounded strangely appropriate to me because marriage is, after all, a marathon. It's a lifelong race in which couples find their pace for the long haul.

According to this verse, there are two vital elements to a lasting marriage.

First, marriage must be respected by all. We can't take it (or one another) for granted. Couples who stay in love express their affection every day. They frequently say those three magic words. They are physically affectionate, holding hands, hugging, cuddling. They express their love sexually. They verbalize their appreciation and admiration. They give little gifts. They create time together. They act as though they love each other regardless of the emotions of any given day, knowing that our feelings usually catch up with our thoughts and choices.

Second, the marriage bed must be undefiled. I've made it a habit through the years to avoid even platonic friendships with members of the opposite sex. We can't isolate ourselves, of course, but most affairs begin as "innocent" relationships that, without either partner realizing it, begin to develop a life of their own.

So guard your marriage, love your spouse, and enjoy the race.

May 5

*Guide me . . . I wait for You **all** day long.*
Psalm 25:5

When geese migrate for the season, they fly by day, but many songbirds travel at night. As we slumber in bed, millions of songbirds are winging their way over our heads under cover of darkness, heading north or south depending on the season.

Take Baltimore orioles, for example (the birds, not the ballplayers). Every fall, they pack their bags, close up their nests, leave the key under the mat, and head south like senior citizens. Weather patterns tell the birds when to move. As cold fronts pass over the eastern U.S., clear skies and north winds usually follow, conditions ideal for migration, allowing the birds to travel with little risk of storms, the wind at their backs, and a clear view of the stars to help them find their way.

The entire trip from North to South America takes two weeks. But the oriole knows its route. Not even our most advanced military technologies have guidance systems so well developed as those in the tiny brains of the smallest migratory birds.

We are more valuable than the birds of the air. If the Lord is pleased to guide them in their migrations, it's a safe bet He also wants to guide our lives too.

∞

To go as I am led, to go when I am led,
to go where I am led . . .
it is that which has been for twenty years
the one prayer of my life.

—*Dr. A. T. Pierson*

May 6

Hallelujah! My soul, praise the LORD.
*I will praise the LORD **all** my life.*

Psalm 146:1–2

Psychology is an academic and applied discipline involving the study of mental processes and behaviors; but the word *psychology* itself comes from a biblical term, the Greek word *psyche,* meaning "soul." This word occurs more than one hundred times in the Greek New Testament. Jesus once said, "Now my soul [psyche] is troubled." The apostle John told Gaius, "Dear friend, I pray that you may prosper in every way and be in good health, just as your soul [psyche] prospers."

Praise is essential to psychological health. It's to the soul what water is to the body. Several years ago, I visited the Egyptian museum in Cairo, and the mummies fascinated me. By definition, a mummy is a person suffering severe dehydration.

To keep from drying up inwardly, we need the hydration of praise and worship; that's what keeps us psychologically healthy and well regulated.

According to Psalm 146, praise is a lifelong commitment. Every single day from now to eternity is an occasion to praise the Lord. Each hour is blushed with colors of praise. Every breath should be for extolling the Lord. Praise is a personal, perpetual attitude of the soul, and how wonderful to think that our last breath on earth and our first breath in heaven would transpire in uninterrupted praise and thanksgiving.

No wonder the psalmist said, "Hallelujah! My soul, praise the Lord. I will praise the Lord all my life; I will sing to the Lord as long as I live."

May 7

*To comprehend with **all** the saints*
what is the length and width,
height and depth of God's love . . .
*so you may be filled with **all** the fullness of God.*

Ephesians 3:18–19

As I write these words, the headlines are about the frenetic campaigns for the presidency. So much depends on steady, sound leadership. The soul, too, needs to be well managed, and Ephesians 3:14–19 is a description of our hearts under wise governance:

- Verses 14–15 announce the *Commander in Chief:* "I bow my knees before the Father from whom every family in heaven and on earth is named." He is head of every authority, the Lord to whom we bow.
- Verse 16 describes the *Treasury Department:* "I pray that He may grant you, according to the riches of His glory." The Bible uses "riches" to describe the endless supply of God's grace. This treasury is never diminished, regardless of our daily withdrawals.
- Verse 16 talks about the *Energy Department:* We are "strengthened with power through His Spirit."
- Then there's the *Department of the Interior:* We are strengthened with power "in the inner man." God's strength flows from His Spirit into our spirits, and we receive interior help for every challenge and opportunity.
- The *Department of Housing* is in verse 17: "that the Messiah may dwell in your hearts through faith."
- And finally, don't forget the *Department of Education* in verses 17–18: "I pray that you . . . may be able to comprehend . . . what is the length and width, height and depth of God's love, and to know the Messiah's love that surpasses knowledge.

May 8

READING: PSALM 119:161–168

I obey Your precepts and decrees,
*for **all** my ways are before You.*

Psalm 119:168

Ways is frequently a code word in the Bible for the modern term *habits*. God is concerned about all our habits, watching carefully to see if all our daily patterns reflect obedience to His precepts.

Horace Mann observed: "Habits are like a cable. We weave a strand of it every day and soon it cannot be broken."

A schoolteacher once took a roll of thread and wrapped it one time around a pupil's wrists, saying, "This represents your doing something one time. Can you break the thread?" The child did so easily. Then she wrapped the thread around his wrists several more times. The effort to break the thread becoming more difficult until finally the pupil was unable to break free at all. "That's what happens," she said, "when acts are repeated until they become habits."

Most of our struggles in life are related to habits—smoking, drinking, oversleeping, nail-biting, cursing, impulsive spending, complaining, pornography, anger, laziness, gossip. According to Hebrews 12:1, these are the sins that so easily ensnare us.

A good first step in replacing bad habits with good ones is memorizing Psalm 119:161–168. It reminds us to fear God's word (v. 161), to rejoice in His promises (v. 162), to hate false habits (v. 163), to praise God seven times a day (v. 164), to rejoice in His abundant peace (v. 165), to carry out His commands (vv. 166–67), and to remember that all our habits are under His constant observation (v. 168).

Habit is overcome by habit.

—Thomas à Kempis

May 9

*I will cleanse you from **all** your impurities and **all** your idols. . . .*
*I will save you from **all** your uncleanness. . . . I cleanse you from **all***
your iniquities . . . . I, the LORD, have spoken and I will do it. . . .
I will respond . . . and do this.

Ezekiel 36:25, 29, 33, 36–37

The legendary broadcaster David Brinkley once described the primitive nature of NBC's first newscasts. Take, for example, this exchange between Brinkley and anchor John Cameron Swayze:

> *Swayze in New York:* Senator Wayne Morse of Oregon announced today he was leaving the Republican Party and becoming a Democrat. Here's David Brinkley in Washington.
> *Brinkley in Washington:* Republican Senator Wayne Morse of Oregon announced today he was switching to the Democratic Party. Here's Senator Morse.
> *Senator Wayne Morse in Washington (on film):* Since the Republican Party no longer represents my views . . . I am switching today to the Democratic Party.
> *Brinkley:* Now back to John Cameron Swayze in New York.[30]

Well, at least viewers got the point.

The Lord never botches the Good News He beams into our hearts, but He does use repetition to get across His point. Ezekiel 36 is a good example. Listen to the resounding drumbeat of emphasis: "I will cleanse you from *all* your impurities and *all* your idols. . . . I will save you from *all* your uncleanness. . . . I cleanse you from *all* your iniquities, . . . I, the LORD, have spoken and I will do it. . . . I will respond . . . and do this."

May 10

No one lights a lamp and puts it under a basket,
but rather on a lampstand,
*and it gives light for **all** who are in the house.*

Matthew 5:15

In his mission to Great Britain in the early 1880s, evangelist D. L. Moody devoted Saturday mornings for children's meetings. He often began by reading Matthew 5:14–16, then he would call an associate to place a candle on an empty table. "Now," boomed Moody, "we will call that light Obedience. Remember that. Mr. Dickson, put Obedience under a bushel."

Immediately Moody's associate would cover the candle with an upturned bushel basket.

"Now," Moody would say, "is that right? No!" He ordered the bushel removed, and Obedience was seen once again.

Moody called for other candles, giving each a name and often telling stories to illustrate the various spiritual qualities he was describing: Obedience, Kindness, Forgiveness, Truth, Peacemaking, Temperance, Faith, Mercy, Patience, Cheerfulness, and so on. By the end of the message, the table was filled with candles that delighted the children and produced on them an effect they never forgot. None were left under the bushel, and the combined light of them illuminated the room.

It's a good lesson for all of us. Our Christianity with all its divine qualities must be constantly displayed. Others should see the purity of our lives, our obedience to Scripture, our cheerfulness, patience, joy, and love.

We should give light to all who are in the house and to all who are in the world.

I am the light of the world. . . .
You are the light of the world.

John 8:12, Matt. 5:14

May 11

The LORD your God has blessed you
in all the work of your hands.
He has watched over your journey.

Deuteronomy 2:7

Recently I had a letter from a descendant of Solomon Ginsburg, looking for more information about this inimitable evangelist of yesteryear. Few know of him today, but his story is incredible, from his birth in 1867 till his death in 1927.

Ginsburg was born to Jewish parents in Poland. He ran away from home at age fifteen and ended up in London, where he was converted after studying Isaiah 53. When he began witnessing to Jewish friends, he was assaulted, beaten, and kicked to unconsciousness. That was the first of many attempts on his life, both in Europe and in South America where he became known as the "Firebrand of Brazil."

In 1912, Ginsburg was traveling from Europe to America. Arriving in Lisbon, he was about to embark for London when telegrams were posted about storms in the Bay of Biscay. He had a stopover ticket that allowed him to delay his journey, but it would cost him a week's time. Praying for guidance, he turned to the calendar he used, which was published by the Women's Missionary Union. The verse for that day was Deuteronomy 2:7—"The Lord your God has blessed you in all the work of your hands. He has watched over your journey."

Ginsburg felt instant peace and proceeded to London, then to America aboard the *Majestic*. Only later did he learn that had he delayed his trip, he would have been a passenger aboard the most famous ocean liner of them all—the *Titanic*.

May 12

*The LORD will protect you from **all** harm;*
He will protect your life.
The LORD will protect your coming and going
both now and forever.

Psalm 121:7–8

This week I flew to Tulsa, and the lines at the security check-points were longer. It's inconvenient, but I put up with it because I want to feel safe while hurtling through high altitudes at five hundred miles an hour in a small, pressurized cigar tube.

Psalm 121 is the "Traveler's Psalm," for it reassures us of "Traveling Mercies." The Lord watches over us on land, sea, and air. He preserves our lives and will let no harm come to us without a hidden purpose.

I began my ministry at a little mountain church with a quaint stone tower and massive bell. Every Sunday, I'd step outside onto the side stoop, reach for the rope, and start pealing the bell. The sound filled the valley and announced the worship hour.

One Sunday nothing happened when I pulled the rope. It seemed stuck. I gave it a little jerk, then a harder yank. I heard a scraping noise above me, and suddenly the bell tumbled out of the belfry. It landed at my feet and cracked the concrete steps. Everyone in the church flew to the windows and looked out at me. There I stood with a limp rope, a broken bell, and the expression of someone whose life had flashed before him.

(Since then I've shuttered at the thought of my preacher buddies conducting my funeral. They're bound to have quoted John Donne's famous poem that says, ask not for whom the bell tolls; it tolls for thee.)

Every day we face a thousand deaths averted. Through all our days and in multiple ways, the Lord watches over us.

May 13

*And **all** things you ask in prayer,*
believing, you will receive.

Matthew 21:22 (NASB)

Some twenty years ago the writer was studying in a theological college. One morning, early, a fellow student—who is today one of England's foremost missionaries—burst into the room holding an open Bible in his hands. . . . He was at that time only a new convert in Christ. . . . The Bible was, comparatively, a new book to him, and as a result he was constantly making "discoveries." On that memorable day on which he invaded my quietude, he cried excitedly—his face all aglow with mingled joy and surprise—"Do you believe this? Is it true?"

"Believe what?" I asked, glancing at the open Bible with some astonishment.

"Why this—" and he read in eager tones St. Matthew 21:21–22: "'If ye have faith and doubt not . . . all things whatsoever ye shall ask in prayer, believing, ye shall receive.' Do you believe it? Is it true?"

"Yes," I replied, with much surprise at his excitement, "of course it's true—of course I believe it." Yet through my mind there flashed all manner of thoughts!

"Well, that's a very wonderful promise," said he. "It seems to me to be absolutely limitless! Why don't we pray more?"

And he went away, leaving me thinking hard. I had never looked at those verses quite in that way. As the door closed . . . I had a vision of my Savior and His love and His power such as I never had before. I had a vision of a life of prayer.

—*From the Kneeling Christian by an "Unknown Christian"*[31]

May 14

The Lord said to her,
"My dear Martha,
*you are so upset over **all** these details!"*
Luke 10:41 (NLT)

Dr. E. Stanley Jones plunged into his work in India with passion, but unbearable heat and hard work shattered his nerves. He was sent home, but Jones returned a year later only to collapse again. In this state, Jones went to the city of Lucknow for meetings. One night, he suddenly felt the Lord asking him: *Are you yourself ready for this work to which I have called you?*

"No, Lord, I am done for," Jones said. "I have reached the end of my resources."

If you will turn that over to Me and not worry about it, I will take care of it.

"Lord," Jones said, "I close the bargain right here." A great peace settled into his heart. "I knew it was done! Life—Abundant Life—had taken possession of me. I was so lifted up that I scarcely touched the road as I quietly walked home that night. . . . I went through the days, working far into the night, and came down to bedtime wondering why in the world I should ever go to bed at all, for there was not the slightest trace of tiredness of any kind."

Jones served more than forty years in India, becoming one of the most famous missionaries of his generation. If we're always worried about "all these details," we'll break down. But if we turn them over to the Lord, He'll take care of them—and of us!

May 15

*I have asked one thing from the L*ORD*;*
it is what I desire:
*to dwell in the house of the L*ORD
***all** the days of my life.*

Psalm 27:4

The phrase *one thing* occurs several times in the Bible, pointing to God's priorities for us. The word *priority* comes from the term *prior,* something coming before something else. Here are some ultimate priorities for us:

- *Worship God!* "I have asked *one thing* from the LORD; it is what I desire: to dwell in the house of the LORD all the days of my life, gazing on the beauty of the LORD" (Ps. 27:4).
- *Put Christ above all else!* "You lack *one thing*: Go, sell all you have . . . . Then come, follow Me" (Mark 10:21).
- *Sit at Jesus' feet studying His Word!* "Martha, Martha, you are worried and upset about many things, but *one thing* is necessary. Mary has made the right choice, and it will not be taken away from her" (Luke 10:41).
- *Tell what Jesus has done for you!* "*One thing* I do know: I was blind, and now I can see!" (John 9:25).
- *Don't look backward but forward!* "*One thing* I do: forgetting what is behind and reaching forward to what is ahead, I pursue as my goal the prize promised by God's heavenly call in Christ Jesus"! (Phil. 3:13–14).
- *Be ready for Christ's return!* "Dear friends, don't let this *one thing* escape you: . . . the Day of the Lord will come like a thief" (2 Pet. 3:8, 10).

Beware lest the *many things* crowd out the *one thing* today.

May 16

*David spoke the words of this song to the LORD
on the day when the LORD rescued him
from the hand of all his enemies . . . .
"The LORD is my rock, my fortress, and my deliverer."*

2 Samuel 22:1–2

As pastor of Toronto's "People's Church," Dr. Oswald J. Smith became a missionary statesman to the world. But as a young man, his ministry almost ended before it began. In 1913, still a student, Smith took a missions trip to Kentucky for evangelistic meetings in an area notorious for its moonshine stills. On Friday night, the building emptied when gunfire erupted.

The preacher was unhurt, but he learned that a gang of ruffians had determined to ambush and kill him. Undaunted, Smith continued the meetings, and at the next service he took his text from 2 Samuel 22: "David spoke the words of this song to the Lord on the day when the Lord rescued him from the hand of all his enemies . . . . 'The Lord is my rock, my fortress, and my deliverer.'"

During the meetings forty-one people came to Christ. But perhaps the biggest impact was on the young preacher himself, for as he saw God's overcoming power, he wrote in his diary: "I am determined that God shall have all there is of Oswald J. Smith."

When God has all there is of us, we're safe in His keeping and useful for His cause, even when we find ourselves in Hog's Hollow.[32]

∞

Plagues and deaths around me fly;
Till He pleases, I cannot die.

May 17

The LORD is my portion; I have promised to keep Your words.
*I have sought Your favor with **all** my heart.*

Psalm 119:57–58

How would you fill in this blank: The Lord is my _____.
Various characters in the Bible answered that question in different ways:

- Moses said, "The LORD is my *strength* and my *song.* . . . The LORD is my *banner*" (Exod. 15:2, 17:15).
- The psalmist said, "The LORD is my *refuge*" (Ps. 94:22).
- Isaiah said, "God is my *salvation*" (Isa. 12:2).
- Jeremiah wrote, "The LORD is my *portion*" (Lam. 3:24).
- The writer of Hebrews said, "The Lord is my *helper*" (Heb. 13:6).
- David said, "The LORD is my *rock,* my *fortress,* and my *deliverer,* my *God,* my *mountain* where I seek refuge, my *shield* and the *horn of my salvation,* my *stronghold*" (Ps. 18:2).
- And we all say, "The LORD is my *shepherd*" (Ps. 23:1).

The old-time Christians had a phrase for all this. When we seek Him with all our hearts, Jesus becomes our "all-in-all." He fills all our lives, meets all our needs, and claims all our affections.

> Jesus only, Jesus ever,
> Jesus all in all we sing,
> Savior, Sanctifier, and Healer,
> Glorious Lord and coming King.
>
> —*A. B. Simpson*

> Only believe, and thou shalt see
> That Christ is all in all to thee.
>
> —*John S. B. Monsell*

May 18

*[His] eyes are on **all** the ways*
of the sons of men
in order to give to each person
according to his ways.

Jeremiah 32:19

Our ways are scrutinized by God, and our smallest deeds are rewarded in due time. I have a small book of ministerial anecdotes from the 1700s. One story involves Rev. John Brown of Haddington, Scotland, who was orphaned early in life. Being a bright child, he taught himself Greek. One day he visited an Edinburgh bookstore for a Greek New Testament.

The proprietor was surprised to find an impoverished child looking for such a book. Pulling one from the shelf, he said, "If you can read it, you shall have it for nothing." The boy read a page, translating it with reasonable ease, and received the book.

Twenty years later, he entered the shop again. "Sir," he said, "I believe I am your debtor. Do you recollect that about twenty years ago a poor boy came in and got a Greek Testament from you and did not pay for it?"

"Yes," said the owner, "I have often thought of it."

"I was that boy. My name is Brown and I live in Haddington."

"Mr. Brown," said the bookseller, "I am glad to see you and have often heard of you. We have here in our shop your books, your *Self-Interpreting Bible,* your *Church History,* etc., which have brought me in much money."

It may take years, even decades, but in due time all our deeds of kindness will come back to bless us.[33]

May 19

*His anointing teaches you about **all** things,*
and is true and is not a lie;
just as it has taught you, remain in Him.

1 John 2:27

One evening a couple of years ago I had a vivid dream. In this dream I was scheduled to speak at a chapel service, and I was late. The students were singing hymns waiting for me. As I arrived, I noticed that I'd forgotten my Bible; so on the way to the platform, I borrowed one from a professor in the audience. But when I got to the pulpit to open it, it suddenly became a moldy, stale loaf of bread.

The recollection of that dream bothered me. "Lord," I prayed, "may I never stand in your pulpit with a dry, moldy, stale message. May my messages from You always be fresh."

After thirty years in ministry, I know my messages will only be fresh if they cycle through my heart in a personal way. I have to sit at the feet of Jesus, listen to His Word, and get His food for my own soul. In the Upper Room, Jesus promised the Holy Spirit would tutor us in the Scriptures if we would prayerfully, quietly, diligently study them in His presence (John 14:26; 15:26; 16:13). Remembering those words, the apostle John later wrote that the Spirit's anointing "teaches you about all things."

It's amazing what fresh insights come as we pour over the Bible for our own nourishment. Only then will our words be fresh and hot, made from scratch and straight from the oven, ready to feed hungry hearts.

Privately, however,
He would explain everything to His own disciples.

Mark 4:34

May 20

The LORD opened the servant's eyes.
He looked and saw that the mountain was covered
*with horses and chariots of fire **all** around Elisha.*

2 Kings 6:17

One night long ago, Dr. H. L. Hastings of Boston was riding horseback through New Hampshire hills, carrying a large sum of money. The moon was bright, and at a particular place Hastings dismounted to fix his stirrups.

Years later Hastings was called to the deathbed of a man who asked if he remembered that instance. Hastings did. The dying man said, "I was lying in wait for you there, and intended to kill you and take that money I knew you had; but I saw another man standing on the other side of your horse, and I was afraid to kill two men, so I did not shoot."

"Why, there was no other man with me," exclaimed Hastings, but the man insisted there was. And only then did Hastings realize the extent of angelic protection all around him.

Something similar happened in 2 Kings 6. Elisha's servant awoke one morning to learn that Syrian forces had surrounded the city. Elisha, however, took the news calmly, knowing that the protecting angels of God also surrounded the city and were watching over him.

I believe angels are around us, too, though in ways we often can't see.

I do not know how to explain it; I cannot tell how it is;
but I believe angels have a great deal to do
with the business of this world. . . .
Angels have much more to do with us than we imagine.[34]

—*Charles H. Spurgeon*

May 21

This good news of the kingdom
*will be proclaimed in **all** the world*
*as a testimony to **all** nations.*
And then the end will come.

Matthew 24:14

In the early days of the Christian and Missionary Alliance, a reporter from the *New York Journal* called on Dr. A. B. Simpson for an interview. They discussed the hundreds of CMA missionaries who were spanning the globe, and the hundreds of thousands of dollars going for their support. Then the reporter abruptly asked, "Do you know when the Lord is coming back?"

"Yes," said Simpson, "and I will tell you if you will promise to print just what I say, references and all."

The reporter nodded and readied his pencil.

"Put this down," said Simpson. "'And this gospel of the kingdom shall be preached in all the world as a witness unto all nations; and then shall the end come'—Matthew 24:14. Have you written down the reference?"

"Yes, what more?"

"Nothing more."

"Do you mean to say you believe that when the gospel has been preached to all nations, Jesus will return?"

"Just that," said Simpson.

"Then," said the reporter, "I think I begin to see daylight."

"What do you think you see?"

"Why I see the motive in this movement."

"Then," said Dr. Simpson, "you see more than some of the doctors of divinity."[35]

May 22

May He incline our hearts toward Him
*to walk in **all** His ways*
and to keep His commands, ordinances, and judgments,
which He commanded our ancestors.

1 Kings 8:58

Some of my best memories are from Myrtle Beach, South Carolina, where my family vacationed when I was a boy. On one occasion, however, I recall my father being upset. I'd been playing in the ocean for an hour or so, and suddenly I saw my dad running through the waves toward me in concern and relief. He pointed to the shoreline and told me to look how far down the beach I was. I was a quarter of a mile from our umbrella, and my folks had lost sight of me. While I'd been body surfing and splashing around, the tide and undertow had carried me down the coastline and I hadn't realized it.

The same thing is happening to our children—and to our churches—today. The currents of our culture are carrying many of us far from our moorings, and it's so subtle we don't even realize it.

The prayer of 1 Kings 8:58 is a revival-prayer, offered by King Solomon as he dedicated the temple in Jerusalem to the Lord. I've made it into a prayer for my own children, having looked it up in several translations. The word *incline* is a powerful verb to use before God's throne: "Lord, incline my children toward You and incline their hearts toward Your Word. Lord, turn all our hearts to You, to walk in all Your ways and to keep Your commands."

Incline our hearts with godly fear
To seek Thy face, Thy Word revere.

—Benjamin Copeland, 1905

May 23

We also pray always for you that our God
would count you worthy of this calling,
*and fulfill **all** the good pleasure of His goodness.*
2 Thessalonians 1:11 (NKJV)

Our society is pleasure-crazed, with vacation advertisements offering "unlimited pleasure," chewing gum designed to double our pleasure, and ads for products enticing us with a thousand suggestive renditions of the word *pleasure*.

It might come as a surprise, then, to discover that God is the inventor of pleasure, the source of pleasure, the secret of pleasure, and that at His right hand are pleasures forevermore (Ps. 16:11).

The ability to enjoy life to its fullest depends on having our souls rightly calibrated. The herb of pleasure has spiritual roots, and only when our hearts are aligned with the Almighty can we appreciate the abundant life. Thus Saint Paul advised us to trust in the living God "who gives us richly all things to enjoy" (1 Tim. 6:17). When our primary blessing is Jesus, we can truly enjoy His secondary blessings and fulfill all the good pleasure of His goodness.

The British pastor and hymnist Philip Doddridge came from a family with a coat of arms bearing the motto, "Whilst we live, let us live." Doddridge converted the motto to a little poem that expressed his philosophy on the matter, saying:

> "Live whilst you live," the epicure would say,
> "And seize the pleasures of the present day."
> "Live whilst you live," the sacred preacher cries,
> "And give to God each moment as it flies."
> Lord, in my views, let both united be;
> I live in pleasure whilst I live in Thee.

May 24

*The LORD is righteous in **all** His ways,*
*gracious in **all** His works.*
*The LORD is near to **all***
who call upon Him, . . . in truth. . . .
*The LORD preserves **all** who love Him,*
*but **all** the wicked He will destroy. . . .*
*And **all** flesh shall bless His holy name.*

Psalm 145:17–21 (NKJV)

In my files is a clipping of a man and his son who hiked up a rugged mountainside to an imposing peak with a magnificent panorama. Gazing in all directions, the dad said, "Jordan, this is a picture of God. His love is as big as all this; it extends as far as we can see or imagine."

"Wow," said the boy, drinking it in, "and to think we're right in the middle of it."

Psalm 145 shows us we're right in the middle of God's love. He is great and greatly to be praised (v. 3). His greatness is unsearchable (v. 3), and we should declare His greatness (v. 6). He is great in mercy, and His compassions are over all His works (vv. 8–9). He upholds all who fall and raises all who are bowed down (v. 14). He provides our needs (v. 16). He is righteous in all His ways and gracious in all His works. He is near to all who call upon Him, and He preserves all who love Him (vv. 17–20).

Reading Psalm 145 is like climbing above the tree line and taking in the breathtaking view of God's compassion, love, and tender mercies—and finding ourselves right in the middle of it all.

May 25

I will make known the LORD's faithful love
and the LORD's praiseworthy acts,
*because of **all** the LORD has done for us—*
even the many good things He has done.

Isaiah 63:7

Isaiah 63:7 talks about all the Lord does for us—all the good things He has done—"based on His compassions and the abundance of His faithful love."

He has promised good for His people (Num. 10:29), and He has promised to work all things for the good of those who love Him (Rom. 8:28). Joseph said to the brothers who had kidnapped and sold him into slavery, "You planned evil against me; God planned it for good" (Gen. 50:20).

Cathy Crawford serves the Lord as a missionary in Europe. She's been diagnosed with multiple sclerosis. Since my wife battles the same disease, I was eager to compare notes when I visited her and her colleagues in France. Cathy told me that some time ago while home on furlough, she found it difficult to drive from church to church. Her retired father offered to be her driver. Mr. Crawford was an unsaved man, and Cathy had prayed for his salvation for many years. As he drove Cathy around, he found himself in church several times a week, listening to his daughter's presentation and often hearing sermons by the preacher of the various services Cathy was attending. You can guess the rest of the story. By the end of the summer, Mr. Crawford had opened his heart to the Lord Jesus Christ.

Whatever happens to you, ask the Lord to turn it for good—and rejoice in all He does for you.

May 26

*To Him be glory in the church
and in Christ Jesus
to **all** generations,
forever and ever. Amen.*

Ephesians 3:21

Legendary Boston pastor A. J. Gordon related an experience that happened early in his ministry. One night he dreamed that as he stepped into the pulpit, the door opened at the back of the church. An usher admitted a fine-looking gentleman, brought him down the aisle, and showed him a seat. Gordon couldn't help noticing him and wondering who he was. Afterward, Gordon sought out the usher and asked about the man. "Oh," came the reply, "didn't you know? That was Jesus Christ. He came into the service and asked that He might sit there. Didn't you realize that?"

Gordon awoke from his dream, but his ministry was changed from that hour. The next time he went into his pulpit, he seemed transformed, refreshed, renewed. He was aware that Jesus was there, in the pew, in the pulpit, and in that place.

Paul felt the same sense of mystery as he wrote Ephesians 3. The concept of the church had not been revealed to the Old Testament prophets, he said, nor was it predicted in their writings (v. 5). But in God's genius, He planned an era between our Lord's ascension and His return during which an entity known as the church, made up of both Jews and Gentiles, would take the gospel to the nations (vv. 6–8).

There's nothing like the church; and every time we gather, Christ is among us. To Him be glory in the church throughout all generations.

May 27

*I will thank the LORD with **all** my heart;*
*I will declare **all** Your wonderful works.*
I will rejoice and boast about You;
I will sing about Your name, Most High.

Psalm 9:1–2

Long ago when Dr. Matthew Hutton was bishop of Durham, he was traveling in the Yorkshire Dales of northern England. Coming to a particular spot, he dismounted, left his horse with an attendant, and retreated a short distance from the road. Kneeling at a particular spot, he prayed for a few minutes, then rose and resumed his journey.

His attendant asked him about it. Years earlier as a poor boy, the bishop explained, he'd been traveling over that same bleak mountain without shoes or socks, and his feet had become so cold he was miserable. Spotting a cow lying at a spot, young Matthew had run toward the animal, frightened him off, and warmed his feet where the cow had been resting. Now, said the bishop, whenever he passed that way, he took time to kneel in the spot and thank God for all the subsequent blessings he had received.[36]

God gave us the capacity of memory, and as we go through life we encounter many sights, sounds, and smells that bring back recollections of bygone days. The psalmist said, "I will thank the LORD with *all* my heart; I will declare all Your wonderful works."

Every memory can become fodder for thanksgiving as we praise God for how He has blessed or delivered or taught us His lessons. The temperature of our spiritual health is measured on the thermometer of thanksgiving.

May 28

*Their message has gone out
to **all** the earth.*

Psalm 19:4

God is the author of two books described in this psalm. The first half of Psalm 19 describes His Book of Creation (vv. 1–6); the last half describes His Book of Scripture (vv. 7–11). Psalm 19 then concludes with a fitting prayer of confession and commitment in verses 12–14.

The psalmist opens with a sweeping appreciation for God's handiwork in the skies. The sun, he said, is a runner who starts a sky-race every morning and completes it each evening. It's a star 93 million miles away, composed of hydrogen and helium, a literal fireball of remarkable energy generated by nuclear fusion reactions, producing 10 million megatons of energy per second. Its temperature is about 10,000 degrees on the surface and approximately 25 million degrees at its center. If it were a little larger, its gravity would pull us into it and we'd burn up; a little smaller and we'd drift off into deadly coldness. If it were a little hotter, we'd be consumed; a little colder and we'd freeze. If it were a little brighter, we'd be blinded; a little dimmer and our world would be perpetually dimmed.

In every way, the sun perfectly matches Earth, making our planet the only known spot in the universe for human life. There's no locale or person on Earth where the sun doesn't shine. God's creation is accessible to all, telling everyone of God's majesty and declaring His glory.

May 29

*David was in a difficult position
because the troops talked about stoning him,
for they were **all** very bitter. . . .
But David found strength
in the LORD his God.*

1 Samuel 30:6

This verse describes a spiritual technique of utmost importance for difficult times. In this passage, all David's men were ready to kill him. Morale was gone, anger was high, and David was utterly distraught. But he knew how to encourage himself in the Lord.

Several years ago, facing a difficult time, I drew a line down the center of the pages of my notebook. On the left side of the line, I listed all the negative emotions I was feeling—discouragement, disappointment, depression, anger, fatigue. I described each attitude as best I could, so my column extended several pages.

Then I started back at the top of the first page and found Bible verses that corresponded to my listed emotions. Beside *depression,* for example, I wrote "Rejoice in the Lord always. I will say it again: Rejoice!" (Phil. 4:4).

When I had filled both columns, I knelt and showed the Lord my pages, explaining to Him that I was on the left side of the page but needed to get into the right column. In the days that followed, I memorized some of the verses God had given me, and in so doing strengthened myself in the Lord.

Are you in a difficult position? There are many techniques for doing it—we all need to learn what works for us—but the key to encouragement is learning how to strengthen ourselves in the Lord as needed.

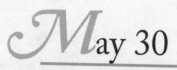# May 30

*But Jesus looked at them and said, "With men this is impossible, but with God **all** things are possible."*

Matthew 19:26

Jesus spoke these words matter-of-factly, declaring a truth of which He had no doubt—that in the realm of God's will, there are no impossibilities. He can do whatever He wants, whenever He wants, for whomever He wants, as He wants; and He can intervene in our lives as He sees fit. He can answer prayer, perform miracles, resolve difficulties, reverse death itself, work all things for good, and reign unrivaled in both time and eternity.

This isn't a randomly mentioned truth in the Bible. It pervades Scripture.

Then the word of the LORD came to Jeremiah: "Look, I am the LORD, the God of all flesh. Is anything too difficult for Me?" . . . Is anything impossible for the LORD? . . . With men it is impossible, but not with God, because all things are possible with God. . . . Father! All things are possible for You. . . . Therefore He is always able . . . , able to do above and beyond all that we ask or think . . . , able to make every grace overflow to you, . . . able to protect you from stumbling . . . . What is impossible with men is possible with God. . . . Mary asked the angel, "How can this be . . . ?" The angel replied . . . : "Nothing will be impossible with God."

Ah, Lord GOD! You Yourself made the heavens and earth by Your great power and with Your outstretched arm. Nothing is too difficult for You!

This is easy in the LORD's sight.[37]

May 31

*He is to read from it **all** the days of his life,*
so that he may learn to fear the LORD his God,
*to observe **all** the words of this instruction,*
and to do these statutes.

Deuteronomy 17:19

In this passage, Moses gave instructions to the future kings of Israel, telling them that when a man was chosen and installed on the throne, he was to write out a copy of the Scripture and keep it with him, reading from it all the days of his life and obeying it carefully.

Learn to read the Bible each day, and learn to read it aloud in private, in your devotions. The psalmist said, "With my lips I proclaim all the judgments from Your mouth" (Ps. 119:13).

The oral reading of God's Word, both in public and private, is almost a lost art. But when we read something aloud, it triples its impact on us. We're not only getting the information through the eye-gate; it's coming through the mouth, then it flies around our heads and enters through the ear-gate. We see it, speak it, and hear it all at once.

The old Puritan Baptist, Octavious Winslow, said 150 years ago: "This precious Word of God has made clear many a perplexity, has illumined many a dark road, has cheered many a lonesome way, has soothed many a deep sorrow, has guided and upheld many a faltering step, and has crowned with victory many a feat of arms in the great battle with Satan, the world, and sin."

June 1

*For just as in Adam **all** die,*
*so also in Christ **all** will be made alive.*

1 Corinthians 15:22

Dr. Bob Hill was a dear friend and a member of my staff at the Donelson Fellowship. He was seventy-two years old, had his degree in gerontology from Oxford, and had longevity in his genes. We assumed he'd live to be a hundred years old.

When his mother passed away at age ninety-three, Bob drove to St. Louis to help conduct the funeral, and he opened the service with these words: "We want to welcome everyone to this memorial service for our mother. This is not a time for grieving but a time for celebration!"

Then Bob slumped to the floor and died of a massive cerebral hemorrhage.

I miss Bob terribly, but I often think of the incredible poignancy of his last words: "This is not a time for grieving, but a time for celebration!"

First Corinthians 15 is the "Resurrection Chapter" of the Bible. Apparently some of the Corinthians had questions about the Resurrection, and Paul tackled them in this glorious chapter. He began by reviewing the historical facts of Christ's resurrection. Then he suggested that the bodily resurrection of Jesus provides the *proof, power,* and *pattern* for our own resurrections.

As in Adam all die, so in Christ all will be made alive, "in a moment, in the twinkling of an eye, at the last trumpet" (v. 52).

Don't worry about dying, and don't over-grieve over loved ones in heaven. Christ arose, and all is well. It isn't a day for grieving, but celebration.

# June 2

Only goodness and faithful love will pursue me
***all** the days of my life.*

Psalm 23:6

The end of Psalm 23 sums up its message, that goodness and mercy follows us throughout life and into eternity. The old divines called them God's two sheepdogs that constantly circle, herd, tend, and protect us every day. Taken altogether, Psalm 23 promises:

- *God's Peace in Life's Meadows:* "The Lord is my shepherd; there is nothing I lack. He lets me lie down in green pastures; He leads me beside the quiet waters. He renews my life."
- *His Plan for Life's Pathways:* "He leads me along the right paths for His name's sake."
- *His Presence in Life's Valleys:* "Even when I go through the darkest valley, I fear no danger, for You are with me; Your rod and Your staff—they comfort me." (Here the pronoun changes to the first person: In verses 1–3, it's "*He* leads . . . *He* restores." In verses 4–6, it's "*You* are with me; *Your* rod and *Your* staff.")
- *His Provision on Life's Tableland:* "You prepare a table before me in the presence of my enemies; You anoint my head with oil; my cup overflows."
- *His Promises for Life's Journey:* "Only goodness and faithful love will pursue me all the days of my life, and I will dwell in the house of the LORD as long as I live."

Goodness and mercy all my life shall surely follow me;
And in God's house forevermore my dwelling place shall be.

—*The Scottish Psalter*

June 3

The Jews demanded of him,
"What miraculous sign can you show us
to prove your authority to do all this?"

John 2:18 (NIV)

While teaching in Sweden, I was approached by a German student named Benjamin who told me that at age eighteen or so he had struggled with doubt. His Christian friends sometimes said things like, "The Lord told me this" and "The Lord showed me that . . . ." But Benjamin didn't know of anything the Lord had ever told him or showed him, and he struggled with doubt. One day he earnestly cried to the Lord, saying, "God, if you are real, if all this is true, please speak to me. Please give me a sign."

He said nothing of this to anyone; but shortly afterward, his father came to him and said, "Benjamin, isn't it wonderful to have faith in Christ! You know, some people are always asking God for signs, but the only sign we need is the cross of Jesus Christ that has already been given, and it is the book He has already provided for us, the Bible. Everything we need is there."

Benjamin realized that God had just given him a sign that his faith shouldn't be propped up by signs but anchored in the cross of Christ and grounded in the Word of God.

Sometimes when we're overwhelmed with problems, we'd like a sign or an audible message from the Lord. But everything we need has already been given in the cross of Christ and in the Word of God. It's a matter of faith.

June 4

The righteous rejoice in the LORD
and take refuge in Him;
***all** the upright in heart offer praise.*

Psalm 64:10

Praise comes naturally to the upright in heart, for they know what it means to rejoice in the Lord. A couple of years ago as I read Philippians 4:4 ("Rejoice in the Lord always"), it dawned on me that Paul wasn't coining a phrase; he was simply repeating Old Testament advice. Doing a little research, I found that the words "Rejoice in the Lord" occur about a dozen times in the Old Testament. The first person identified with them was Hannah, who said, "My heart rejoices in the LORD . . . . There is no one besides You!" (1 Sam. 2:1–2).

Referring to King Jehoshaphat, 2 Chronicles 17:6 says, "His mind rejoiced in the Lord's ways."

The Psalms talk four times about rejoicing in the Lord; Isaiah uses the phrase twice, Zechariah once, and Habakkuk has the most profound testimony of all. He says that even if the fig trees blight, the olives fail, the economy crashes, and all goes wrong, yet he can still rejoice in the Lord (Hab. 3:16–19).

In these Old Testament passages, the primary Hebrew word used for rejoice is *simhah,* which has as its root meaning "to shine, to be bright." So the biblical phrase "Rejoice in the Lord" could well be translated "Brighten up in the Lord always; and again I say brighten up!"

We may not be able to rejoice in our circumstances, but we can rejoice in the Lord and brighten up in God our Savior. All the upright in heart offer praise.

June 5

Peter answered and said to Him,
*"See, we have left **all** and followed You."*
Matthew 19:27 (NKJV)

David Livingstone was one of the most famous men on earth when he disappeared in darkest Africa. After months without word from him, the *New York Herald* sent its overseas correspondent, Henry Stanley, to search for him. When Stanley asked how much the paper was willing to invest, he was told to spend whatever it took, but FIND LIVINGSTONE. He did find Livingstone and greeted him with the famous words "Dr. Livingstone, I presume."

Sometime later, pressing further into Africa, Stanley wrote a letter that included "King M'tesa of Uganda has been asking about the white man's God. . . . Oh that some practical missionary would come here."

Stanley entrusted the letter to a French soldier, Colonel Linant de Ballefonds, but the colonel was slain at the Nile. English soldiers discovered his body shortly afterward, and while burying him they pulled off his long boots and found Stanley's letter inside, stained with the dead man's blood. The letter was forwarded to the English general in Egypt, who sent it to a newspaper in London.

On December 12, 1875, while traveling in Berlin, Alexander Mackay picked up a copy of the *Edinburgh Daily Review,* and as he read the letter a thrill shot through his heart. He knew he was the man. God instantly called him to Uganda, and Mackay left all, followed the call, never looked back, and spent fourteen years evangelizing Uganda before dying of malarial fever.

We need heroes today more than ever who will leave all and follow Him.[38]

June 6

READING: LUKE 5:1–11

"Master," Simon replied,
*"we've worked hard **all** night long and caught nothing!*
But at Your word, I'll let down the nets."

Luke 5:5

After a futile evening in his boat, Peter was skeptical but obedient when Jesus told him to lower his nets for a catch. The nets suddenly filled to the breaking point. "Don't be afraid," said Jesus (with a smile, I like to think). "From now on you will be catching people."

Sometimes we toil through the night with little to show for it, but in the end Jesus will bless our efforts and fill our nets. William Carey labored seven years in India before baptizing his first soul. Someone once observed that while the number of actual conversions directly attributable to Carey is quite small, the number indirectly attributable to him is innumerable.

America's first missionary, Adoniram Judson, labored seven years in Burma before seeing a convert. Robert Morrison, the founder of Protestant missions in China, labored seven years before his first convert. Mr. and Mrs. Henry Nott toiled for twenty-two years in Tahiti before baptizing their first convert on May 16, 1819.

Allen Gardiner traveled repeatedly to South America to evangelize the islands of Patagonia and Tierra del Fuego. He died of starvation without seeing a single soul saved, but the South American Missionary Society he founded has been saving souls for more than 150 years.

We're doing more good than we know, but we'll only see the full results when we get to heaven. So we work by faith, lower the nets in obedience, and trust God for the catch.

June 7

*Therefore, just as sin entered the world
through one man, and death through sin,
in this way death spread to **all** men,
because **all** sinned.*

Romans 5:12

I read of a man walking a beach when he found a magic lantern. Picking it up, he remembered the fairy tale of his childhood and gave it the obligatory rub. To his surprise, a genie appeared in a flash of smoke and offered to obey the man's any wish. Thinking quickly, the man asked for a copy of the newspaper dated one year in advance. Instantly the newspaper was in his hand, and he turned to the stock market report. Knowing the stock listings a year in advance would guarantee him unlimited wealth. But after pouring over the business section, he turned the page and was surprised to see his own name staring back at him—in the obituaries.

The Bible teaches that God created us to be eternal beings—we have eternity in our hearts (Eccles. 3:11). But from the days of Adam and Eve, we've sinned against God and fallen short of His glory (Rom. 3:23). Sin separates us from God, for God is altogether pure and perfect; and being separated from God means death. Fame, glamour, wealth, status, and pleasure all evaporate in a moment, and without Christ all our relationships end in inevitable separation and ultimate despair.

That's why Jesus came. That's why He died in our stead.

∞

Lord Jesus, I believe You died and rose again for me. I receive the gift of eternal life by faith. Help me live for You from this day forward.

June 8

My mouth will tell
about Your righteousness
*and Your salvation **all** day long,*
though I cannot sum them up.

Psalm 71:15

In her book *Ethel Waters: Finally Home,* Juliann DeKorte tells of caring for the ailing gospel singer and of sitting by her bed and reading Psalm 71 to her. The heading under the chapter in Ethel's Bible was "A Prayer for Old Age." It was of everlasting comfort during her final illness, but according to Mrs. DeKorte, Ethel had discovered this psalm long before.

"Well, honey, it goes way back," Ethel once explained. "It was one of the lowest points of my life. I was lonely, desperate, and bitter from wrongs committed against me—a long string of them, too painful to mention. One night I sat alone in my hotel room, feeling terribly sorry for myself. I was discouraged and fearful, and my heart was breaking, while off in the distance I heard people laughing and having fun at a party.

"In desperation I turned to a Bible sitting on the table—this was before I committed my life to Jesus. I cried out to God to help me, and I opened the Bible at random to the Psalms. My eyes fell on Psalm 71. It was a turning point in my life! The words fit my situation exactly and they spoke to my heart and comforted me in such a wonderful way that I felt they were written especially for me. Ever since then, it has been *my* psalm."[39]

It can be our psalm too.

June 9

All the words of my mouth are righteous . . . .
All of them are clear to the perceptive,
and right to those who discover knowledge.

Proverbs 8:8–9

Miss Wisdom is the speaker in Proverbs 8. She calls out from the hillsides over life's thoroughfares and at the city gates, exhorting us to hear, to think, and to fear the Lord. "All the words of my mouth are righteous," she says. "All of them are clear . . . . Accept my instruction instead of silver, and knowledge rather than pure gold."

When we study the wise words of Scripture, it makes us wise in all areas of life. In my files is a clipping about the famous African-American scientist George Washington Carver. He was born into slavery in Missouri and kidnapped and sold to another owner in Arkansas. At age ten, he gave his heart to Jesus Christ, and he grew up to become a world-famous botanical researcher, specializing in the peanut.

Once before a Senate committee, he was asked, "Dr. Carver, how did you learn these things?"

"From an old Book," he replied.

"What book?"

"The Bible."

"Does the Bible talk about the peanut?" asked the chairman.

"No, Mr. Senator," Carver said, "but it tells about the God who made the peanut. I asked Him to show me what to do with the peanut, and He did."

Our heavenly Father, being omniscient, possesses total knowledge, and He reflected His knowledge in every page of His Book, which, like a wise woman, calls on us to learn about all of life from her.

June 10

You are a holy people belonging to the LORD your God.
The LORD your God has chosen you to be His own possession
out of all the peoples on the face of the earth.

Deuteronomy 7:6

In his wonderful little book *Christian Living*, F. B. Meyer points out that God has chosen us as His own possessions of all the peoples on earth, and we belong to Christ in *four* ways.

1. First, we are His by *Creation*, for Psalm 100:3 says, "He made us, and we are His."
2. We are His by *Purchase*. "You are not your own," says 1 Corinthians 6:19–20, "for you were bought at a price."
3. We are also His by *Deed of Gift*, for the Father has given us to Christ. Jesus prayed in John 17, "They were Yours, You gave them to Me . . . . Father, I desire those You have given Me to be with Me where I am" (vv. 6, 24).
4. Finally, we are His by *Conquest*, for we have freely surrendered ourselves to Him as Lord and Master, gladly making Him our rightful King and Ruler.

"Ah," wrote Meyer, "it is impossible to escape the fact that in the thought of God, we are the absolute property of Jesus Christ, our Lord: and that He thinks much of that fact."

He has dearly bought my soul;
Lord, accept, and claim the whole!
To Thy will I all resign,
Now, no more my own, but Thine.

—*John Newton, 1779*

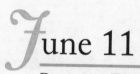

June 11

*With **all** humility and gentleness, with patience.*
Ephesians 4:2

In his little volume *Christian Living*, Dr. F. B. Meyer wrote that full surrender to Christ isn't enough; we must also appropriate Him by faith. Christian living isn't just imitating Jesus; He must live His supernatural life through us by His Holy Spirit.

A little group of earnest men were gathered not long ago around a fire, eagerly discussing the methods of a holy life, and reciting their own experiences of the grace of God. One had recently entered upon the gladness of a life of entire consecration, and spoke fervently of his new-found joys. But when his story was told, a venerable clergyman expressed his disappointment at an experience which was only negative, and told so little of the positive side of the appropriation of Christ.

Years before, when engaged in a gathering of unruly and noisy children, he had been suddenly driven to claim from the Savior the gift of His own gentle patience with the words, "Thy patience, Lord!" And instantly so divine a calm filled his spirit that he realized that he had made a great discovery. And from that moment he had retained the extremes of his brief petition, inserting between them the graces, the lack of which was hurrying him to sin.

In a moment of weakness, "Thy strength, Lord!" or in moments of conscious strength, "Thy humility, Lord!" When assailed by unholy suggestions, "Thy purity, Lord!" or when passing through deep waters of trial, "Thy resignation and restfulness, Lord!"

What is this but a living example of the appropriation of Christ!

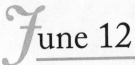# June 12

The skies will yield their dew. I will give the remnant
*of this people **all** these things as an inheritance.*

Zechariah 8:12

Perhaps you've never thought of it, but dew is one of God's ingenious inventions. On clear nights, water vapor in the air gathers around each blade of grass, condenses, and forms billions of water droplets to refresh plants and to water the earth. When the Lord wanted to impress Job with His creative energy, He asked him, "Who fathered the drops of dew?" (Job 38:28). The promise of dew represented a free blessing that would come upon the Jewish people every day (Gen. 27:28; Deut. 33:13, 28). In Palestine it rains little from April to October, and if it weren't for the dew, all vegetation would perish during summer months. The rabbis taught that rainfall in Israel was dependant on the moral behavior of the people, and times of drought were considered disciplinary actions to correct disobedience. The dew, however, wasn't dependant on moral behavior. It was just a free, constant blessing from God.

The morning dew is God's way of telling us that every morning is a fresh start, and every day is sprinkled with His compassions.

Thou art our Morning and our Sun,
Our work is glad, in Thee begun;
Our foot worn path is fresh with dew,
For Thou createst all things new.

—*Lucy Larcom, 1892*

Let my teaching fall like rain and my word settle like dew.

Deuteronomy 32:2

June 13

*I will give You thanks with **all** my heart;*
I will sing Your praise.

Psalm 138:1

A cholera epidemic swept through Asia following World War I, but experts noticed that it did not penetrate China. The reason? The cholera germ cannot survive boiling water, and the Chinese drink tea almost exclusively.

When the epidemic threatened to wrack the Philippines, doctors ordered people to boil their water. But the cholera continued. Investigating, the doctors found that the population had misunderstood their instructions. Every day Filipinos would boil some water and take two or three teaspoons like medicine, then drink their ordinary water as usual!

That's the way we sometimes think of thanksgiving. We take a spoonful every now and then, sometimes at meals or annually on Thanksgiving Day. But a thankful spirit isn't a matter of spoonfuls; it's a constant state of mind.

Remember the story of the ten lepers Jesus healed? Afterward only one returned to thank Him. I have a theory the one leper had a life-orientation toward thanksgiving; and had you seen him the day before his healing, you would have found a thankful person. He would have told you, "Well, it's true I have this disease, but praise God anyway. Let me tell you about all these blessings . . . ." Having a mind-set of thanksgiving already, it was only natural for him to thank Christ for healing him.[40]

The other nine were grouches before they were healed and unthankful afterward.

One in ten! Are the same proportions true today? Ninety percent of us negative? Let's give thanks with all our hearts, not by the spoonful.

June 14

Those who make [idols] are just like them,
*as are **all** who trust in them.*

Psalm 115:8

Psalm 115 warns against serving an idol, which is anything we love more than we love Jesus. We're internally wired to become like whatever we're worshipping, but the Lord wants to spare us the tragic fate of worshipping the wrong gods.

The *Gideon* magazine recently told of a man named Guille Zapata who received a New Testament at an engineering university and after reading it received Christ as his Lord. He was hired as a petroleum engineer in a small town in Peru known for being superstitious and occultish.

Guille put up a sign offering free Bible lessons, but no one seemed interested. One day, the rain came in torrents and the water seeped into Guille's house. As he frantically tried to bail out the water, a filthy dog suddenly darted through the open door. The animal grabbed Guille's New Testament, turned on his paws, and dashed back out into the rain.

Throwing down his buckets, Guille raced after the dog but was unable to retrieve his Bible. The dog, meanwhile, ran into the shack of a well-known witch doctor named Leoncio Guerrero.

Two weeks later, this man knocked on Guille's door to enroll in Bible lessons. Leoncio explained that one evening an ugly dog had brought a little blue book into his house. He opened it to Psalm 115 and started reading about the sin of idolatry and realized something was missing from his life. Guille was able to lead him to faith in Christ.[41]

June 15

> *All* were judged . . . .
> *This is the second death, the lake of fire.*
> **Revelation 20:13–14**

"There are some ministers who never mention anything about hell," Charles Spurgeon once noted. "I heard of a minister who once said to his congregation, 'If you do not love the Lord Jesus Christ, you will be sent to that place which it is not polite to mention.' He ought not to have been allowed to preach again, I am sure, if he could not use plain words. Now, if I saw that house on fire over there, do you think I would stand and say, 'I believe the operation of combustion is proceeding yonder'? No; I would call out, 'Fire! Fire!' and then everybody would know what I meant."

C. S. Lewis once heard a young minister bring his sermon to a close by saying, "And now, my friends, if you do not believe these truths, there may be for you grave eschatological consequences." Afterward, Lewis asked the man, "Did you mean that they would be in danger of hell?"

"Why, yes," he answered, to which Lewis replied, "Then why in the world didn't you say so?"

Evangelist Vance Havner pastored a country church early in his ministry. Once when he preached about hell, an old farmer upbraided him, saying he should preach instead about the meek and lowly Jesus.

"That's where I got my information about hell," said Havner.

Jesus died to save us from God's righteous wrath, and how shall we escape if we neglect such a great salvation?

June 16

*Trust in Him at **all** times, you people;*
pour out your hearts before Him.
God is our refuge.

Psalm 62:8

There's a sermon in every line of this verse. Notice the first word of each phrase:

- *Trust.* The writer of Psalm 62 was evidently beset by difficult people (vv. 3–4, 9–10). My own reaction to troubling people swings from anxiety to anger, but the psalmist advises faith. We must trust our Lord at all times. Right now, create a mental image of some person causing you anxiety, and, like the giant crane swinging around a load of care, transfer that individual to God's hands. Make this a regular habit. Do it *at all times*, advises David.

- *Pour.* Three times in the Psalms, prayer is likened to *pouring* our hearts out to God (Pss. 42:4, 62:8, 142:2). This is a picturesque word comparing our hearts to pails filled with water. We're brimming with weariness, weakness, and worry. Take this bucket and pour it out like water before the Throne of Grace. Do it verbally, do it audibly, do it in prayer. Then proceed to the third word:

- *God.* Thomas à Kempis once described God as "unflappable, unfluffable, indecipherable, indescribable."[42] Here in Psalm 62, David described Him in even better terms, presenting God as our Rock, our Salvation, our Defense, our Expectation, our Glory, the Rock of our Strength, and our Refuge.

Visualize Him enclosing you within the boundaries of His grace, for there's no safer place to be. Trust Him at all times and pour out your heart to Him, for He is your refuge.

June 17

All the promises of God in Him are Yes,
and in Him Amen,
to the glory of God through us.

2 Corinthians 1:20 (NKJV)

God's promises are sprinkled throughout Scripture like jewels on velvet—more than seven thousand of them—for when we're impoverished, sad, confused, guilty, at wit's end, and at death's door. There are even promises in the Bible *about* God's promises. Here in 2 Corinthians, Paul was defending himself against critics who accused him of being fickle. The apostle said, in effect, "I am not *yes* one day and *no* the next. I try to keep my promises. But it's God who is perfectly consistent. He is always *Yes!*"

Then he wrote this wonderful promise about promises: "For no matter how many promises God has made, they are 'Yes' in Christ. And so through him the 'Amen' is spoken by us to the glory of God" (NIV).

In other words, "Lord, have You promised to never leave us or forsake us, and to work all things for our good?" He says, "Yes!" and we say, "Amen—then so be it!"

"Have You promised to hear and answer our prayers? To watch over us and deliver us from evil? To give peace and strength as needed?" He says, "Yes!" and we say, "Amen!"

"Have you promised us an eternal home in heaven, where sin, sickness, and sorrow can never intrude?" He says, "Yes!" and we say, "Amen!"

That equation works for all God's promises. For no matter how many promises God has made, they are all *Yes* in Christ, and through us is the *Amen* for the glory of God.

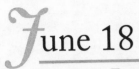

June 18

> *Then God spoke **all** these words.*
> **Exodus 20:1**

With that, the Bible gives us the greatest "to do" list in all of human history—the Ten Commandments (Exod. 20:1–17). In this little record, the eternal God summarizes His sinless character, codifies it into a list of requirements for mankind, and provides us a basis for spiritual life and ethical conduct.

The Ten Commandments have fallen out of favor in our society, and great legal wars are being fought over its right to adorn courtroom walls and public spaces. But think how horrible it would be to live in a world in which the Ten Commandments didn't exist. One Holocaust survivor, reflecting on the unspeakable horrors of Auschwitz, said that it was like a world in which all the Ten Commandments were reversed.

If you'd like an easy way to memorize the Ten Commandments (or to help your children do so), here's an old British school poem that will help:

> Above all else love God alone;
> Bow down to neither wood or stone.
> God's name refuse to take in vain;
> The Sabbath rest with care maintain.
> Respect your parents all your days;
> Hold sacred human life always.
> Be loyal to your chosen mate;
> Steal nothing, neither small nor great.
> Report, with truth, your neighbor's deed;
> And rid your mind of selfish greed.

June 19

*In that day when He comes to be glorified by His saints
and to be admired by **all** those who have believed.*

2 Thessalonians 1:10

Some people actually dread the thought of heaven. They think it'll be boring, a never-ending church service, but the Bible teaches no such thing. We'll have physical bodies on a New Earth doing normal human things, including:

- *Service.* Revelation 22:3 says His servants will serve Him. We'll have meaningful jobs and purposeful activity.
- *Responsibility.* We'll hold positions of authority and responsibility, perhaps over groups or cities on the New Earth (Luke 19:17, Rev. 22:5).
- *Fellowship.* In Luke 16:19–31, the former beggar, Lazarus, was step-in-step with Abraham, enjoying his fellowship. We're told in 1 Thessalonians 4:13–18 not to despair over loved ones who pass away. We'll enjoy their company throughout eternity.
- *Learning and Travel.* God is omniscient and omnipresent, but we'll always have the capacity to learn and to go.
- *Eating and Drinking.* We'll feast with the patriarchs (Matt. 8:11) and with Jesus Himself, who ate and drank after the resurrection (Acts 10:41).
- *Rest.* (Rev. 14:13).
- *Worship.* We'll gather around the Throne in downtown New Jerusalem and Crystal River (Rev. 22:1–3). Our Lord will be glorified by us and admired by all who have believed.

What's not to look forward to?

June 20

All authority has been given to Me . . . .
Go therefore and make disciples of all the nations,
baptizing them in the name of the Father
and of the Son and of the Holy Spirit,
teaching them to observe all things
that I have commanded you;
and lo, I am with you always.

Matthew 28:18–20 (NKJV)

The Great Commission begins with Christ's *power. All authority* is His, and we operate by His authorization. Whether it's sharing our testimony, teaching a lesson, evangelizing on campus, or entering a restricted-access country, it's His command; we simply obey.

The Great Commission fulfills His *purpose,* to make disciples in *all nations.* Every country is a potential mission field, and every person a potential disciple.

It outlines Christ's *plan,* to reach the world by evangelizing and baptizing and by teaching these new believers to obey *all* He has spoken.

The Commission reassures us of Christ's *presence.* He is with us at *all* times as we go, even to the end of the age. I tell my congregation that I want to lie down at night knowing that someone somewhere in the world is getting up to continue the work, sent out by our church, supported by our dollars, and sustained by our prayers. I want to be a part of a cause bigger than I am, something wider than the walls of my church and vaster than the boundaries of my town. I want to be involved in a harvest of global proportions at the twilight of history.

That only happens if we are Great Commission Christians in a Great Commission church.

# June 21

> *Be strong and courageous,*
> ***all** you who put your hope in the* LORD.
>
> **Psalm 31:24**

Lord, I've waited so long and prayed so hard for the answer to my need, but it hasn't come and You haven't heard. I'm weary with waiting.

> *Be strong, and let your heart take courage,*
> *all you who wait for the Lord!*
>
> **Psalm 31:24 (ESV)**

I'm trying to be strong, but I'm discouraged. There's no sign of breakthrough, and I feel like giving up.

> *Wait for the* LORD; *be courageous and let your heart be strong.*
> *Wait for the* LORD. . . . *Take delight in the* LORD, *and He will give*
> *you your heart's desires. Commit your way to the* LORD;
> *trust in Him, and He will act . . . . Be silent before the* LORD
> *and wait expectantly for Him.*
>
> **Psalm 27:14; 37:4–5, 7**

How long, Lord?

> *Though it delays, wait for it,*
> *since it will certainly come and not be late.*
>
> **Habakkuk 2:3**

But, Lord . . . !

> *Calm down and be quiet. Don't be afraid or fainthearted . . . .*
> *If you do not stand firm in your faith,*
> *then you will not stand at all.*
>
> **Isaiah 7:4, 9**

Lord, I believe! Help Thou mine unbelief.

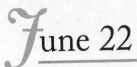

June 22

*Job was the greatest man
among **all** the people of the east.*

Job 1:3

When you think of the biblical character of Job, you probably think of trials, troubles, and tribulations. But there's another side to Job; his life teaches dual lessons, showing us:

1. *Integrity comes from trusting God in prosperity.* Job is called the greatest man in the east and a man of perfect integrity. In chapter 29, Job described how he treated people with respect, helped the unfortunate, and cared for all he met. In chapter 31, he spoke of his sexual integrity. He made a covenant with his eyes not to look lustfully at women, and he made a personal commitment never to covet another man's wife. In verses 24–28, he testified that despite his vast wealth he had never placed any confidence in gold or trusted in money. His integrity came from trusting God in prosperity.

2. *Maturity comes from trusting God in adversity.* Despite his spotless character, Job encountered a catastrophic series of disasters, and we see a different man at the end of the book than at the beginning. Some lessons are learned only in the furnace, and by the final chapter of Job we have a man with a message that has spanned the ages: We trust God when things go well—that's integrity. We trust Him when things go badly—that's maturity.

*Take the prophets who spoke in the Lord's name
as an example of suffering and patience. . . . You have heard of Job's
endurance and have seen the outcome from the Lord.*

James 5:10–11

June 23

Blessed be the God and Father of our Lord Jesus Christ . . .
*the God of **all** comfort.*

2 Corinthians 1:3

Praise God for pressure! That unexpected concept opens the book of 2 Corinthians, the most autobiographical of Paul's writings. Here the great apostle confessed he wasn't an iron man but was subject to "struggles on the outside, fears inside" (7:5). "We were completely overwhelmed—beyond our strength—so that we even despaired of life" (1:8). Yet in his opening paragraph (2 Cor. 1:3–11) he listed seven reasons for praising God for pressure:

1. Pressure lets us discover God as the God of all comfort (1:3). He has just the right medicine for every affliction.
2. Pressure allows us to comfort others with the comfort we ourselves receive (v. 4). The Lord believes in recycling; He wants us to pass along His comfort to others.
3. Pressure develops in us the quality of endurance (v. 6).
4. Pressure matures our faith (v. 9). Paul said that his afflictions came to teach him not to "trust in ourselves, but in God who raises the dead."
5. Pressure cultivates in us the quality of hope (v. 10).
6. Pressure spurs us on to prayer and to recruit the prayers of others (v. 11a).
7. Pressure leads to thanksgiving as God intervenes and answers (v. 11b).

Be not dismayed, but go to Him who is the God of all comfort,
who comforteth all those that are bowed down,
and He will give you a word which shall heal your wounds,
and breathe peace into your spirit.

—Charles H. Spurgeon

June 24

A woman suffering from bleeding for 12 years,
*who had spent **all** she had on doctors*
yet could not be healed by any, approached from behind
and touched the tassel of His robe.
Instantly her bleeding stopped.

Luke 8:43–44

Eusebius, the church historian born just a hundred years after the apostles, provides fascinating details about the woman who touched Christ's robe in Luke 8. According to his sources, she was a Gentile from Caesarea Philippi, a town in the far north of Israel at the headwaters of the Jordan River. After she returned home from being healed, her grateful townspeople commissioned a statue of Jesus—the only lifelike image of Jesus ever crafted.

Eusebius wrote, "Her house was pointed out in the city, and amazing memorials of the Savior's benefit of her were still there. On a high stone [base] at the gates of her home stood a bronze statue of a woman on bent knee, stretching out her hands . . . . Opposite to this was another of the same material, a standing figure of a man clothed in a handsome double cloak and reaching his hand out to the woman . . . . This statue, they said, resembled the features of Jesus and was still extant in my own time: I saw it with my own eyes when I stayed in the city."[43]

We don't know what became of the statue; but we can still touch the hem of His garment.

∽

He turned with "Daughter, be of good comfort,
Thy faith hath made thee whole!"
And peace that passeth all understanding
With gladness filled her soul.

—*George F. Root*

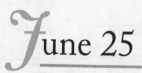

June 25

All the days of the oppressed are miserable,
but a cheerful heart has a continual feast.
Proverbs 15:15

As I write these words, I'm warding off an anxiety attack by doing things I usually do when spiraling into worry—journaling, praying, calling my girls, listening to my wife, trying to sing, getting busy, and attempting to rechannel my thoughts. I'm so glad I found this verse tonight. Proverbs 15:15 warns that we can succumb to the oppression of anxiety and depression, or we can choose to be cheerful with the unsinkable joy of Jesus.

*Anxiety in a man's heart weighs it down, but a good word **cheers** it up.*
Proverbs 12:25
And is there a better word than God's Word?

*A **cheerful** heart is good medicine.*
Proverbs 17:22 (NIV)
And there are no co-pays or pharmacy costs!

*You give him blessings forever; You **cheer** him up with joy in Your presence.*
Psalm 21:6

*God loves a **cheerful** giver.*
2 Corinthians 9:7
Cheerful giving is an outgrowth of cheerful living.

*Be of good **cheer**; your sins are forgiven you. Be of good **cheer** . . .*
*your faith has made you well. Be of good **cheer**! It is I; do not be*
*afraid. . . . Be of good **cheer**, I have overcome the world.*
Matthew 9:2, 22; 14:27; John 16:33 (NKJV)

When doubts filled my mind,
*your comfort gave me renewed hope and **cheer**.*
Psalm 94:19 (NLT)

June 26

Honest balances and scales are the LORD's;
all *the weights in the bag are His concern.*
Proverbs 16:11

In his book *Shadows on the Wall*, published in 1922, the inimitable writer F. W. Boreham tells of a small store in his childhood town. It was run by Mrs. Blundell, a soft-spoken soul with stooped shoulders and spectacles; and it wasn't for ordinary groceries. It was a sort of convenience store. Very often, young Boreham was sent with a short list of things needed, and he relished those trips. "I liked being alone with Mrs. Blundell," he wrote. "On the table by the window she had a bowl of goldfish . . . . Then there was Mrs. Blundell's big tortoise-shell cat: I liked to hear her tell of the mice he had caught in the storeroom at the back."

One day, to his delight, he was allowed behind the counter. There he saw lots of things he later forgot and one thing he never forgot. On the back of the scales where sugar and flour and cocoa were weighed was a little sign, with the words of Proverbs 11:1—

A false balance is abomination to the Lord
but a just weight is His delight.

"There," said Mrs. Blundell, "you can keep saying that to yourself all the way home, can't you? Never mind the long words in the first part, but remember: 'A just weight is His delight.'"

"Don't forget," she called as he turned the corner for home. And he never did:

All the weights in the bag are His concern. . . .
A just weight is His delight.[44]

June 27

*I will gather **all** the nations*
against Jerusalem for battle.
Zechariah 14:2

Each time I've been in Israel, I've visited Armageddon, a word that literally means *The Mount of Megiddo.* Today the ancient site of Megiddo lies in ruins, but from the hilltop is one of the most fantastic views on earth—a vast, fertile, fruited valley, twenty-four miles long and fourteen miles wide. It's the only level ground in Israel where a million soldiers could muster.

This is where Joshua fought in Joshua 12, where Deborah battled the Moabites in Judges 5, where Gideon and his three hundred men beat the Midianites in Judges 7, and where Saul was defeated in 1 Samuel 31. This is where King Josiah was slain in 2 Chronicles 35.

In a book entitled *The Battle of Megiddo,* the Egyptologist Harold Nelson asserts that the battle of Megiddo on May 15, 1479 BC, is the first battle in history in which we can study in any detail the military maneuvers and tactics. It forms the starting point for military science. More recently, this is where General Allenby defeated the Turkish Army and liberated Palestine in 1918, paving the way for the reestablishment of the state of Israel in 1948.

I believe the Bible teaches that the armies of the world will gather here on the Last Day, spilling over the landscape in all directions. "I will gather all the nations against Jerusalem for battle. . . . Then the Lord will go out to fight against those nations . . . . On that day His feet will stand on the Mount of Olives" (vv. 2–4).

And Jesus will win.

June 28

READING: 2 CHRONICLES 16:7–10

*The Lord searches **all** the earth for people*
who have given themselves completely to Him.
2 Chronicles 16:9 (NCV)

About one hundred years ago, a college student in Wales named Evan Roberts felt a passion for revival. Returning to his village of Loughor, he preached to seventeen people, and his sermon had four points:

- Confess any known sin to God and put away any wrong done to others.
- Put away any doubtful habit.
- Obey the Holy Spirit promptly.
- Confess faith in Christ openly.

By the end of the week, sixty people had been converted, igniting a revival. Within three months one hundred thousand converts were added to the churches in Wales. It spread around the globe and the years of 1905 and 1906 became revival years in this world. I remember hearing my Uncle Walter tell of the revival that spread through the Tennessee Mountains in 1905. My grandfather was a circuit preacher in the hills, and everywhere he went, scores of people were converted. When you drive through the mountains today, there are little churches in every hollow and up every road, and many of them were started in the 1905 revival.

If you read missionary biographies from Asia during these years, you'll read of the 1905 revival—the last worldwide revival that this earth has experienced. And almost everyone traces it back to a college student named Evan Roberts.

The Lord is looking for such a person today, for the eyes of the Lord range throughout the earth to show Himself strong for those whose hearts are completely His.

June 29

*My God will supply **all** your needs*
according to His riches in glory in Christ Jesus.
Philippians 4:19

Not just some of your needs, but all of them. And not just your financial needs, but your emotional, spiritual, and relational needs as well.

In the old book *The Kneeling Christian*, the author tells of an incident that occurred in the life of Hannah Whitall Smith. A friend who occasionally paid her visits of two or three days was a great trial. Her personality and demands grated on Hannah's nerves. The time came when this critical woman was planning a visit for a whole week, and Hannah felt that nothing but a night of prayer could fortify her for this great testing. She prepared a plate of cookies and went to her bedroom, ready to spend the night fortifying her soul for this impending visit. No sooner had she knelt by her bed than Philippians 4:19 flashed to mind: "God will supply all your needs according to His riches in glory in Christ Jesus."

"When I realized that," said Hannah Smith, "I gave Him thanks and praised Him for His goodness. Then I jumped into bed and slept the night through. My guest arrived the next day, and I quite enjoyed her visit."[45]

PS: This promise is connected to our generosity in giving to missionaries. In the verses that precede it, the apostle Paul thanked the Philippians for providing for his support. They had provided for the missionary's needs, so God promised that He would meet all their needs as well.

June 30

Now may the God of hope fill you
*with **all** joy and peace in believing,*
so that you may overflow with hope
by the power of the Holy Spirit.

Romans 15:13

The word *benediction* describes prayers that end a worship service or conclude an event. The actual term comes from a Latin word meaning "to speak well," and it's a pronouncement of blessing. There are many benedictions in the Bible, but this is one of the best because it tells how the Lord wants to invigorate our attitude. The God of hope longs to fill us with all joy and all peace as we rely on Him, resulting in an overflowing life.

Recently I read of a woman in Central America who was afflicted with amoebas. The doctor prescribed medicine and hormones and told her to quit nursing her eleven-month-old baby. She did so, but while taking the treatments she discovered she was pregnant again. The doctor advised an abortion because the medicine and hormones are contraindicated during pregnancy. They could cause serious birth defects.

Going home greatly troubled, this woman picked up her devotional book, and Romans 15:13 jumped off the page at her with divine reassurance. She said, in effect, "Lord, you knew all about my illness, my medications, and my pregnancy. You've given me new life, and I'm going to rejoice in it whether there are birth defects or not." She was so bolstered by that verse that she carried the baby to term. "Twenty-four years have passed since that time," she wrote. "Today our daughter, Rebecca, is a short-term missionary."[46]

July 1

All we like sheep have gone astray;
we have turned, every one, to his own way;
and the LORD has laid on Him the iniquity of us all.

Isaiah 53:6 (NKJV)

This verse begins and ends with an *all*. "*All* we like sheep . . . the Lord has laid on Him the iniquity of us *all*." The preceding verse explains how it happened: "He was wounded for our transgressions, He was bruised for our iniquities; the chastisement for our peace was upon Him, and by His stripes we are healed."

These words have led thousands to Christ, including the great Reformer, John Calvin. According to G. A. Neilson in his book *Twelve Reformation Heroes*, Calvin was born in France in 1509, and was eight years old when Martin Luther posted his Ninety-five Theses on the cathedral door in Wittenberg, Germany, sparking the Protestant Reformation. As time went by, John traveled to Paris for university studies. News of the Reformation hit Paris with an excitement hard to describe, and Calvin's cousin, Olivetan, was passionate about spreading the news. He frequently spoke to John of being justified by grace through faith.

At first, Calvin resented his cousin's witness, but when he saw a Protestant being burned at the stake, he was convicted. "These men have a peace which I do not possess," he said. "I will take my cousin's advice and search the Bible."

As he studied Isaiah 53, he realized he was a sheep who had strayed far from the Good Shepherd. He humbly acknowledged that God had laid on Christ all his iniquities, and he trusted Christ alone for eternal salvation.

The "alls" of Isaiah 53:6 reach you and me too: "All we like sheep have gone astray." He bore the iniquity of us all.

# July 2

*May you be strengthened with **all** power,*
*according to His glorious might, for **all** endurance and patience,*
with joy giving thanks to the Father.
Colossians 1:11–12

My favorite devotional books are the older ones, like Mrs. Cowman's *Streams in the Desert* and *Springs in the Valley*. Dr. A. B. Simpson has a volume with 365 installments entitled *Days of Heaven on Earth*. My favorite devotionalist is Mary W. Tileston, who put together the classic *Daily Strength for Daily Needs*. Just the title of the latter volume encourages me. That's what we need—daily strength for daily needs. Our energy gives out, and we often discover that our physical strength is interwoven with our emotional and spiritual enthusiasm. The distresses, disappointments, and conflicts of life sap us both inwardly and outwardly. Here's what the Lord has to say about daily strength for daily needs:

> May you be strengthened with all power, according to His glorious might, . . . strengthened with power through His Spirit in the inner man . . . . May . . . your strength last as long as you live.
>
> Be strengthened by the Lord and by His vast strength. . . .
>
> Take hold of My strength. . . .
>
> The LORD is my strength and my shield; my heart trusts in Him, and I am helped. Therefore my heart rejoices, and I praise Him with my song. . . .
>
> The LORD gives His people strength; the LORD blesses His people with peace. . . .
>
> Youths may faint and grow weary, and young men stumble and fall, but those who trust in the LORD will renew their strength.[47]

# July 3

*To the pure, **all** things are pure, but to those
who are corrupted and do not believe, nothing is pure.
In fact, both their minds and consciences are corrupted.*

Titus 1:15 (NIV)

Recently my friend's elderly mother passed away. Her attitude had grown critical and sour over the years, but Keith had done his best to care for her. Some time after her funeral, he dreamed of her. He walked into the dining room and there she was, sitting in her regular spot waiting for supper. "Mom," Keith exclaimed, "You're here. You're back."

She nodded. He said, "You passed away and went to heaven." She nodded again.

"Mom, if you've been to heaven and seen it, you know what it's like. You can tell us all about heaven."

She said curtly, "I didn't like it!"

Titus 1:15 gives us an inviolable principle—we see life through the eyeglasses of our own attitudes. The way we perceive things has more to do with perspective than with circumstances. Through the years I've had people at my church—every pastor has this crowd—who are easily disgruntled about one thing or another. I tell my staff that if someone has a genuine concern in any one area, we need to take it seriously. But if someone is unhappy about everything, the real problem is likely in that person's heart.

To the joyful, all things are joyful. To the unhappy, all things are disagreeable. To the angry, all things are provoking. To the patient, all things are patient.

The fault-finder will find faults even in paradise.

—*Henry David Thoreau*[48]

July 4

I proclaimed a fast . . .
that we might humble ourselves before our God
and ask Him for a safe journey for us, our children,
*and **all** our possessions. . . . I was ashamed to ask the king*
for infantry and cavalry to protect us . . . since we had told him,
*"The hand of our God is gracious to **all** who seek Him,*
*but His great anger is against **all** who abandon Him."*

Ezra 8:21–23

Here's a Fourth of July devotion.

In 1604, John Robinson became pastor of St. Andrew's Church in Norwich; but King James was making it impossible for Puritans to serve in the English church, so Robinson became a Separatist and fled to the Netherlands, where he pastored a congregation in Leyden. The church, located near the university, numbered several hundred—many of them exiled English Separatists.

In 1619, the congregation made a decision to relocate—not across the street or even across the city, but around the world—to America. The first wave of thirty-five members, led by one of the church's elders, William Brewster, packed their bags and prepared to sail on the *Mayflower*. The church gathered for a solemn service to send them off, and Robinson selected Ezra 8:21 as the text for his sermon. It was Ezra's prayer, beseeching God for safety and blessing on a group of His children who were pilgrims heading for a new home.

Robinson intended to lead the next wave of pilgrims, but he became ill on February 22, 1625, and died a few days later. But he's famous today as the Pilgrim's Pastor whose sermon from Ezra 8 launched the Christians who launched a nation.

July 5

Turn away from your idols;
*turn your faces away from **all** your abominations.*

Ezekiel 14:6

I have a friend named Ted Seymore who grew up just south of London. As a teenager, he became a ruffian and hung out with a street gang. In 1953, when Ted was fifteen, an evangelist named Charles Kingston came to town for a tent revival. One night Ted and his buddies decided to break up the meeting by sneaking around the outside of the tent, pulling up the tent stakes, and causing the tent to collapse on those inside. They were caught in the act, but instead of being marched to the police station, the boys were ushered into the meeting.

There were two big signs hanging inside the tent. One was John 3:16: "For God so loved the world that He gave His only begotten Son, that whosoever believeth in Him should not perish, but have everlasting life." The other was Romans 6:23: "For the wages of sin is death, but the gift of God is eternal life through Jesus Christ our Lord."

Those verses became the theme of Kingston's sermon; and as he preached repentance, young Ted realized God loved him, that Jesus had died for him, and that he was facing an eternal decision about accepting or rejecting the Savior. That night changed his life forever, and Ted Seymour has since devoted a half century to serving God in remarkable ways around the world.

When we meet Christ, we've come to that place in life when we turn from our idols and from all our abominations and find our meaning in Him.

July 6

Offer yourselves to God,
*and **all** the parts of yourselves to God*
as weapons for righteousness.
For sin will not rule over you.

Romans 6:13–14

We live in the most addiction-prone society in history. The mobility of our population, the breakup of the family, the loss of spiritual roots, the entertainment orientation of our culture, the accessibility and increasing potency of addictive agents—these create a social atmosphere as suited for addictions as the jungle is for snakes.

I have a theory about addictions. I believe our sadistic enemy, the devil, aims to destroy us, and he gets pleasure in manipulating us into destroying ourselves. If there is anything he loves more than the destruction of human life, it is the self-destruction of a life.

According to Romans 6, addiction isn't just a personality dysfunction or hang-up. It's spiritual slavery and bondage to sin. Lasting recovery is based on the freedom of Christ.

> For we know that our old self was crucified with Him in order that sin's dominion over the body may be abolished, so that we may no longer be enslaved to sin . . . . Consider yourselves dead to sin, but alive to God in Christ Jesus. Therefore do not let sin reign in your mortal body, so that you obey its desires. And do not offer any parts of it to sin as weapons for unrighteousness. But as those who are alive from the dead, offer yourselves to God, and all the parts of yourselves as weapons for righteousness. For sin will not rule over you, because you are not under law but under grace. (6:6, 11–14)

July 7

All *the Israelites complained.*
Numbers 14:2

There was a boy named Grumble Tone who ran away to sea.
"I'm sick of things on land," he said, "as sick as I can be;
A life upon the bounding wave will suit a lad like me!"

The seething ocean billows failed to stimulate his mirth,
For he did not like the vessel, nor the dizzy, rolling berth,
And he thought the sea was almost as unpleasant as the earth.

He wandered into foreign lands, he saw each wondrous sight,
But nothing that he heard or saw seemed just exactly right;
And so he journeyed on and on, still seeking for delight.

He talked with kings and ladies fair; he dined in courts, they say,
But always found the people dull, and longed to get away
To search for that mysterious land where he would like to stay.

He wandered over all the world, his hair grew white as snow;
He reached that final bourne[49] at last where all of us must go,
But never found the land he sought. The reason you would know?

The reason was that north or south, where'er his steps were bent,
On land or sea, in court or hall, he found but discontent;
For he took his disposition with him everywhere he went.

—*Ella Wheeler Wilcox, 1892*

July 8

Not wanting any to perish,
*but **all** to come to repentance.*

2 Peter 3:9

Once when Bishop John Sharp (1643–1714) was traveling by horseback, he was accosted by a good-looking young man who held a pistol in trembling hands. Sharp asked him to lower his weapon and, with evident concern, inquired as to his condition. "Sir, sir," cried the young man, "No words—'tis not the time—your money instantly!"

"You see I am an old man," replied the bishop, "and my life is of very little consequence; yours seems far otherwise. I am named Sharp, and am archbishop of York. . . . Tell me what money you want, and who you are, and I will not injure you, but prove a friend."

He then gave the young man some money and asked him to call on him at his house later in the week. The fellow actually showed up, and Sharp counseled him earnestly.

Nothing more transpired for a year and a half, then one day the young man knocked on the bishop's door again.

"My lord," he said, sinking to his knees, "you cannot have forgotten the circumstances at such a time and place; gratitude will never suffer them to be obliterated from my mind. . . . You have saved me in body and soul! You have saved a dear and much-loved wife, and a little brood of children, whom I regarded dearer than my life. Here are the fifty pounds, but never shall I find language to testify what I feel."[50]

When we reflect the burden of Jesus Christ—who wants all to come to repentance—every encounter becomes an opportunity.

July 9

*I will praise the LORD at **all** times.*

Psalm 34:1

As a young man, Dr. J. Edwin Orr traveled the globe for Christ, and the Lord seemed to perform miracle after miracle in provision and guidance. On one occasion, however, things went badly. Dr. Orr arrived in Madrid with little money, and he was reduced to eating a penny roll and sleeping on a park bench. In the middle of the night, he awoke. Feeling for his wallet, he realized he'd been robbed. At 3:00 a.m., he again awoke to find himself surrounded by thugs who wanted to pick the rest of his pockets. Orr threatened to create a scene that would bring the police, and the men slunk off into the night. But the evangelist was disheartened and very downcast.

Presently a thought flashed to mind. He told himself, in effect, "I've traveled around the world without provision or purse, and nothing like this has ever happened before. I should be grateful God has allowed it to happen now to show me how wonderfully He has cared for me in the past."

A spirit of thanksgiving rose in his heart, and he lay back on his stone bench and slept till morning. Awakening, he sang a hymn and told himself the tide had turned. Later that day, he met some people who opened their homes and churches to him, affording him a fruitful revival ministry during his stay in that city.[51]

The tide always turns when we praise the Lord at all times!

> The Lord I will at all times bless,
> My mouth His praises shall express;
> In Him shall all my boasting be,
> While all the meek rejoice with me.

> *—The 1912 Psalter*

July 10

*The love of money is a root of **all** kinds of evil,*
and by craving it, some have wandered away from the faith
and pierced themselves with many pains.

1 Timothy 6:10

Some time ago CNN carried a report of a man who was rushed to the emergency room of Cholet General Hospital in western France, suffering severe stomach pain. Doctors were awed when they viewed the X-rays. This man had an enormous opaque mass in his stomach that weighed twelve pounds—as much as a bowling ball—and was so heavy it forced his stomach down between his hips. The man, who had a history of major psychiatric illness, had swallowed 350 coins (worth $650), along with assorted pieces of jewelry. The doctors opened his stomach and removed the contents, but he died twelve days later from complications.[52]

As grotesque as it sounds, the same illness is afflicting millions of people in another sense. A craving for money can clog our souls with tragic results; it's the root of all kinds of evils.

The Bible presents a balanced view of worldly wealth. We're told to be wise stewards and to enjoy what God gives us, remembering that He's the one who gives the power to gain wealth and that we should plan wisely for future needs. On the other hand, we should give generously, tithe faithfully, and realize that money is a temporary tool God entrusts to us for our welfare, for the sake of others, and for the extending of His kingdom. It's dangerous when craved, and deadly when swallowed.

Solomon got more hurt by his wealth
than he got good by his wisdom.

—*Puritan Thomas Brooks*

July 11

Command your children to carefully follow
***all** the words of this law.*

Deuteronomy 32:46

The theme of Deuteronomy is obedience to God's law, and its constant refrain is—teach your children, pass down to them the importance of carefully following all God's commands. We should talk about God's Word when we get up in the morning and when we go to bed at night, when we sit at home and when we travel the road, and we're to write the words of the Bible on our walls and gateposts (Deut. 6:6–9).

I once heard of a woman whose sons all went off to sea. They became sailors, and the woman was unhappy about it. One day she realized that on the living room wall was a picture of a majestic clipper ship, flags waving, ploughing the waves. No one had ever said anything about that painting, but now she realized its unspoken influence in the home.

A mother in our church told me that her young son had a problem with night fears. He was unable to sleep at night because of various worries. One Sunday in a message I quoted the verse that says God has not given us a spirit of fear, but of love, of power, and of a sound mind (1 Tim. 1:7). That impressed the boy, and his mother purchased some glow-in-the-dark paint, and inscribed that verse along the top of the wall opposite his bed so he could see it as he fell asleep at night. It did the trick.

If we do nothing else as parents, let's help our children follow all the wonderful words of God's Book.

July 12

> *There is not Greek and Jew,*
> *circumcision and uncircumcision,*
> *barbarian, Scythian, slave and free;*
> *but Christ is **all** and in **all**.*
>
> **Colossians 3:11**

An old nursery rhyme says:

> I do not like thee, Dr. Fell,
> The reason why I cannot tell;
> but this one thing I know full well:
> I do not like thee, Dr. Fell.

There are some people we just don't like; but simply put, that's prejudice. And it's forbidden in this passage. The original Greek here is very strong: In Christ there is *no such thing as* artificial distinctions among God's people. We're brothers and sisters in Christ regardless of nationality (Greek or Jew), religious background (circumcision or uncircumcision), cultural distinctions (barbarian or Scythian), or economic status (slave or free). Christ is *all*—He is everything to us, and He is *in all* of us.

We're to live as prescribed here in Colossians 3, putting off our old attitudes of pride and prejudice (v. 10), putting on new attitudes of love and acceptance (v. 11), and treating others with compassion, kindness, gentleness, and patience (v. 12). We accept and forgive each other (v. 13), displaying a love that promotes unity (v. 14). We should have such peaceful personalities that our homes and churches are harmonious places (v. 15). So we can say:

> I've learned to like thee, Dr. Fell,
> The reason why I'm glad to tell:
> The Christ who saved my soul from hell
> Now helps me love thee, Dr. Fell.

July 13

Don't be afraid of what they fear;
do not dread those things.
*But remember that the LORD **All**-Powerful is holy.*
He is the one you should fear.

Isaiah 8:12–13 (NCV)

In the days when Christian stalwarts in Scotland were being hunted down like dogs, agents of the infamous Thomas Bell burst into the home of William Veitch and dragged him away as his children watched in horror. William's wife, Marion, calmed the youngsters by reading Scripture to them, but she herself was inwardly alarmed. As soon as she could, Marion arranged to visit her husband in prison; but the trip, occurring in the dead of winter, was treacherous and bitterly cold.

After visiting William, Marion went to a friend's house and broke down in tears, knowing her husband was facing execution for his faith in Christ. She opened her Bible and read the words of Isaiah 8:12–13. Those verses imparted instant strength as she realized that in fearing the All-Powerful God, she had nothing else to fear.

Meanwhile, as he planned Veitch's execution, Thomas Bell visited a friend and lingered late into the night over alcohol. His friend tried to dissuade him from returning home that evening, for it was deadly cold, but Bell insisted on leaving. He was never seen alive again, and his body was found two days later standing up to his arms in a block of ice in the river.

William Veitch was soon freed, and the restored couple worked side by side for the next forty years, reminding their parishioners that when we fear the Lord, we dispense with all other fears.[53]

July 14

*We will not **all** fall asleep,*
*but we will **all** be changed.*

1 Corinthians 15:51

I've seen this verse posted at the entrance to church nurseries, evoking a smile. But how much greater our joy at its true meaning: Most Christians throughout history will have fallen asleep before our Lord returns. But there will be a generation of Christians—it may be us!—remaining on earth to greet our Lord when He comes. Regardless of whether we're dead-and-buried or alive-and-kicking, we'll all be changed.

Our mortal, perishable, aging, decaying bodies will undergo instant metamorphosis, as Jesus did at the moment of His resurrection. We'll become physically whole, eternally young and strong, immune from illness, incapable of dying—imperishable, incorruptible, and immortal.

This change will be sudden and instantaneous. Verse 52 says it will happen in a flash. The Greek term was *atomo*, from which we get the words *atom* and *atomic*. It conveys the idea of a tiny particle of matter of time that is indivisible, inseparable. In other words, this physical transformation will occur during a moment so quick it cannot be divided. It is instantaneous, an atomic moment, in the twinkling of an eye.

A parallel text, Philippians 3:21, says that Jesus will "transform the body of our humble condition into the likeness of His glorious body, by the power that enables Him to subject everything to Himself." The risen body of Jesus is the pattern, promise, and proof of our own resurrection.

Listen! I tell you a mystery. We will not all sleep, but we will all be changed!

July 15

*I rejoice in the way revealed by Your decrees
as much as in **all** riches.*

Psalm 119:14

After an accident left her a near-invalid at her mission station in Dohnavur, India, Amy Carmichael wrote messages each day to her co-workers. One of her communiqués said: "When reading your Bible have you not often noticed that some word has shone out and seemed to speak in a new, direct, clear way to you? It has been as though you had never read it before. You cannot explain the freshness, the life in it, the extraordinary way it has leapt to your eye—to your heart."[54]

I've frequently had such experiences when my heart was downcast. Even the most familiar passages of Scripture can take on new life as we read them day by day. Sometimes a verse or word will leap off the page as if catapulted by the Holy Spirit.

Other days the experience isn't so dramatic; it's more like eating a balanced meal and finding sustenance for the day. In either case, it's a rich experience.

The psalmist said that he rejoiced in God's word as much as in all riches. A single word from God can bring more joy than the total wealth of the world. Are you as excited about the sustaining power of God's Word as you are about the purchasing power of American dollars?

Money is temporary, and wealth eventually loses its luster. But the words of Scripture impart the affluence of His glorious inheritance in us and the incomparable prosperity of His grace.

July 16

*Praise Him, **all** His angels;*
*praise Him, **all** His hosts.*

Psalm 148:2

If all the angels were to praise God at once, how many would that be? Have you ever wondered about the number of angels? We don't have an exact census, but the Bible gives us several hints.

In Matthew 26:52–53, Jesus told Peter in the Garden of Gethsemane, "Put your sword back in place . . . . Do you think that I cannot call on my Father, and He will provide Me at once with more than 12 legions of angels?" A Roman legion numbered about six thousand soldiers, so Jesus claimed instant access to the protection of seventy-two thousand angelic soldiers, had He but asked.

Revelation 5:11 confirms that number, saying, "[I] heard the voice of many angels around the throne, and also of the living creatures, and of the elders. Their number was countless thousands, plus thousands of thousands." The Greek says literally, "numbering myriads of myriads and thousands of thousands."[55] The New Living Bible translates it as "thousands and millions of angels."

Hebrews 12:22 sums it up talking about "innumerable angels in festal gathering" (NRSV).

Angels as far as the eye can see and the mind can imagine. Think of the praise! Imagine being part of the celebration!

Angels holy,
high and lowly,
Sing the praises of the Lord!

—*A canticle from the Septuagint*

July 17

READING: EZEKIEL 3:10–15

*Son of man, listen carefully to **all** My words
that I speak to you and take them to heart.*

Ezekiel 3:10

Ruthless Babylonians had interred thirty-year-old Ezekiel in a refugee camp and he was embittered, but God gave him visions and words of hope. "Son of man," said the Lord, "listen carefully to all My words that I speak to you and take them to heart."

That's a vital practice for us all.

Isabel Fleece, wife of the former president of my alma mater, wrote a little book entitled *Not By Accident* following the death of her teenage son. Here's how she described the comfort of hearing from the Lord:

> [I learned] that the Word of God is an anchor to the soul, and to flee to it is to find strong consolation from God. As the hours dragged their weary way across the stillness of that first night, it seemed as if time had ceased, and we were held suspended in deep despair. No rest or sleep, no quietness or light—nothing but the deep, deep pain—nothing but that and God. As our senses began to take in what had happened, and we began to believe that Ned was gone, I closed my eyes and asked for help. And the great Lover of our souls, our blessed Savior who is Himself the Eternal Word, poured into my listening heart the sweetness of the Word of God, and I was quickened . . . . It was as though Jesus Himself drew near and spoke to me, for my mind poured over verse after verse.[56]

How wonderful to listen to all that God speaks to our hearts!

July 18

*In **all** things grow up into him who is the Head, that is, Christ.*
Ephesians 4:15 (NIV)

Eighteenth-century pastor and hymnwriter John Newton wrote many hymns that aren't as famous as his renowned "Amazing Grace." One of his most honest and unusual hymns tells of what happened when he prayed to grow up in Christ in all things:

> I asked the Lord that I might grow
> In faith, and love, and every grace;
> Might more of His salvation know,
> And seek, more earnestly, His face.
>
> 'Twas He who taught me thus to pray,
> And He, I trust, has answered prayer!
> But it has been in such a way,
> As almost drove me to despair.
>
> I hoped that in some favored hour,
> At once He'd answer my request;
> And by His love's constraining pow'r,
> Subdue my sins, and give me rest.
>
> Instead of this, He made me feel
> The hidden evils of my heart;
> And let the angry pow'rs of hell
> Assault my soul in every part.
>
> Lord, why is this, I trembling cried,
> Wilt thou pursue thy worm to death?
> "'Tis in this way," the Lord replied,
> "I answer prayer for grace and faith.
>
> These inward trials I employ,
> From self, and pride, to set thee free;
> And break thy schemes of earthly joy,
> That thou may'st find thy all in Me."

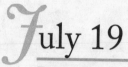

July 19

*My house will be called a house of prayer for **all** nations.*

Isaiah 56:7

I belong to a weekly Bible study that opens each session with prayer requests. The other day as we compiled our sick list and jotted down the needs of our missionaries, I wondered what the Lord would say if we asked Him for His prayer requests. Later as I researched the matter in the Bible, I found God asking us to pray for world leaders in 1 Timothy 2. We're told in Psalm 122:6 to pray for the peace of Jerusalem. And in Isaiah 56:7, the Lord describes His house as a "house of prayer for all nations."

There are 194 countries in the world (including Vatican City and Taiwan), and all of them need prayer; but how often do we mention any of them during our prayer times at church?

Katrina and I once attended Sunday night services at All Souls Church in London. That evening, a woman stood in the pulpit to lead the church in prayer. She prayed for the upcoming elections in various countries, for famine relief in others, for victims of a natural disaster in another, and for freedom for oppressed Christians in yet another part of the world. Her prayer literally covered the globe—and it made me ashamed that I haven't led more Pastoral Prayers like that in the church I pastor in Nashville.

Learn to pray globally, for God's house is a house of prayer for all nations.

> All the world for Jesus
> Let each one pray and give,
> Until remotest nations
> Shall look to Him and live.
>
> —*Grace W. Davis, 1894*

July 20

*Since **all** these things are to be destroyed in this way,*
it is clear what sort of people you should be
in holy conduct and godliness.

2 Peter 3:11

I love planet Earth. My favorite spot is atop Roan Mountain in eastern Tennessee, with its far-famed rhododendron gardens, grassy balds, and windswept crags. The Lord created Earth as a dazzling and perfectly designed "MySpace" for humanity. Placing Adam and Eve in the Garden of Eden, He told them to "dress and keep it"—to cultivate and care for it. He wants His natural creation to reflect His glory. Of all people on Earth, then, Christians should appreciate the beauty of this planet, marvel at God's creative genius, and care for what He has entrusted to our keeping.

All Christians are, therefore, ecologists.

But another point must be made. There's an inevitable day of ultimate global warming that cannot be avoided. "The present heavens and earth are held in store for fire . . . . The Day of the Lord will come like a thief; on that day the heavens will pass away with a loud noise, the elements will burn and be dissolved, and the earth and the works on it will be disclosed" (2 Pet. 3:7, 10).

Spiritual health depends on knowing what's temporary and what's eternal. God is preparing a new universe, a new earth, and a New Jerusalem (Rev. 21–22). Our passion should be cast in that direction. And Peter asks a most practical question: Since all these things must be dissolved in this way, what sort of people should we be?

The answer: We should be people of holy conduct and godliness.

July 21

And whatever you do,
whether in word or deed,
*do it **all** in the name of the Lord Jesus,*
giving thanks to God the Father through Him.

Colossians 3:17 (NIV)

This verse uses an interesting phrase: "in the name of the Lord Jesus." That means as though it were Him!

Yesterday I had a medical procedure requiring that I be put to sleep. The hospital wanted to know if I had a durable power of attorney, and they asked me who would make a decision in my name should a crisis arise. The person who acts in my name does so with full legal authority as though I myself were making the decision.

This verse tells us that whatever we say in life, we're to say it as though Christ were saying it. Whatever we do in life, we're to do it as though Christ were doing it. Whatever we do, whether in word or deed, we're to do it in the name of the Lord Jesus.

And we're to do it with thanksgiving.

That means we're to thank God for the opportunity of talking each day, and of doing so in His name. We're to be thankful for our work as we go through our daily deeds, for we're privileged to be continuing and carrying on His mission.

We're honored people, and even our smallest tasks have the touch of eternity on them. That's why six verses later we read another "whatever you do" verse that says: "Whatever you do, work at it with all your heart, as working for the Lord, not for men" (Col. 3:24 NIV).

July 22

Know the God of your father,
and serve Him with a loyal heart and with a willing mind;
*for the LORD searches **all** hearts*
*and understands **all** the intent of the thoughts.*

1 Chronicles 28:9 (NKJV)

The older devotional writers often talked about cultivating a "quiet mind," a mind that abides in Christ without fear, flurry, or fretting. Missionary Amy Carmichael wrote,

> Lord, Grant to me a quiet mind
> That trusting Thee, for Thou art kind,
> I may go on without a fear,
> For Thou, my Lord, are always near.

St. Francis de Sales counseled: "Never be in a hurry; do everything quietly and in a calm spirit. Do not lose your inward peace for anything whatsoever, even if your whole world seems upset. Commend all to God, and then lie still and be at rest in His bosom. Whatever happens, abide steadfast in a determination to cling simply to God . . . . Maintain a holy simplicity of mind, and do not smother yourself with a host of cares, wishes, or longings, under any pretext."[57]

And an anonymous poet of an earlier century said:

> I've many a cross to take up now,
>   and many left behind;
> But present troubles move me not,
>   nor shake my quiet mind.
> And what may be to-morrow's cross
>   I never seek to find;
> My Father says, "Leave that to me,
>   and keep a quiet mind."[58]

July 23

You still lack one thing:
sell all that you have and distribute it to the poor,
and you will have treasure in heaven.
Then come, follow Me.

Luke 18:22

Jesus wasn't telling everyone to sell all they have. This was His counsel to the rich young ruler, and for two reasons. First, the Lord pinpointed the young man's surrender point; his wealth had become his "god." Second, this encounter occurred days before the crucifixion, and the early Christians would soon be scrambling for their lives and scattered to the ends of the earth (Acts 8:1). Jesus knew this young man needed to be liberated from the shackles of his fortune.

For you or me, the "you-still-lack-one-thing" might be in a different area.

In the late 1700s, a revival swept through Finland, greatly stirring the heart of a young man named Paavo Ruotsalainen. He began reading the Bible with earnestness, along with Luther's Shorter Catechism and the writings of John Bunyan; but his heart longed for something deeper than he had hitherto experienced.

Ruotsalainen heard of a godly blacksmith named Jacob Hogman, two hundred kilometers away. Setting out to visit the blacksmith, he begged for food and lodging en route. Hogman saw him gladly and simply said to him: "One thing you lack and therewith you lack all else: the inner awareness of Christ."

Those words changed his heart forever, and Paavo Ruotsalainen went on to become a giant in Finish church history whose ministry ushered in a great period of revival and blessing.

What "one thing" is lacking in your devotion to Christ?

July 24

The seed cast in the weeds represents
the ones who hear the kingdom news but are overwhelmed
*with worries about **all** the things they have to do*
*and **all** the things they want to get.*
The stress strangles what they heard,
and nothing comes of it.

Mark 4:18–19 (MSG)

Today's *New York Post* has an article titled "Stress Mess in U.S." about a study by the American Psychological Association finding that 48 percent of Americans can't sleep at night because of stress. Seventy-five percent of Americans worry constantly about two things—money and work. Half of us are also stressed about paying our rent or mortgage. According to the report, stress and worry are taking a toll, leading us to fight with family members, drink, smoke, and gulp junk food like starving fools. It's leading to obesity, hypertension, heart disease, and cancer.[59]

In His parable of the sower, Jesus warned that too much stress can also damage us spiritually. When we're overwhelmed by all our tasks and desires, the stress strangles the Word in our hearts and hinders the crop. The biblical antidote is a simpler lifestyle, a deeper trust, and a daily walk with Christ. As the psalmist said, "As pressure and stress bear down on me, I find joy in Your commands" (Ps. 119:143 NLT). For starters, here's an old prayer that may help:

Drop Thy still dews of quietness,
Till all our strivings cease;
Take from our souls the strain and stress,
And let our ordered lives confess
The beauty of Thy peace.

—*John Greenleaf Whittier, 1872*

July 25

Instruct those who are rich in the present age
not to be arrogant or to set their hope
on the uncertainty of wealth, but on God,
*who richly provides us with **all** things to enjoy.*

1 Timothy 6:17

Years ago I invited British pastor Geoffrey King to preach at my church. Rev. King, now in heaven, ranks among the top expositors I've ever known, but he was eccentric. He dressed peculiarly, had odd views on hygiene, and constantly set me into spasms of laughter without meaning to. While in Nashville, he had two requests. He wanted to play all the organs in town and ride all the roller coasters.

One day I took him to Opryland theme park and, despite his age, he headed right to the big coaster. As we barreled down the first drop, he turned to me and shouted, "Rob, Rob, never grow up! Remember that God has given us richly all things to enjoy!"

It was my one and only sermon on a roller coaster, but I've never forgotten it.

This verse doesn't give us permission to wrongfully indulge our appetites, but it means that God has given a universe of blessings for our enjoyment and welfare. Happiness isn't found in things, but in Him who helps us enjoy all things.

Jesus wants us to enjoy life more abundantly. He surrounds us with goodness and mercy every day of our lives, and from the fullness of His grace we have all received one blessing after another (John 10:10, Ps. 23:6, John 1:16).

When we learn to enjoy God, we get all other joys to boot!

July 26

Look up and see: Who created these?
He brings out the starry host by number;
*He calls **all** of them by name.*

Isaiah 40:26

Isaiah 40, one of the Bible's greatest chapters, is addressed to homeless exiles in Babylonian refugee camps, people devastated by national and personal calamity. The message of this chapter is simple: "Say to the cities of Judah, 'Here is your God!'" (v. 9).

Your God measures the waters in the hollow of His hand (v. 12). If you make a little cup with your palm and think of the vast, rolling oceans that cover most of Earth's surface, they're no more than a spoonful of water in the hollow of God's hand.

He has marked off the heavens with the span (v. 12), which is the distance between your thumb and fifth finger. The universe with its vast uncharted reaches fits nicely, as it were, in the span of God's omnipotent hand.

The nations are a drop in a bucket to Him (v. 15). The next time you water your plants, turn the bucket upside down and shake out the last drops. They're equivalent to America, Russia, China, India, and all the nations of the world in God's sight.

And the stars! "Look up and see: who created these? He brings out the starry host by number; He calls them all by name" (v. 26).

The conclusion:

> Do you not know?
> Have you not heard?
> Yahweh is the everlasting God,
> the Creator of the whole earth.
> He never grows faint or weary;
> there is no limit to His understanding.
> He gives strength to the weary. (vv. 28–29)

July 27

Joash took it to heart to renovate the LORD's temple.
So he gathered the priests and Levites and said,
"Go out to the cities of Judah
*and collect money from **all** Israel*
to repair the temple of your God
as needed year by year, and do it quickly."

2 Chronicles 24:4–5

The Bible encourages us to give at least 10 percent of our income to the Lord, but the average Christian in America gives about 2 percent. Of every dollar God sends to us, we give just over two pennies back to Him.

When I look at those numbers, I feel like the great British preacher Charles Haddon Spurgeon, who once spoke before a group of people to raise money for his ministries. At the end of his talk, he took his hat and passed it around for the offering. No one put anything in it, and it came back to Spurgeon empty. The people wondered what the famous preacher would do next. Spurgeon simply bowed his head and prayed: "I thank You, O Lord, that at least these old skinflints have given me my hat back."

In 2 Chronicles 24, Joash expected all Israel to contribute toward needed renovations in the temple, and those who gave were blessed. The Lord still expects all His people to be faithful stewards today.

Earn all you can, save all you can,
and then give all you can. Never try to save out of God's cause;
such money will canker the rest. Giving to God is no loss;
it is putting your substance into the best bank.

—*Charles H. Spurgeon*[60]

July 28

All bitterness, anger and wrath, insult and slander
must be removed from you, along with *all* wickedness.
And be kind and compassionate to one another.

Ephesians 4:31–32

Let me open this devotional with the image of a clogged-up commode.

Suppose you go into a restroom to find a commode that's been used again and again without anyone having bothered to flush it. The drain is so clogged that the water has backed up, spilling the entire mess across the floor. That's a picture of a human heart that refuses to flush away anger, resentment, and bitterness. The unhealthy debris builds up and backs up until the person's life becomes toxic and repulsive, and then it spills into the lives of others.

True love overlooks the many small, daily offenses that are bound to occur. We sometimes rub each other the wrong way or get miffed at each other. But as we grow in the Lord Jesus, we learn to flush away small, daily offenses. Paul said about such offenses, "What does it matter?" (Phil. 1:18).

Peter said, "Above all, keep your love for one another at full strength, since love covers a multitude of sins" (1 Pet. 4:8).

Proverbs 12:16 is my favorite verse on this subject because it's so plainspoken: "A fool's displeasure is known at once, but whoever ignores an insult is sensible."

The grace of God is a plunger that can unclog the heart, clear the pipes, and convey the fresh waters of the Holy Spirit. Perhaps today the Lord will give you the blessing of overlooking an insult.

July 29

I sought the LORD, and He answered me
*and delivered me from **all** my fears.*

Psalm 34:4

When our children were little, one of our daughters was deathly afraid of the car wash. She thought our car was being attacked by giant instruments while we were trapped inside. Intense blasts of pelting water struck every side, creating a cacophony of confusion and sound. Strange balls of spinning terror fell from above and battered the car, while monster-like devices reached out and assailed the doors and windows. She screamed bloody murder.

As for myself, I wasn't a bit afraid because I knew that three minutes and forty-five seconds later I'd be leaving with a cleaner car.

Now that I'm older, I wonder if I'm not like my little girl—so afraid of things that pose no alarm whatsoever for my heavenly Father.

God is incapable of fear, for nothing can harm Him or alarm Him. When we're in His care, nothing can harm us either, unless He allows it for purposes we may not understand at the time. The writer of Psalm 34 wrote: "I sought the Lord, and He answered me and delivered me from all my fears. Those who look to Him are radiant with joy; their faces will never be ashamed. This poor man cried, and the Lord heard him and saved him from all his troubles. The angel of the Lord encamps around those who fear Him, and rescues them" (vv. 4–7).

If you're in God's car—in His care—you needn't fear the noise.

July 30

*Besides **all** this,*
it's the third day since these things happened.

Luke 24:21

On the first Easter, two bewildered souls, trudging back to their home in Emmaus, met a Stranger on the road. The risen Lord Himself drew alongside and walked with them, but somehow He disguised Himself and they didn't realize who He was. The two related what they knew about the events of the day, then said, "Besides all this, it's the third day . . . ," and they recalled Jesus' prediction to rise from the dead.

The Stranger began talking to them, giving them an amazing overview of Old Testament prophecies. He showed them from every part of the Hebrew Scriptures—Law, Psalms, and Prophets—the panoply of predictions about His mission. He quoted promises given hundreds of years in advance that He had fulfilled to the last detail. Then at the supper table that night, He revealed Himself visually and suddenly disappeared.

Why did Jesus preach this sermon in disguise? He wanted them to be intellectually convinced of the Resurrection, not just by eyewitness proof, but on the basis of the miracle of fulfilled prophecy.

Hundreds of specific promises in the Old Testament describe in detail all aspects of our Lord's birth, life, ministry, death, and resurrection. Though we haven't yet seen Jesus with our physical eyesight, we can see Him on every page of the Old Testament; and through the miracle of fulfilled prophecy, we know He's risen!

The New is in the Old Contained;
the Old is in the New Explained.

July 31

From the days of John the Baptist until now,
the kingdom of heaven has been suffering violence . . . .
*For **all** the prophets and the law prophesied until John.*
Matthew 11:12–13

Alexander Mackay arrived in Uganda from Scotland in 1878, eager to win the powerful tribal king, M'tesa, to Christ. In his journal he wrote, "Sunday, January 26, 1879. Held service in court. Read Matthew 11:1–30, about Jesus and John the Baptist. The Spirit of God seemed to be working. I have never had such a blessed service."

John the Baptist was Mackay's favorite Bible character, and that day he quoted John while preaching before King M'tesa, warning him to repent and to prepare the way for the Lord. A tall Arab gentleman was there with bales of cloth and guns to barter for slaves. With the courage of John the Baptist, Mackay warned the king, saying, "O King M'tesa, the people of this land made you their king and look to you as their father. Will you sell your children, knowing that they will be chained, put into slave ships, beaten with whips; that most of them will die of mistreatment . . . ?"

Mackay knew his life was in jeopardy, but to his delight the king turned and told the Arab, "The white man is right. I shall no more sell my people as slaves."

In Mackay's journal: "Afternoon. The King sent a message with a present of a goat, saying it was a blessed passage I read today."

A blessed passage![61]

May the Lord give us all the courage of John the Baptist and Alexander Mackay.

August 1

*In that He died, He died to sin once for **all**;*
but in that He lives, He lives to God.

Romans 6:10

Jesus died to sin once for all.

Does that mean once for all *time*, or once for all *people?*

The Greek word *ephapax* is like our English phrase "once and for all." I remember my mother tackling projects, saying, "I'm going to get this job done once and for all."

Our Lord's one moment of sacrifice on the cross is effective for all time. Hebrews 7:27 says: "He doesn't need to offer sacrifices every day, as high priests do . . . . He did this once for all when He offered Himself."

Hebrews 9:12 adds: "He entered the holy of holies once for all . . . by His own blood."

Hebrews 10 talks about "the offering of the body of Jesus Christ once and for all. . . . For by one offering He has perfected forever those who are sanctified" (vv. 10, 14).

Peter said, "For Christ also suffered for sins once for all, the righteous for the unrighteous, that He might bring you to God" (1 Pet. 3:18). Jude chimes in, too, writing about "the faith that was delivered to the saints once for all" (Jude 3).

Jesus saw our need, left His glorious throne, and descended to the world, saying, "I'm going to get this job done once and for all." And in six hours one Friday, He accomplished all that ever needs to be done for our eternal welfare.

> Once, only once, and once for all,
> His precious life He gave;
> Before the cross in faith we fall,
> And own it strong to save.

> —*William Bright, 1865*

ugust 2

All who had diseases
were pressing toward Him to touch Him.
Mark 3:10

I read about a woman who told her husband, "Orson, I've been watching that young married couple across the street. Every morning when the husband leaves the house he kisses his wife good-bye, and every evening when he gets home he kisses her again and hugs her affectionately. Now why can't you do that?"

Orson replied, "Well, honey, I can't do that. I hardly know her."

He missed the point, but a lot of us miss the point. Sometimes my wife will say to me, "Robert, you haven't hugged me or kissed me all day."

I always delight to repair the damage.

There was once a lonely man who passed a bookstore while walking down the street. Looking in the window, he saw a book with the title *How to Hug.* He rushed in to buy the book, but to his chagrin he discovered it was the seventh volume of a dictionary. It covered all the words from "How" to "Hug."

Our church is a "hugging church," but not all churches are like that. I have a friend who died of Lou Gehrig's disease. He'd once belonged to my church in Nashville but moved away. He loved his new church, but the people there were more reserved in expressing their affection. "Sometimes," he told me, "I just need a hug."

Jesus knew how to have and to hold, so everyone wanted to touch Him. He knew the power of an appropriate, affectionate human-to-human touch. Make a point today to hug your spouse, your kids, or even a friend who needs a spot of love.

August 3

READING: 2 CORINTHIANS 9:10–12

He will always make you rich enough
*to be generous at **all** times, so that many will thank God*
for your gifts which they receive from us.
2 Corinthians 9:11 (TEV)

Our seven-year-old granddaughter, Chloe, has a purse that's seldom out of her sight, and we never know what to expect when she opens it because it's the depository for all sorts of strange treasures, from rocks and insects to coins to toys. The other day as our daughter was hauling her brood of six across town in the van, one of the children was picking at her ear and it started bleeding. "Don't pick at it anymore, Christiania," said her mother, "and when we get to our destination, I'll get a piece of ice for you to hold against it."

Whereupon, to everyone's surprise, Chloe opened her purse and pulled out a piece of ice!

When asked why she had ice cubes in her purse, Chloe simply explained, "I was afraid I'd get thirsty on the trip."

I'll bet if you'd open your purse, you'd have something there to help someone too. God provides for us in advance so that we'll have what we need to meet another's needs. If you're the recipient of some blessing, perhaps God is supplying you with something to give away. The apostle Paul promised that God would always make us rich enough to be generous at all times, so that many would thank God for the gifts received.

God gives His mercies to be spent.
—*William Cowper*

August 4

*The angel of the LORD encamps **all** around*
those who fear Him, and delivers them.

Psalm 34:7 (NKJV)

After I read missionary Darlene Deibler Rose's memoirs, *Evidence Not Seen: One Woman's Faith in a Japanese P.O.W. Camp*, it was hard not to use her stories to illustrate every sermon I preached. Talk about a page-turner!

Early in her book, Darlene told of a night when, as a rookie missionary in Indonesia, she was awakened by what she thought were rats. She tried to ignore them until she heard a book slam onto the floor, whereupon she jumped out of bed and jerked the bedroom door open. Facing her was a rat of a different sort—a Boegis bandit who, seeing her, drew his machete and prepared to strike. Without thinking, Darlene rushed at him. The man inexplicably turned, ran down the hall, and out of the house with Darlene in hot pursuit.

Suddenly the full realization of her situation hit her like a hammer. "Lord," she whispered, "what a stupid thing for me to do." Instantly Psalm 34:7 came to mind as though the Lord was quoting it to her: "The angel of the Lord encamps all around those who fear Him, and delivers them."

In the days that followed, Boegis bandits combed the area but never again did one of them bother her.

Years later, Darlene had a conversation with a Boegis acquaintance. She asked why the bandits had never again entered the house. His answer: "Because of those people you had there—those people in white who stood about the house."[62]

# August 5

You observe my travels and my rest;
*You are aware of **all** my ways.*

Psalm 139:3

John Quincy Adams, sixth president of the United States, was a brilliant, well-traveled, and cantankerous man who still fascinates historians. Here are two bits of trivia you probably don't know about him.

Adams was the first president to be interviewed by a woman reporter—but you wouldn't believe the circumstances. Every morning in the summer, Adams walked from the White House to the Potomac and stripped naked for swimming. Journalist Anne Royall, whose requests to interview Adams had been refused, allegedly went to the river and gathered up Adam's clothes while he swam, and she sat on them until she had her interview with the president, who was standing helplessly chest deep in the water.

The other interesting detail about John Quincy Adams is that he was a hymnist. One of his best hymns is based on Psalm 139, titled "O Lord, Thy All-discerning Eyes." It says, in part:

> O Lord, Thy all-discerning eyes
> My inmost purpose see;
> My deeds, my words, my thoughts, arise
> Alike disclosed to Thee:
> My sitting down, my rising up,
> Broad noon, and deepest night,
> My path, my pillow, and my cup,
> Are open to Thy sight.
>
> Before, behind, I meet Thine eye,
> And feel Thy heavy hand:
> Such knowledge is for me too high,
> To reach or understand.

August 6

*Shout triumphantly to the LORD **all** the earth. . . .*
*His faithfulness endures through **all** generations.*
Psalm 100:1, 5

This great psalm of joy is affectionately called "The Old 100th."
It's short enough to memorize, exuberant enough to reinvigorate
us every day, wide enough to cover all the earth with its message,
and long enough to bless God's people through all generations.

Stanza 1 (vv. 1–3) is devoted to *Gladitude*. We're to shout triumphantly to the Lord and to serve Him with gladness. Stanza 2
(vv. 4–5) is about *Gratitude*. We're to enter His gates with thanksgiving and His courts with praise, giving thanks to Him and praising His name.

A sixteenth-century hymnist put it to music in the classic "All
People That on Earth Do Dwell," sung to the tune usually associ-
ated with the Doxology.

> All people that on earth do dwell,
> Sing to the Lord with cheerful voice.
> Him serve with fear, His praise forthtell;
> Come ye before Him and rejoice.
>
> The Lord, ye know, is God indeed;
> Without our aid He did us make;
> We are His folk, He doth us feed,
> And for His sheep He doth us take.
>
> O enter then His gates with praise;
> Approach with joy His courts unto;
> Praise, laud, and bless His Name always,
> For it is seemly so to do.

August 7

*The Lord will rescue me from **all** evil and take me safely
into His heavenly Kingdom. To Him be the glory forever.*
2 Timothy 4:18 (TEV)

More people are crowded onto this planet now than ever before in history, yet loneliness is pandemic. Morris West, in his book *The Devil's Advocate*, wrote, "It comes to all of us sooner or later. Friends die, family dies, lovers and husbands too. We get old; we get sick . . . . In a society where people live in impersonal cities or suburbs, where electronic entertainment often replaces one-to-one conversation, where people move from job to job, and state to state, and marriage to marriage, loneliness has become an epidemic."[63]

Four categories of people are especially lonely: singles, people in ministry, those whose friends forsake them, and prisoners on death row. The apostle Paul fit into all those categories at once. In his last recorded chapter, 2 Timothy 4, he's clearly bothered by the cold weather (v. 13), his lack of reading material (v. 13), the fickleness of his friends (vv. 10, 16), and his legal problems (v. 16). But Paul stayed busy, wrote letters, and remembered that God was going to deliver him from all evil.

Through all the changing scenes of life, we have an unassailable basis for optimism. It's Christ Himself, who will rescue us from all evil. Reject self-pity. Learn to dispel loneliness. Stay busy, be positive, and keep looking upward!

> Through all the changing scenes of life,
> In trouble and in joy,
> The praises of my God shall still
> My heart and tongue employ.
>
> Of His deliverance I will boast,
> Till all that are distressed
> From my example courage take
> And soothe their griefs to rest.
>
> —*Nahum Tate and Nicholas Brady, 1698*

August 8

How countless are Your works, Lord!
*In wisdom You have made them **all**.*

Psalm 104:24

All that's good, and great, and true,
All that is and is to be,
Be it old or be it new,
Comes, O Father, comes from Thee.

Mercies dawn with every day,
Newer, brighter than before;
And the sun's declining ray
Layeth others up in store.

Not a bird that doth not sing
Sweetest praises to Thy Name;
Not an insect on the wing
But Thy wonders doth proclaim.

Every blade and every tree
All in happy concert ring,
And in wondrous harmony
Join in praises to their King.

Fill us, then, with love divine;
Grant that we, though toiling here,
May in spirit, being Thine,
See and hear Thee everywhere.

May we all, with songs of praise,
Whilst on earth Thy Name adore,
Till with angel choirs we raise
Songs of praise forevermore.

—*Godfrey Thring, British clergyman, 1863*

August 9

Look unto me, and be ye saved,
***all** the ends of the earth:*
for I am God, and there is none else.
Isaiah 45:22 (KJV)

This text wrought one of the most famous conversions in history. When Charles Haddon Spurgeon was fifteen, he was driven by a snowstorm into a little Primitive Methodist church where a handful of faithful members had braved the blizzard. The pastor didn't show up, but at length an old fellow rose without preparation and chose Isaiah 45:22 as his text.

Spurgeon later recalled: "He had not much to say, thank God, for that compelled him to keep on repeating his text, and there was nothing needed—by me, at any rate—except his text. I remember how he said, 'My dear friends, this is a very simple text indeed. It says, Look! Well, a man needn't go to college to learn to look. You may be the biggest fool, and yet you can look.'"

Spotting Charles in the back of the room, the man added, "Young man, you look very miserable. And you always will be miserable—miserable in life and miserable in death—if you don't obey my text; but if you obey now, this moment, you will be saved." Then he shouted at the top of his voice: "Young man, look to Jesus Christ. Look! Look! Look! You have nothing to do but to look and live!"

I owe my conversion to Christ to an unknown person,
who certainly was no minister in the ordinary acceptation
of the term; but who could say this much, "Look unto Christ
and be saved, all ye ends of the earth."

—Charles H. Spurgeon

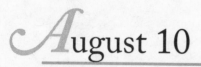# August 10

*Indeed, we have **all** received grace after grace.*
John 1:16

John 1:16 is perhaps my favorite verse on grace in the Bible, but when you read it in the King James Version, it has a strange ring to it, as though something has been left out: "And of his fullness have all we received, and grace for grace."

The actual Greek says that out of His fullness we have all received *charin anti charitos*—grace *anti* grace. The word *anti* is a Greek preposition that sometimes means "against," but it can have several other meanings along the lines of "opposite of . . . instead of . . . in place of."

Literally, this verse says that out of the fullness of His own infinite goodness, God gives us grace in the place of grace, grace upon grace. Think of ocean waves, each coming upon the other in endless succession, each rolling into and replacing the next. In other words, God gives endless waves of blessings to His children. One manifestation of His grace has barely receded when another comes, grace on top of grace. It's His goodness and mercy following us all the days of our lives. The New International Version puts it: "From the fullness of his grace we have all received one blessing after another."

G.R.A.C.E. is <u>G</u>od's <u>R</u>iches <u>A</u>vailable to <u>C</u>laim <u>E</u>veryday.

Blessed be the God and Father of our Lord Jesus Christ, who has blessed us with every spiritual blessing in the heavens, in Christ.
Ephesians 1:3

Grace is flowing from Calvary,
Grace as fathomless as the sea,
Grace for time and eternity,
Grace, enough for me.
—Edwin O. Excell, 1905

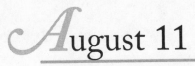

August 11

He is the image of the invisible God,
*the firstborn over **all** creation . . . .*
***All** things have been created through Him and for Him.*
*He is before **all** things,*
*and by Him **all** things hold together. . . .*
*God was pleased to have **all** His fullness dwell in Him.*

Colossians 1:15–17, 19

A couple of months ago, two men came to my house wanting to convert me to their cult. They claimed to be Christian, but denied that Jesus Christ is the eternal God, coequal with the Father. They showed me Colossians 1:15 and alleged that Jesus was a created being—the firstborn of God's creation.

I pointed out that Colossians teaches quite the opposite, that Jesus is God Himself, the visible image of the invisible One, the eternal Creator. By saying "He is the image of the invisible God," Paul was telling us that Jesus is the visible manifestation of the invisible Father, even as Christ claimed when He said, "The one who has seen Me has seen the Father" (John 14:9).

When Jesus is called "the firstborn over all creation," it refers to His priority and supremacy over the cosmos, as is seen by the context. The whole point of the passage is that Jesus Christ is Lord. He existed before the creation, made all that has been made, and rules over all that is. The New Living Translation captures this: "Christ is the visible image of the invisible God. He existed before God made anything at all and is supreme over all creation."

Jesus is before all, beyond all, above all. In Him all creation holds together, and in all things He must have the preeminence.

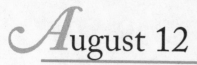# August 12

For the grace of God that brings salvation
*has appeared to **all** men.*
It teaches us to say "No" to ungodliness and worldly passions,
and to live self-controlled . . . lives in this present age.

Titus 2:11–12 (NIV)

Titus was Paul's troubleshooter. Every time we see him in the New Testament, he's tackling a difficult problem for the apostle Paul. In the letter bearing his name, Titus was on the island of Crete, which was known for its laziness, lying, and gluttony (Titus 1:12). Paul had sent him to straighten out things in the church (1:5).

One of the hallmarks of the letter is its emphasis on self-control and self-discipline. For an interesting Bible study, read through these three short chapters, looking for every reference to personal discipline and self-control. In Titus 2:11–12, Paul says that the same grace of God that has appeared to all people with salvation also has the power to enable us to say no to temptation and to live with self-control.

What kind of self-control do you need? With your credit cards? With anger or anxiety? With tobacco or alcohol use? With gambling temptations? With your thought life? With your diet or eating habits? With exercise? Profanity? Pornography? Sexual immorality in its various forms? Laziness? Entertainment and diversions?

Louisa May Alcott wrote: "A little kingdom I possess, / Where thoughts and feelings dwell; / And very hard the task I find / Of governing it well."

We cannot govern our own hearts, but the grace of God can do it.

The fruit of the Spirit is . . . self-control.

Galatians 5:22

# August 13

Seek the LORD,
all *you humble of the earth,*
who carry out what He commands.

Zephaniah 2:3

Humble people are those who obey God faithfully without worrying about whether or not they're noticed. They even rejoice if someone else gets the fame and acclaim. It's interesting to me that behind every famous "name" in Christian history is an obscure one.

For example, perhaps you've heard of Martin Luther, the fiery German Reformer who changed the world by nailing a list of his beliefs and convictions to the door of the cathedral in the little village of Wittenberg, Germany.

But have you ever heard of Johann von Staupitz?

Staupitz was born in the late 1400s—no one knows the exact date—in Motterwitz, Germany. He became a respected theologian who met young Martin Luther while the latter was a struggling young monk plagued by doubts and deadly depression. Luther felt he could confess all his sins to Dr. Staupitz, and he once spent six long hours in one session. Von Staupitz pointed the young man to the blood of Christ and to the love of God.

It was also Von Staupitz who later appointed Luther as professor of theology at Wittenberg. Taking up his responsibilities there, Luther lectured on Romans and Galatians and in the process discovered the truths of justification by grace through faith.

Martin Luther later said, "If it had not been for Dr. Staupitz, I should have sunk in hell."

Our significance isn't found in fame or fortune, but in knowing that we have been links in God's chain. Our faithfulness to Him, even in obscurity, will yield results that can only be calculated in eternity.

August 14

Moses was faithful as a servant
*in **all** God's household,*
as a testimony to what would be said.

Hebrews 3:5

My friend Lee Hollaway gave me an e-mail from a military chaplain in Iraq who'd been upset by a change in his travel plans. He was bumped from an afternoon Kuwait-to-Iraq flight and rescheduled for a 3:30 a.m. transport.

"I got pretty frustrated as I realized that I wasn't going to get any sleep and spent the day a little bitter," he wrote.

Going back to his tent, he found a soldier sitting on the cot reading a Bible. "I'd been setting out Bibles in the tents and they'd been going fast," recalled the chaplain. "When I asked the soldier what he was reading, he responded, 'The Bible, sir. I'm trying to read through the Psalms.'

"I asked him if he'd ever read the Bible before and he had not. I directed him to the Gospel of John and he got pretty excited. We're going to get back together and talk about what he read, so please be praying for him as I plan to share the gospel with him."

The chaplain continued, "Shortly after this encounter I started crying as I realized how I'd complained that things didn't go my way. If I'd been on that earlier flight, I'd have missed that opportunity with the soldier. I decided at that point to start trusting in God more, especially when things don't go as planned. I know He is sovereign and will daily place me where He wants me to be. Nothing makes me happier than knowing this."

Our only duty in life is to be faithful to all the work the Lord assigns.

# August 15

*You gave Him authority over **all** flesh;*
*so He may give eternal life to **all** You have given Him.*
This is eternal life: that they may know You, the only true God,
and the One You have sent—Jesus Christ.

John 17:2–3

Age and illness settled over John Knox like a thick Scottish mist, and at last the craggy old Reformer of Scotland approached the end of his journey. Taking to his deathbed, he called for his wife, and the scene was later described by Knox's servant, Richard Bannatyne.

On November 24, 1572, John Knox departed this life to his eternal rest. Early in the afternoon, he said, "Now, for the last time, I commend my spirit, soul, and body"—pointing upon his three fingers—"into thy hands, O Lord!" Thereafter, about five o'clock, he said to his wife, "Go, read where I cast my first anchor!" She did not need to be told, and so she read the seventeenth of John's evangel:
"Thou hast given Him power over all flesh, that He should give eternal life to as many as Thou hast given Him; and this is life eternal, that they might know Thee, the only true God, and Jesus Christ whom Thou hast sent."

God the Father has given our Lord Jesus Christ authority over all flesh, and with that authority Jesus gives eternal life to all who are His own.

Here we may cast our anchor.

August 16

READING: ECCLESIASTES 9:7–10

Enjoy life with the wife you love
***all** the days of your fleeting life.*

Ecclesiastes 9:9

Several years ago I salvaged a desk from a house reportedly abandoned by the Russian mafia, and my wife claimed it for the corner of the bedroom. Now every morning she rolls her wheelchair to it as I bring her coffee, and there she spends the morning in Bible study and prayer. Meanwhile, I do the same at my own desk. If you ask us the secret of a long and happy marriage, that's it. We've learned to enjoy each other's presence because we've learned to enjoy the presence of the Lord who bestows all the love, joy, peace, and patience needed for a happy home.

At the marriage of Queen Elizabeth II to the Duke of Edinburgh in 1947, the archbishop of Canterbury, Geoffery Francis Fisher, said, "The ever-living Christ is here to bless you. The nearer you keep him, the nearer you will be to one another."

The contrary is also true. I've found that when there's tension between Katrina and me, the problem isn't usually between the two of us but between the Lord and me. If I confess and straighten out my spiritual life, the trouble with Katrina disappears.

That's why in the mornings we have our individual Quiet Times, then at bedtime we pray together. The old adage is today largely untried but it's still true: The couple that prays together stays together. For when we walk in the light, as He is in the light, we have fellowship with one another (1 John 1:7).

"Go, show your love to your wife."

Hosea 3:1 (NIV)

August 17

You will seek Me and find Me
*when you search for Me with **all** your heart.*
Jeremiah 29:13

On October 10, 1821, Charles Finney, twenty-nine, became convicted about his eternal condition, and he walked into the woods to settle the matter. He tried to pray, but he couldn't seem to manage it. A driving sense of guilt and depression hammered his heart.

Suddenly Jeremiah 29:13 dropped into his mind "with a flood of light . . . . The Spirit seemed to lay stress upon that idea in the text, When you search for me with all your heart." Finney was wonderfully converted, sparking a revival that propelled him to become one of the greatest evangelists in American history.

Sundar Singh was born in North India in 1889, the son of a wealthy Sikh. When as a youth he came into contact with the gospel, he publicly burned the Bible in fury. But one day, his eyes fell on Jeremiah 29:13: "You will . . . find Me when you search for Me with all your heart." During the night, he saw a globe of light in the room, and the Living Christ appeared to him as in a dream. "My heart was immediately filled with joy and I was changed for all eternity," he said. Sundar Singh later became one of the greatest evangelists in Indian history.

Oh, do let Jesus have all of your heart!
He will give you such a fullness of joy in Himself
that will far more than repay you for any earthly pleasure
you may think you may miss because of it.
—*Hannah Whitall Smith*

August 18

*All Scripture is inspired by God
and is profitable for teaching,
for rebuking, for correcting,
for training in righteousness.*

2 Timothy 3:16

The original Greek New Testament says, *Pasa Graphe Theopneustos:* "Every Scripture *Theopneustos*." That last term comes from two smaller words: *Theos,* meaning God; and *pneuma,* with a silent *p.* This is the word from which we get our English words *pneumonia* and *pneumonic.* It means "wind, air, or breath." As a verb, it means "to exhale."

All Scripture is God-breathed or breathed out by God.

When we open our mouths to speak, we're simply exhaling, using ours lips and tongue to form sounds (called words) with our exhaled breath. In the same way, every word of the Scripture has been breathed out, spoken out, by God.

Peter adds: "No prophecy of Scripture comes from one's own interpretation [origination], because no prophecy ever came by the will of man; instead, moved by the Holy Spirit, men spoke from God" (2 Pet. 1:20–21).

This doesn't mean God dictated the Bible like a boss to a transcriber. The authors of the various books of the Bible wrote with their own personalities, insights, backgrounds, and life-circumstances. Yet the original documents of the Bible were written by those who, though permitted to exercise their own gifts and literary skills, wrote under the control and guidance of the Holy Spirit so that their recorded words were totally correct, infallible, inerrant, unfailing, and true.

That's the miracle of inspiration, and that's why the Bible is able to equip us for every good work.

August 19

*Talk ye of **all** his wondrous works.*
Psalm 105:2 (KJV)

For several years I've had the joy of writing for and with Dr. David Jeremiah, and the other evening my wife and I had supper with him at Nashville's Opryland Hotel, which is near our home. The three of us spent the evening talking about discoveries we'd made in the Bible and about wonderful verses that amazed us. As we departed, Dr. Jeremiah said, "This has been so refreshing. When Christians get together, we don't do this enough. We talk about everything but the Lord. It's been wonderful tonight just talking about the Lord and His Word."

Deuteronomy 6 instructs us to talk about God's Word when we rise in the morning and when we retire at night, when we sit at home and when we walk along the way.

Malachi 3:16 says, "Then those who feared the Lord talked with each other, and the Lord listened and heard. A scroll of remembrance was written in his presence concerning those who feared the Lord and honored his name" (NIV).

Is your conversation sprinkled with the things of the Lord and seasoned with the salt of Scripture?

∞

In one of the streets of that town I came where there were
three or four women sitting at a door in the sun, talking about
the things of God. And being now willing to hear what they
said, I drew near to hear their discourse. . . . Their talk was about
a new birth—the work of God in their hearts.

—*John Bunyan,*
author of Pilgrim's Progress,
in describing the events that led to his conversion

# August 20

If we confess our sins,
He is faithful and righteous to forgive us our sins
*and to cleanse us from **all** unrighteousness.*

1 John 1:9

If you could reverse the clock and do it over, you wouldn't have said those words, hurt that person, or made that blunder. But we cannot turn back the hands of time, and sins once committed cannot be uncommitted. Our lives are littered with failure, guilt, and shame, and there's nothing we can do to expunge the record.

But He can.

> If we confess our sins, He is faithful and righteous to forgive us our sins and to cleanse us from all unrighteousness. . . . The blood of Jesus His Son cleanses us from all sin. . . . He forgives all your sin; He heals all your diseases. . . .
>
> You have thrown all my sins behind Your back. . . . Blot out all my guilt.
>
> I will purify . . . I will forgive all the wrongs.[64]

To forgive ourselves we have only to grasp the extent of God's forgiveness in Christ. The power of His blood enables us to shut all our shameful moments in a locked box and bury them forever at the foot of the cross.

> Gone, gone, gone, gone,
> Yes, my sins are gone.
> Now my soul is free and in my heart's a song.
> Buried in the deepest sea,
> Yes, that's good enough for me.
> I shall live eternally;
> Praise God! My sins are gone!

# August 21

Your eyes saw me when I was formless;
***all** my days were written in Your book*
and planned before a single one of them began.

Psalm 139:16

On September 11, 2001, Jill Briscoe was in the air, traveling from Europe to Chicago, when her plane landed in Newfoundland. Because of the terrorist attack on the World Trade Center, air traffic was suspended, and Jill found herself stranded with 250 other passengers in a Salvation Army center for several days. One morning a woman in the coffee line turned to Jill and said, "I want to go home. I just want to go home."

Jill took a deep breath and said quietly, "I am home."

When the woman looked up startled, Jill said, "Home is the will of God. I happen to believe that for those who love the Lord, nothing can happen that He doesn't allow."

Jill went on to explain that when the pilot had made the announcement that there had been a national emergency and the airspace and borders of the United States were closed but giving no other explanation, a verse of Scripture came to her mind. It was Psalm 139:16: "All my days were written in Your book and planned before a single one of them began."

That meant every day—even September 11, 2001.[65]

We have a preordained life! Nothing can happen to us that God hasn't known about from eternity. No evil can overtake us that He has not foreseen. The blessings of this day are pre-appointed, His plan is written in loving letters, and Home is the will of God.

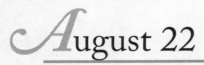# August 22

*The widow who is . . . left **all** alone puts her hope in God and
continues night and day to pray and to ask God for help.*
1 Timothy 5:5 (NIV)

Even when we're all alone, the Lord is near to help us—and what
a wonderful little four-letter word is that term *help*, appearing
more than two hundred times in the Bible. A couple of years ago,
I put together a booklet listing many of the great "help" passages.
Here's a sampling for today's devotion:

"Lord, *help* me!" . . . I rise before dawn and cry out for *help* . . . .
Hurry to *help* me, Lord . . . for human *help* is worthless.

Since He Himself was tested and has suffered,
He is able to *help* those who are tested. . . .
Will not God grant justice to His elect
who cry out to Him day and night?
Will He delay to *help* them?

Where will my *help* come from? My *help* comes from the Lord,
the Maker of heaven and earth. . . . The Lord *helps* all who fall.

For I, the Lord your God, hold your right hand and say to you:
Do not fear, I will *help* you.

Happy is the one whose *help* is the God of Jacob,
whose hope is in the Lord his God, the Maker of heaven
and earth . . . . Therefore let us approach the throne of grace
with boldness, so that we may receive mercy
and find grace to *help* us at the proper time.[66]

August 23

READING: 1 CHRONICLES 29:10–20

All things come from You,
and of Your own we have given You.
1 Chronicles 29:14 (NKJV)

Sometimes I give my wife a box of chocolates—or she gives one to me. Opening it, the first thing we do is to offer a piece to the other. We offer back something of what we have received to the one who gave it.

In 1 Chronicles 29, King David launched a campaign to raise funds for the temple. He gave from his own resources, then encouraged others to do the same. "Now, who will volunteer to consecrate himself to the Lord today?" he asked in verse 5, meaning: "Who is willing to be a generous giver to this God-inspired project?"

"Then the leaders of the households, the leaders of the tribes of Israel, the commanders . . . and the officials in charge of the king's work gave willingly. . . . The people rejoiced because of their leaders' willingness to give, for they had given to the Lord with a whole heart" (vv. 6, 9).

When the money came in, David offered a great prayer of praise, and in the middle of it he hit on the underlying truth of stewardship. Everything we have comes from God. When we contribute to His work, we're simply giving back a portion of what He has generously given us.

We give Thee but Thine own,
Whate'er the gift may be;
All that we have is Thine alone,
A trust, O Lord, from Thee.

—*William W. How, 1864*

August 24

All things were created through Him,
and apart from Him not one thing was created
that has been created.

John 1:3

The prologue of John's Gospel (John 1:1–18) is arguably the deepest and most beautiful preamble in all literature. It's also packed with doctrine. Think of what John's opening words tell about Christ:

- Christ is eternal: *In the beginning.*
- Christ is God's communiqué to the world: *was the Word.*
- Christ is equal with God: *The Word was with God.*
- Christ IS God: *And the Word was God.*
- Christ is the Creator of the Cosmos: *All things were created through Him, and apart from Him not one thing was created that has been created.*
- Christ is the Source of life: *Life was in Him.*
- Christ is the Source of hope: *And that life was the light of men.*

The Bible consistently tells us that God the Son was the agent of creation (Col. 1:16, Heb. 1:2). God the Father may have designed the universe, but it was God the Son who flipped the switch. To put it plainly, it was God the Son who spoke the words that brought the universe into being.

Without being dogmatic, I believe if we could have heard the voice saying "Let there be light" in Genesis 1 and the voice saying "Blessed are the pure in heart" in Matthew 5, we would have recognized the same voice.

"All things were made through Him, and without Him nothing was made that was made" (NKJV).

August 25

They were astonished beyond measure,
*saying, "He has done **all** things well."*

Mark 7:37 (NKJV)

One day over lunch this week, I asked my wife a strange question. It was sort of out of the blue, and she didn't know what
to make of it. I asked her, "How would you react if a good friend
came up to you and sliced you open with a knife?"

"Well," she said, shocked, "that would be terrible."

"Yes," I said, "but what if that friend were a surgeon and he
was performing an operation that would save your life?"

Well, that's different, isn't it? We still wouldn't like it at the
time, but we'd be grateful for a friend with enough skill to help us
at a critical moment.

There are times when the Lord allows things to happen that
we don't like at the time, but we know He intends all things for
our good, that He does all things well, and that in all things we
are more than conquerors. So, as Job put it, "Though He slay me,
yet will I trust Him."

Our friend Jesus is the Great Physician, who will never harm
us but will always do us good. Goodness and mercy follow us all
the days of our lives. And even if it appears for a moment that He
is harming us, we know it's in appearance only and not in reality,
for it will inexorably turn for our good. We can trust Him completely and joyfully, for He does all things well.

> Praise God who works all things for good
> For those who love His name.
> His providential care shall turn
> All blessings into gain.

> —RJM

August 26

*Woe to you when **all** men speak well of you.*

Luke 6:26 (NIV)

When James K. Polk was president of the United States, his wife Sarah took a very visible role in the nation's capital. She was outspoken, bold, and well-informed. As a result, she became a controversial First Lady, and some people even tried to use the Bible to denounce her influence. One day at a White House reception, a Southern visitor approached and said, "Madame, I have long wished to look upon a lady upon which the Bible pronounces a woe!"

Conversation stopped as everyone waited to see how Mrs. Polk, a devout Presbyterian, would respond. Looking at her critic, she replied, "Does not the Bible say, 'Woe unto you when all men speak well of you?'"[67]

That's a good verse to bear in mind because taking a stand for Christ is increasingly unpopular in our pagan and pluralistic society. If you believe that God created the world, that He is a God of both love and holiness, that Jesus died and rose again for our sins and is the only way to heaven, and that we have a responsibility to take that message to a needy world—those beliefs will vilify you in many segments of our society. Our world is determined to intimidate, marginalize, and silence Christians.

But our goal isn't popularity; it's to know Him and make Him known. We shouldn't be needlessly offensive, but we shouldn't be afraid of the "offense of the cross." These are exciting days in which to bear a witness for our Savior!

August 27

After three days, they found Him in the temple complex . . . .
***All** those who heard Him were astounded at His understanding*
and His answers. When His parents saw Him, they were astonished,
and His mother said to Him, "Son, why have You treated us like this?
Your father and I have been anxiously searching for You."

Luke 2:46–48

One of my daughters went missing once. It was only for a few minutes in a department store—she had wandered to a nearby aisle—but I was in sheer panic, and my heart was racing a thousand beats a minute. I can't imagine losing a child in a large city for three days. Mary's outburst was understandable: "Son, why have You treated us like this?" After all, the twelve-year-old seemed in no hurry to be found. He was soaking up the atmosphere in the temple, asking and answering questions with the rabbis and astonishing all who heard Him.

Almost with a shrug, He said to His mother, "Why were you searching for Me? . . . Didn't you know that I had to be in My Father's house?" Or as the older translations put it: "about My Father's business?" He went home with them obediently, but "His mother kept all these things in her heart" (v. 51).

Twenty-one years later, it was "déjà vu all over again":

Same city—Jerusalem
Same time—The Passover
Same anguish—Jesus is gone!
Same duration—Three days
Same reaction at His appearance—Astonishment!
Same rationale—He was about His Father's business.

There was nothing accidental about His twelve-year-old adventure. It was a prophetic preview, and we are still astonished at His understanding and answers.

August 28

All these blessings will come and overtake you,
because you obey the LORD your God.
Deuteronomy 28:2

The blessings coming from obedience encompass all the blessings of God, including the blessing of usefulness. How terrible to live a useless life. How wonderful to be usable, useful, and a blessing to God and others.

I once heard of a retired general who, as soon as he opened his eyes in the morning, prayed: "Your orders today, Lord!" My own oft-offered prayer is: "Your agenda today, Lord!"

Several years ago, I found Anna Waring's prayer about this; and though I'm finding it harder to memorize things, this poem inscribed itself on my brain almost as soon as I read it. It expresses the joy of knowing that our times are in His hands (Ps. 31:15):

> I love to think that God appoints
> My portion day by day;
> Events of life are in His hand,
> And I would only say,
> Appoint them in Thine own good time,
> And in Thine own best way.

If we are really and always and equally ready
to do whatsoever the King appoints, all the trials and vexations
arising from any change in His appointments, great or small,
simply do not exist. If He appoints me to work there,
shall I lament that I am not to work here?

—*Frances Havergal*

What may be my future lot, high or low concerns me not;
This doth set my heart at rest: What my God appoints is best.

# August 29

You saw in the wilderness
how the LORD your God carried you
*as a man carries his son **all** along the way*
you traveled until you reached this place.

Deuteronomy 1:31

Several years ago, I became so upset about a particular situation that I couldn't sleep. Switching on the light, I turned to the book of Deuteronomy to see if there might be some word there to relax my mind. Deuteronomy is an underestimated book.

Straightaway I came to this passage in chapter 1 where Moses was recounting to the younger Israelis the terrible sin that condemned their parents' generation to forty years in the wilderness. The text says, in essence, "I carried you out of Egypt, across the Red Sea, and toward the Promised Land like a man carries his little boy in his arms, yet you still would not trust Me. You feared that I couldn't lead you. You grumbled when you should have trusted and obeyed."

Reading those words, I realized that the underlying sin of the Israelites was the sin of worry—of fear, panic, and unbelief. Worry occurs when we distrust His promises, disregard His power, and discount His presence. Worry believes that our problems are greater than His power. Worry fears that God may, while carrying us, drop us.

But He will not drop us. He carries us all the way until we reach our heavenly home.

Hidden in the hollow of His blessed hand,
Never foe can follow, never traitor stand;
Not a surge of worry, not a shade of care,
Not a blast of hurry touch the spirit there.

—*Frances Havergal*

# August 30

READING: 2 TIMOTHY 4:1–7

*I've run hard to the finish, believed **all** the way.*
***All** that's left now is the shouting.*
2 Timothy 4:7 (MSG)

Have you ever heard of the jockey who started the race on one horse, ended on another, and didn't know the difference?

It happened on a rainy night in West Virginia in 1970. James Thornton was riding Native Bird. Thundering around the track in the middle of the pack, he was side by side with a powerful thoroughbred named Kandi Arm. He raised his whip to urge on Native Bird, but accidentally struck Kandi Arm across the nose. It startled her so badly that she bumped into Native Bird, and the jockey riding Kandi Arm flew off the horse.

The collision tossed Thornton straight up into the air, and he came down between the two animals. He desperately grabbed a handful of mane and wound up under the horse's neck. Somehow he managed to pull himself onto the back of the thoroughbred and back into the saddle to finish the race in sixth place. Only then did he realize he wasn't riding Native Bird at all. He was on the back of Kandi Arm. He had finished the race on the wrong horse.

Someday soon we're going to finish the race and come to the end of our earthly lives. I wonder if only then will some realize they were riding the wrong horse, were driven by the wrong passions, were living for the wrong purposes.

May we be able to say with Paul, "I have finished the race, I have kept the faith."

> May I run the race before me
> Strong and brave to face the foe.
> Looking only unto Jesus
> As I onward go.
>
> —*Kate Wilkinson*

# August 31

If it is possible, as much as depends on you,
*live peaceably with **all** men.*
Romans 12:18 (NKJV)

In the early 1970s, I was working with the Billy Graham team in Norfolk, and I was amazed at how critical some were toward Dr. Graham. One group took out full-page ads in the newspaper with a banner reading: "The Bible or Billy!" I went to the crusade office and discussed it with Dr. Graham's advisors, but they just smiled and shrugged it off. "Dr. Graham has a policy of not responding to criticism," they told me. "He says that if you wrestle with skunks, even if you win, you lose."

I've never forgotten that, and many times when I've been criticized in ministry I've just shrugged it off. Too often we get our feelings hurt, we let ourselves get upset, or we take offense too easily. But do you remember how Jesus was rejected in Nazareth? They took Him to the brow of the hill to push Him off. But the Bible laconically says that "passing through the midst of them, He went His way."

The dogs bark but the caravan passes.

Proverbs 12:16 says, "A fool's displeasure is known at once, but whoever ignores an insult is sensible."

The apostle Paul said in Romans 12:18, "Live peaceably with all men." But he attached two qualifiers: (1) if it be possible and (2) as far as it depends on you.

Occasionally we have to respond to an insult or answer our critics, but usually the best response is no response. Wrestling with skunks isn't a recommended sport.

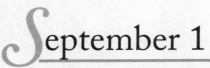

September 1

Sing to Him; sing praise to Him;
*tell about **all** His wonderful works!*
1 Chronicles 16:9

There's an old joke about a minister whose route to work every day took him through a park where an old fellow habitually sat on a bench. One day the minister, feeling a surge of compassion for the fellow, handed him an envelope containing ten dollars and a note saying "Never Despair." As he passed the next day, the man handed him back an envelope containing sixty dollars. The old codger explained, "Never Despair was in the money, paying six to one in the second race."

We always win when we make up our minds to Never Despair, as we repeatedly learn from studying the life of King David. In 1 Chronicles 16, David composed a hymn of praise as the ark of the covenant was brought into Jerusalem. It began: "Give thanks to the LORD; call on His name; proclaim His deeds among the peoples. Sing to Him; sing praise to Him; tell about all His wonderful works!"

Singing is one of God's greatest antidotes to despair. It affects us in four ways: In body, as we tap our feet, clap our hands, dance, or sway. In mind, as we soak in the great theology contained in the historic hymns. In emotion, as we experience the feelings engendered by the melodies and harmonies. And in soul, as we lift our hearts and minds in praise to God.

From Genesis to Revelation, the Bible is filled with psalms, hymns, and spiritual songs. We're holier, healthier, and happier people when we sing of all His wonderful works.

September 2

Reflect on what I am saying,
for the Lord will give you insight into all this.
Remember Jesus Christ.

2 Timothy 2:7–8 (NIV)

I've just checked out of a motel in Tulsa, and my room was an icebox. The air-conditioner was one of those under-the-window units, and no matter how I adjusted the setting, it still blew out cold air. I didn't want maintenance staff tromping through my room, so I just endured it. This morning as I prepared to check out, I noticed another thermostat, this one on the wall, set in the low sixties. When I adjusted it, the air-conditioner responded immediately. Evidently when the room was updated, the controls were switched.

Our emotions are like that. They blow hot and cold, unresponsive to our efforts to adjust them. Sometimes when I'm angry, depressed, or anxious I try to adjust my mood, but it doesn't cooperate. The real thermostat is my brain, and the best way to adjust my emotions is by adjusting my thoughts. If I can start thinking differently, my feelings respond. That's why the Bible puts so much emphasis on our minds.

In 2 Timothy 2, Paul addressed Timothy's insecurities, telling him to change the way he was thinking. "Think of yourself, not as a timid soul endangered by persecution, but as a soldier for Christ, a hard-working farmer, and a disciplined athlete. Meditate on those images, and focus your mind on Jesus Christ." We control our emotions by controlling our thoughts, and we do that with the Word of God.

September 3

*I am now going the way of **all** the earth,*
*and you know with **all** your heart and **all** your soul that*
none of the good promises the LORD your God made to you has failed.
Everything was fulfilled for you; not one promise has failed.

Joshua 23:14

Katrina and I made a trip to Florida to visit an elderly friend named Antoinette Johnson. At ninety-one and living in a retirement home in Juno Beach, she loves the Lord with great devotion, is a diligent student of Scripture, and can hardly wait to see Him face-to-face.

When we entered her apartment, we saw a big sign reading: "DNR"—"Do Not Resuscitate." She explained, "I don't want some paramedic dragging me back when I'm just about to meet my Lord!"

Over her bed was a framed picture of the Mount of Olives. She said, "That's the place to which He is going to return, and every night I literally sleep with that thought hanging over my head."

How like Joshua.

He was aged when he spoke the words of chapter 23, and when he said he was going the way of all the earth, he was confessing he was near the portals of death; but his heart was resting on God's promises, none of which had ever failed him.

How wonderful to retire each evening under the shadow of the Mount of Olives, to sleep with a promise for a pillow, and to awaken with the thought that soon we'll awaken in His glorious presence forever.

Not one of His promises can ever fail.

September 4

*His spirit was refreshed by **all** of you.*

2 Corinthians 7:13

I recall hearing Ruth Graham once talk about Philemon, who refreshed the hearts of Paul and others (Philemon 7, 20). Mrs. Graham advised us college students to learn how to refresh others. In this passage in 2 Corinthians, Paul said that the weary spirit of Titus was refreshed by "all of you"—by his visit with the entire Corinthian congregation.

A recent study indicated that people living in the same house as someone exhibiting signs of depression die seven years sooner than the average. The report wasn't that the depressed person died earlier but the loved ones living with him or her. It's hard to live with someone suffering a mental illness. But how wonderful to live with those whose hearts overflow with the joy of Jesus, and how influential are those who learn to refresh themselves that they might refresh others. A cheerful look brings joy to the heart of others (Prov. 15:30).

It is prayer, meditation, and converse with God
that refreshes, restores, and renews the temper of our minds,
at all times, under all trials, after all conflicts with the world. . . .
As our day, so is our strength. Without this healing and refreshing of spirit, duties grow to be burdens, the events of life chafe
our temper, employments lower the tone of our minds,
and we become fretful, irritable, and impatient.

—Henry Edward Manning,
nineteenth-century British archbishop

He who refreshes others will himself be refreshed.

Proverbs 11:25 (NIV)

September 5

READING: 2 CORINTHIANS 11:26–33

*Not to mention other things,
there is the daily pressure on me:
my care for **all** the churches.*

2 Corinthians 11:28

Some people think a pastor's job is easy—a thirty-minute work-week—but hours of preparation go into that half-hour sermon; and between Sundays are countless visits to hospitals, nursing homes, and shut-ins. Plus phone calls and e-mails from friends and foes, staff meetings, deacons' meetings, funerals, weddings, denominational affairs, counseling sessions, budget meetings, mission trips, paperwork, reference forms, community functions, baptisms, and prospect follow-up. Not to mention soul-winning and disciple-making.

We expect a pastor to be an orator, a biblical scholar, a student of the popular culture, a skilled administrator, a trained counselor, a conflict negotiator, a one-person complaint department, an evangelist, an educator, a PR spokesperson, and a change agent who can make improvements without altering anything. We want our pastor to be young enough to have energy and vision, yet old enough to keep the senior adults happy. We want our pastor to be innovative enough to change things, but traditional enough to keep things the same.

And take it from me—a small number of demanding, critical, negative, and vocal people can drown out a thousand encouraging words. I've found it more difficult to get saved people happy than to get lost people saved.

All of which is to say this—pray for your pastor and love your pastoral staff. Disagree with them rarely, quietly, and discretely. Remember to say thanks.

They depend on your encouragement in bearing the daily pressure of all the church.

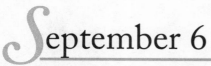

September 6

READING: 2 TIMOTHY 4:6–8

*In the future, there is reserved for me
the crown of righteousness,
which the Lord, the righteous Judge,
will give me on that day,
and not only to me,
but to **all** those who have loved His appearing.*

2 Timothy 4:8

Every generation has wanted the Lord to come back soon. One of our earliest documents, the *Didache*, says, "Let not your lamps be quenched, nor your loins unloosed; but be ready, for you know not the hour in which our Lord will come."

St. Cyril wrote in the fourth century, "Let us wait and look for the Lord's coming upon the clouds from heaven."

Augustine expected the Lord to return around the year AD 1000. In the 1300s, John Wycliffe concluded that the end of the world and the second coming of Christ should be expected immediately. In the sixteenth century, John Calvin advised, "Hunger after Christ until the dawning of that great day when our Lord will fully manifest the glory of His kingdom."

In the eighteenth century, John Wesley said, "The Spirit in the heart of the true believer says with earnest desire, 'Come, Lord Jesus.'" In the twentieth century, evangelist Billy Graham said: "Many times when I go to bed at night I think to myself that before I awaken Christ may come."

When He comes, He'll have a special reward for all who have longed for His appearing—the crown of righteousness. Let's train ourselves to think of our Lord's return whenever we see a sunrise or sunset. Every time clouds and sun merge in spectacular form, let's remember to pray, "Even so, come, Lord Jesus."

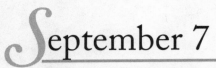

September 7

*One God and Father of **all**,*
*who is above **all** and through **all** and in **all**.*

Ephesians 4:6

The Ponte Fabricio is the oldest bridge in Rome, built before the days of Christ. It's sometimes called the "Bridge of Four Heads" because Pope Sixtus V commissioned four renowned architects to restore the bridge in the sixteenth century. The project was marred, however, by arguments and fistfights between the four. Finally Sixtus had them beheaded on the bridge, and there he erected a monument to them—four heads carved into one block of stone. "Now," he said, "for eternity they are committed to a peaceful and quiet unity."[68]

Our homes and churches should be bridges to happiness, but squabbling and division sometimes mar them. In Ephesians 4, the Bible appeals for unity, telling us we must work hard to avoid dissension. With all humility and gentleness and patience, we accept one another in love, keeping the unity of the Spirit (vv. 2–4).

The reason? We're one family—there is one body and one Spirit, one hope, one Lord, one faith, one baptism, one God and Father of all, who is . . .

- *Over* all: He holds sovereign control over our lives.
- *Through* all: He manifests Himself in this world through us.
- *In* all: He lives within us by His Spirit, and our bodies are His earthly temples.

Ours is a church of one Head, from whom the whole body, fitted and held together by every supporting ligament, grows and builds itself up in love as each part does its work (v. 16).

September 8

*To **all** who are in Rome, loved by God, called to be saints. . . .*
*I thank my God through Jesus Christ for **all** of you*
*because the news of your faith is being reported in **all** the world.*
Romans 1:7–8

Knowing he could be martyred at any time, the apostle Paul stopped outside Corinth at the villa of friend Gaius, and there he wrote the book of Romans. His purpose was (1) to prepare Christians in Rome for his intended visit, and (2) to deposit with them a treatise of his doctrine of justification by faith so that, should he die, a digest of his theology would be on record in the center of the Roman Empire, where it could influence all the world and all of history.

The book of Romans is made up of sixteen rich chapters, and it cannot be read too often or studied too much.

The golden-mouthed preacher John Chrysostom had this epistle read to him twice a week, and his sermons changed the world.

A pagan philosopher and prodigal named Aurelius Augustine was converted when his eyes fell on the book of Romans, and he became one of the greatest leaders in the history of Christianity.

A distraught German monk named Martin Luther discovered the book of Romans and set the world on fire.

A confused Anglican named John Wesley, sitting in a Moravian meetinghouse in London's Aldersgate Street and listening to a reading of Luther's preface to Romans, felt his heart strangely warmed. It sparked a revival that changed history.

As F. F. Bruce said, "There's no telling what may happen when people begin to study the Epistle to the Romans."

It takes about twenty minutes to read straight through Romans, but it's time well spent. It takes a lifetime to absorb the book of Romans, but it makes a well-formed soul.

September 9

*Give thanks in **all** circumstances,*
for this is God's will for you in Christ Jesus.
1 Thessalonians 5:18 (NIV)

This verse gives us the true secret of a healthy heart. It doesn't tell us to give thanks *for* all circumstances, but *in* all circumstances, because God is with us through all the circumstances of life. His mercies are new every morning, His compassions never fail, and He causes all things to work for the good of those who love Him.

I recently read of a young would-be journalist who moved to Manhattan, where his career sputtered and stalled. He grew so depressed that one cold and damp Saturday he wanted to stay in bed all day. But he had to pick up a photograph across town, so he set out walking. Somehow it came to his mind specifically to look for things that seemed pleasing to him—a baby in a buggy, the sizzling smells wafting from a bistro, a jet piercing the clouds. He never forgot his "thanksgiving walk," and it transformed his outlook.

Psychologists have studied the psychological effects of gratitude, and a new science of thanksgiving is emerging. People who approach life by seeing and counting their blessings each day are less depressed, less envious, and less anxious. They feel better about their lives, they're more optimistic and energetic, they exercise more, have stronger immune systems, encounter fewer illnesses, get more sleep, enjoy greater life expectancy, and have happier homes.

Give thanks in all circumstances today, for this is God's will for you in Christ Jesus.

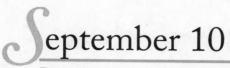

September 10

The LORD does whatever He pleases in heaven and on earth,
*in the sea and **all** the depths.*

Psalm 135:6

We were crowded in the cabin,
    Not a soul would dare to sleep,
It was midnight on the waters,
    And a storm was on the deep.

"'Tis a fearful thing in winter
    To be shattered by the blast,
And to hear the rattling trumpet
    Thunder, "Cut away the mast!"

So we shuddered there in silence,
    For the stoutest held his breath,
While the hungry sea was roaring
    And the breakers talked with Death.

As thus we sat in darkness,
    Each one busy with his prayers,
"We are lost!" the captain shouted
    As he staggered down the stairs.

But his little daughter whispered,
    As she took his icy hand,
"Isn't God, upon the ocean,
    Just the same as on the land?"

Then we kissed the little maiden.
    And we spoke in better cheer,
And we anchored safe in harbour
    When the morn was shining clear.

—*James T. Fields, "The Captain's Daughter"*

September 11

*They are filled with **all** unrighteousness,*
evil, greed, and wickedness.

Romans 1:29

In 1954, President Eisenhower, responding to a reporter's question about Indochina, said, "You have . . . what you would call the 'falling domino' principle. You have a row of dominoes set up, you knock over the first one, and what will happen to the last one is the certainty that it will go over very quickly. So you could have a beginning of a disintegration that would have the most profound influences." This became known as the famous "Domino Theory" that led to the Vietnam War.

Historians still debate the merits of the Domino Theory, but the Bible has a Domino Theory of its own, except that it's no theory. Romans 1:18–32 is a perceptive analysis of any society—be it Sodom, Greece, Rome, or America—that collapses spiritually. It begins with a rejection of God as Creator (vv. 18–21). That leads to idolatry, for if we don't recognize the Creator we have to find substitutes (vv. 22–23). That leads to immorality because the restraints of holiness are removed (vv. 24–25). That leads to rampant homosexuality and to the homosexualization of the culture (vv. 26–27). That eventually leads to total moral breakdown as people become filled with all unrighteousness, evil, greed, and wickedness (vv. 28–32).

These dominos are falling, and our one prayer and hope is REVIVAL.

O Breath of life, come sweeping through us,
Revive Thy church with life and power;
O Breath of life, come, cleanse, renew us,
And fit Thy church to meet this hour.

—Bessie Head, c. 1914

September 12

READING: PSALM 104:24–35

*I will sing to the LORD **all** my life.*
Psalm 104:33

This week I received a letter from a woman who had read my book *Then Sings My Soul*. She said she awakens almost every morning with a song in her heart, and usually it's a hymn. During her devotions, she looks up that hymn and sings it. But recently she awoke with anxiety. Some doors had opened that seemed too big for her. She had been asked to be the keynote speaker at a conference and felt overwhelmed. The first thought upon awakening was, *I can't do this*. During her devotions, the anxiety wouldn't leave. She'd been working for several years to cultivate peace with God, but now all that work seemed undone in a single morning.

Suddenly the words of an old hymn came to mind: "My faith has found a resting place, not in device or creed. / I trust the Ever-living One—His wounds for me shall plead. / I need no other argument, I need no other plea; / It is enough that Jesus died, and that He died for me." And this woman discovered once again that anxiety can't exist in the soul that is resting in simple faith in the Lord Jesus.

Nor can it exist in the souls of those who sing the Lord's songs all their lives.

I wonder if you feel as I do about the heavenliness of song.
I believe truly that Satan cannot endure it,
and so slips out of the room—
more or less!—when there is true song.

—*Amy Carmichael*[69]

September 13

*Go into **all** the world
and preach the gospel to the whole creation.*

Mark 16:15

In a cemetery at Yale University is the grave of a remarkable missionary named Hiram Bingham. As a young man, he felt impressed that the "Go" in Mark 16:15 was meant for him, and it resonated like this: "Go to the Sandwich Islands [modern Hawaii] and preach the gospel to every creature there."

Arriving there in 1819, Bingham found the inhabitants with no written language. They were hardened gamblers, thieves, and alcoholics who practiced raw immorality and human sacrifice. Children were routinely killed, torture was widespread, and disease was rampant.

Bingham studied the language, reduced it to writing, translated the New Testament, established schools, and taught hygiene to the people. After four years, the first native convert was baptized. A revival swept over the islands that resembled the Pentecostal days of Acts.

On February 10, 1822, after preaching to huge crowds from Mark 16:15, Bingham wrote, "I discoursed on the great commission given by Christ to His disciples to proclaim His gospel in all the world, as the grand reason of our coming to them and of their attending to the message of His ambassadors."

It's the Grand Reason for our lives too.

PS: Hiram's son, Hiram Bingham II, also became a missionary in Hawaii. His grandson, Hiram Bingham III, was an explorer who became a U.S. Senator and the governor of Connecticut. His great-grandson, Hiram Bingham IV, became American vice-consul in Marseille, France, during World War II, and rescued Jews from the Holocaust.

September 14

*"Come, for **all** things are now ready."*
*But they **all** with one accord began to make excuses.*
Luke 14:17–18 (NKJV)

One Sunday I ended my message with a story from the autobiography of the frontier evangelist Peter Cartwright, who tried earnestly to lead a young man to faith in Christ. But the fellow kept putting off the decision. Then he suddenly fell ill, and it became apparent he was dying. When Cartwright tried to witness to him a final time, the young man screamed, "It's too late. I'm lost! I must make my bed in hell! Lost! Forever lost!"

I then closed with the verse that says, "Seek the Lord while He may be found; call to Him while He is near" (Isa. 55:6). As I gave the invitation, I saw a woman hurry out of her seat and come down the aisle to kneel at the altar. With heartfelt tears, she prayed and gave her heart to the Lord Jesus. We rejoiced with her.

Two days later, she went to pick up her son's bicycle at the home of her estranged husband. The man came out of the house and pumped her full of bullets as she got out of her car.

I prayed with her on Sunday and preached her funeral on Friday.

What if she had put off her decision?

∽

A burden weighs my soul I can no longer bear;
Unless removed this night, 'Twill sink me into despair.
It must be settled tonight, I can no longer wait,
Peace with my God I now must have,
Tomorrow may be too late.

—*C. B. Kendall, 1881*

September 15

READING: DEUTERONOMY 14:1–2

The LORD has chosen you to be His special people
*out of **all** the peoples on the face of the earth.*
Deuteronomy 14:2

In this verse, Moses is telling the young Israelite nation that of all the nations in history, they are set apart and special. From their tribes would come the Messiah, God's channel of redemption for all the earth. The King James Version uses the phrase *His peculiar people,* and in 1 Peter 2:9, Christians are described in the same way: *But ye are . . . a peculiar people.*

I sort of like the word *peculiar.* With the kind of world we face, the idea of being peculiar for the Lord isn't so bad. It's like the man hauled before the emperor. "If you don't recant your faith," threatened the monarch, "I'll throw you in prison."

"Then I'll have a whole new group to preach to in the jail," said the man.

"I'll kill you," roared the emperor. But the man replied, "I have eternal life through Christ."

"I'll have you tortured," said the emperor, to which the man said, "Then I'll be following in the steps of my Lord, for He, too, was tortured, and in the process He redeemed the world."

"I'll condemn you to slavery!"

"I'm already a slave to Christ."

"I'll burn you at the stake."

"You threaten me with flames that burn for a moment, but you're facing hell."

The emperor finally released the Christian, shaking his head and saying, "What do you do with a man like that?"

Isn't that what the world should say of us?

September 16

*Do you not know that the runners in a stadium **all** race,*
but only one receives the prize?
Run in such a way that you may win.

1 Corinthians 9:24

In 1904, a Cuban mail carrier named Felix Carvajal boasted he was going to the Olympics in St. Louis and win the marathon for Cuba. He had no money or backing; but, quitting his job, he managed to catch a boat to New Orleans and hitchhike to St. Louis, where the American team took pity on him and gave him food and a bed.

Felix had neither uniform nor running shoes, nor training or experience. Cutting off his pants above the knees, he appeared at the starting line in street shoes. The heat was withering that day and the humidity was oppressive. Most of the runners collapsed, and one nearly died. But Felix was from Cuba—the heat and humidity put him right at home. He laughed, joked, and talked all the way until he was within two miles of the prize, and far ahead of all challengers.

Then he spotted an orchard alongside the road, and he stopped to eat an apple. Then another, and another. The apples were green, and suddenly Felix doubled over with stomach cramps and could only watch as three men overtook him.

Of the thirty-one starters that day, only fourteen finished the race. Felix came in fourth, but he should have been first, which brings us to Paul's exhortation: The Christian life is a marathon. All the runners run, but it takes self-discipline to finish the race.

Don't stop too soon.

September 17

All that is in the world—
the lust of the flesh, the lust of the eyes, and the pride of life—
is not of the Father but is of the world.
1 John 2:16 (NKJV)

Rev. Charles Spurgeon was counseling a girl about loving the world or loving Christ. They were standing in the Metropolitan Tabernacle, and Spurgeon advised her to this effect: "There are three things you can do, and I will explain those three things by using an illustration. When you leave the Tabernacle today, you'll walk onto the street and a streetcar will come by. You can go up to the streetcar, put one foot in the car, and leave the other on the ground. But if you don't have a tumble, I'll be very surprised. That's what happens to people who try to keep in touch with the world and in touch with Christ at the same time. They have a terrible fall before long.

"Or you can stand there and let the streetcar pass by. You see it, hear its bell, and notice the people on board, but you stay where you are. That's a picture of those who love the world and stand in the mud of their sins.

"The third option is to step totally off the street into the car, entrust your full weight and being to it, and let it take you where it's going. And that's what I recommend. Give yourself fully to Christ. Jump in with both feet. Let the Conductor guide you along the tracks of holiness until at last He brings you to the terminal of His glory."

Take myself, and I will be
ever, only, all for Thee.

—Frances Havergal, 1874

September 18

READING: ACTS 19:11–20

*Then fear fell on **all** of them,*
and the name of the Lord Jesus was magnified.

Acts 19:17

When I was a boy, my dad took an overnight trip and returned with a truckload of army surplus materials left over from World War II. There were tents and hammocks and canteens, which we used on camping trips. He even returned with two jeeps, which became orchard vehicles. But to me the greatest treasures were several pairs of binoculars. He gave me a set, and I have them to this day. I remember gazing in amazement at the distant moon. I could see its landscape and features so much more clearly, and my childlike wonder was boundless.

I think of those binoculars whenever I encounter this word *magnify* in the Bible. It's a praise word and describes how we should worship the Lord. For example, the psalmist said, "I will . . . magnify Him with thanksgiving," and the Virgin Mary said, "My soul magnifies the Lord" (Ps. 69:30, Luke 1:46 NKJV). In Acts 19, Paul's exercise of apostolic authority caused fear to fall on all the people, and the name of the Lord was magnified.

Magnifying something does not increase its size—my binoculars didn't make the moon any bigger. But it became bigger in my eyes. I saw it more clearly, and my wonder increased in direct proportion. Worship and thanksgiving are the binoculars by which the Lord Jesus Christ is magnified in our eyes and we see Him more nearly as He is.

Oh, magnify the Lord with me, and let us exalt His name forever (Ps. 40:16).

Let your name, not mine, be praised.
Let your work, not mine, be magnified.

—Thomas à Kempis

September 19

READING: 2 CHRONICLES 8:12–16

*All of Solomon's work was carried out from the day
the foundation was laid for the LORD's temple until it was finished.
So the LORD's temple was completed.*

2 Chronicles 8:16

George Herbert, the great seventeenth-century British poet,
studied the biblical descriptions of Solomon's temple, the
cathedrals of his own day, and his own local church. One day
while gazing at the floor of one of them, he thought of the analogy
between it and his own soul, which he described in his brilliant
poem *The Church Floore*.

> Mark you the floore? that square and speckled stone,
>   Which looks so firm and strong,
>   Is PATIENCE:
> And th' other black and grave, wherewith each one
>   Is checkered all along,
>   HUMILITIE:
> The gentle rising, which on either hand
>   Leads to the quire above,
>   Is CONFIDENCE:
> But the sweet cement, which in one sure band
>   Ties the whole frame, is LOVE
>   And CHARITIE. . . .
>
> Blest be the Architect Whose art
> Could build so strong in a weak heart!

*You yourselves, as living stones,
are being built into a spiritual house.*

1 Peter 2:5

September 20

*So rid yourselves of **all** . . . envy.*

1 Peter 2:1

The twentieth-century composer John W. Peterson wrote such classics as "It Took a Miracle" and "Heaven Came Down and Glory Filled My Soul." He was one of Christianity's beloved musicians, yet he once acknowledged that he fell victim to jealousy toward other composers. He was afraid that newer, younger artists would rise through the ranks and invade his "territory." Whenever anyone would sing something by another popular composer such as Ralph Carmichael, it would frustrate him.

But Peterson acknowledged his sin of envy before God and prayed for deliverance. One night at two or three in the morning, unable to sleep, he finally came to grips with it and confessed his sin of pride. Then he began to pray for those whom he had envied. "Lord, bless Ralph Carmichael. Bless Kurt Kaiser. Bless Otis Skillings—he's been writing some wonderful music. Bless Bill Gaither. . . ."

Peterson said that although the temptation hasn't gone away completely, he has achieved a breakthrough in his attitude through prayer. Now "when Satan lights his fires of resentment and jealousy, I can put them out by thanking God for my fellow writers, asking Him to bless them, and taking delight in their success."

Whatever our temptations, there is victory when you approach them seriously, with determination, and in the power of Jesus Christ. The Bible tells us to reckon ourselves dead to sin and to rid ourselves of envy—and it's hard to be jealous of others when you're praying for God's blessings on their lives.[70]

September 21

Therefore the LORD is waiting to show you mercy,
and is rising up to show you compassion,
for the LORD is a just God.
*Happy are **all** who wait patiently for Him.*

Isaiah 30:18

My friend Joe Henderson fought in World War II and Korea. Afterward he went into business and came to faith in Christ through the influence of an aunt. He was later appointed executive director of one of the largest global ministries on earth, the Gideons.

In the early days of his Christian life, Joe was burdened for a half brother, who was heir to a vast fortune worth 850 million dollars. Joe witnessed to him aggressively—too aggressively—resulting in a broken relationship.

Still Joe prayed for his brother day after day, year after year, for fifty-seven years. Finally, when both men were in their eighties, the brother had a stroke and Joe called on him. Joe cautiously asked if he could pray, and the other man was willing. On the next visit, the brother brightened up and said, "Joe, I am born again!"

It had taken fifty-seven years—nearly six decades—of prayer.

Isaiah 30:18 says that God is *waiting* to show mercy on us, and that we must all *wait* patiently for Him. Sometimes He doesn't answer prayers as promptly as we'd like. It takes time to align all the circumstances for the best outcome. It takes time for faith to develop and deepen. It takes time for the human heart to soften or heal.

So keep praying, and wait patiently for Him.

September 22

A time is coming
*when **all** who are in the graves will hear His voice.*
John 5:28

Grace Coolidge was one of America's most popular First Ladies, but her world fell apart when her son Calvin Jr., sixteen, died following an injury on the White House tennis courts. President Calvin Coolidge never recovered from the tragedy, later writing, "When he went, the power and the glory of the Presidency went with him." Grace, however, strengthened herself in the Lord and anticipated the day of reunion. Out of the experience, she wrote a poem entitled "The Open Door," one of only a handful of poems ever published by a First Lady.

> You, my son,
> Have shown me God.
> Your kiss upon my cheek
> Has made me feel the gentle touch
> Of Him who leads us on.
> The memory of your smile, when young,
> Reveals His face,
> As mellowing years come on apace.
> And when you went before,
> You left the gates of Heaven ajar
> That I might glimpse,
> Approaching from afar,
> The glories of His grace.
> Hold, son, my hand,
> Guide me along the path,
> That, coming,
> I may stumble not,
> Nor roam,
> Nor fail to show the way
> Which leads us—Home.

September 23

READING: 1 THESSALONIANS 5:19–28

*Test **all** things. Hold on to what is good.*
Stay away from every form of evil.
1 Thessalonians 5:21–22

My old professor Dr. Otis Braswell once assigned to me a book by F. B. Meyer called *The Christ Life for Your Life,* the thesis of which is that our external behavior isn't based on rules and reforms, but on the reality of Christ who lives within. Because of the indwelling Christ, we're sensitive to the Holy Spirit's presence, and we modify our attitudes and behavior as He convicts us of sin. We test all things and cleave to the good.

Dr. Meyer gave this illustration: "I was staying with another man, a pastor. I had said nothing about smoking—I never do single out sins—I had not alluded to the habit; but one day we were walking along a street that led over a river, and to my surprise as we got to the apex of the bridge, he took his tobacco pouch and pipe and threw them over, and said, 'There, I have settled that.' Turning to me, he said, 'I know, Mr. Meyer, you have said nothing about it; but for the last few months God has been asking me to set a new example to my young men. . . . God was searching me, and I was fighting Him; but it is all settled now, sir, it is all done now.'"

This man made an internal, Spirit-guided decision based on prolonged conviction, externalized it by symbolically and literally throwing his pipe in the river, and confessing it publicly to another person.[71]

The old commentator Matthew Henry gives us good advice: "We should therefore abstain from evil, and all appearances of evil, from sin, and from that which looks like sin, leads to it, and borders upon it."

September 24

*Then **all** the people would come early in the morning
to hear Him in the temple complex.*
Luke 21:38

In college I discovered the habit of rising early to hear His voice. My school required students to rise at 6:15, and, after showering and dressing, to devote a half hour to personal devotions before breakfast. I resisted at first, but it gradually became an ingrained habit.

British army chaplain Bishop Taylor Smith testified, "As soon as I awake each morning, I rise from bed at once. I dress promptly. I wash myself, shave, and comb my hair. Then fully attired, wide-awake and properly groomed, I go quietly to my study. There, before God Almighty and Christ my King, I humbly present myself as a loyal subject to my Sovereign, ready and eager to be of service to Him for the day."

***Early in the morning** Abraham went to the place
where he had stood before the Lord.*
Genesis 19:27

***Early in the morning** Jacob took the stone that was near his head and set
it up as a marker. He poured oil on top of it and named the place Bethel.*
Genesis 28:18–19

*Very **early in the morning,** while it was still dark, He got up, went
out, and made His way to a deserted place. And He was praying there.*
Mark 1:35

*Very **early in the morning,** on the first day of the week,
they went to the tomb at sunrise.*
Mark 16:2

Early in the morning my song shall rise to Thee.
—*Reginald Heber*

September 25

The LORD of Hosts will prepare a feast
*for **all** the peoples on this mountain . . . .*
On this mountain He will destroy the burial shroud . . .
*over **all** the peoples, the sheet covering **all** the nations;*
He will destroy death forever.

Isaiah 25:6–8

Centuries before Christ, Isaiah predicted that one day on a mountain God would (1) satisfy the spiritual hunger of the world, (2) rip away the shroud of death over humanity, and (3) destroy death forever. Verse 10 adds, "For the LORD's power will rest on this mountain."

When did God accomplish this? He did it on Mount Calvary when Jesus was crucified. Thank God for that mountain!

I saw in my dream, that the highway up which
Christian was to go was fenced on either side with
a wall, and that wall was called Salvation. Up this
way, therefore, did burdened Christian run, but not
without difficulty, because of the load on his back.
He ran thus till he came to a place ascending; and
upon that place stood a cross, and a little below, at
the bottom, a sepulcher. So I saw in my dream, that
just as Christian came up with the cross, his burden
loosed from his shoulders and fell from off his back,
and began to tumble, and so continued to do till it
came to the mouth of the sepulcher, where it fell in,
and I saw it no more. Then was Christian glad and
lightsome, and said with a merry heart, "He hath
given me rest by His sorrow, and life by His death."

—*John Bunyan in Pilgrim's Progress*

September 26

We do not have a High Priest
who cannot sympathize with our weakness,
*but was in **all** points tempted as we are,*
yet without sin.

Hebrews 4:15 (NKJV)

Some buildings are so substantial that we can't receive mobile phone service in them. Radio waves have a hard time penetrating the walls and the electronic fields of the building, so we have to walk outside into the open air to make a call.

Think of it as an illustration. When you're in the center of Christ, it's hard for the devil's radio waves to reach you. They're weakened by His overwhelming power. The more enclosed we are in the Lord, the stronger we'll be over temptation.

Jesus Himself, though tempted in all points like us, was absolutely sinless. He had no trouble resisting temptation in the Gospels, and He has no trouble now. When we say, "Not I, but Christ," reckoning ourselves dead to sin but alive to Him, we find that He Himself resists temptation through us.

Our ability to trounce temptation is in direct proportion to our fellowship with Christ. If we're walking with the Lord each day, having our daily quiet time, memorizing His Word, praying without ceasing, and enjoying unbroken fellowship with Christ—if we are abiding in Him—temptation will lose much of its power.

There's no temptation to which we're immune; but there's no temptation over which Jesus isn't victorious. So when the devil knocks, let Christ open the door.

> Tempted in all points as we are,
> and yet without sin was He found;
> God-man, our frailties He knows,
> and His grace doth to sinners abound.
>
> —*Leila N. Morris, 1911*

September 27

I declare the end from the beginning,
and from long ago what is not yet done, saying:
My plan will take place, and I will do **all** *My will.*

Isaiah 46:10

When I order plants from a nursery catalog, a little box notes, "If we're out of the item you want, may we substitute one of equal or greater value?" When we make our requests to God, we should always say, "Yes, Lord, You may substitute. You may grant an alternative answer of equal or greater value." If He says no to our requests, it's because His plan is better. His delays are not denials, and His denials are but disguised blessings.

But You, taking Your own secret counsel and noting the real point of her desire, did not grant her what she was then asking in order to grant to her the thing that she had always been asking.

—Augustine about his mother's earnest prayers that he not go to Italy.
(He went anyway, and there he was converted to Christ.)

How often has God said no to my earnest prayers
that He might answer my deepest longings,
give me something more, something better.

—Ruth Bell Graham

God wants us to trust him, no matter what He does. There is a heavenly carelessness that leaves it all with Jesus and doesn't become upset when He does things contrary to what we expected.

—Vance Havner

And so I thank Him from my heart, for what His love denies.

—Fanny Crosby

September 28

READING: JOHN 18:28–38

*I find in Him no fault at **all**.*
John 18:38 (KJV)

Not even Pontius Pilate while condemning Him could find fault in the sinless Son of God. Jesus was as pure as Adam before the fall and as holy as Almighty God in eternity. Though He had mixed and mingled with humanity for thirty-three years in dusty towns and jostling cities, and though Satan himself had tested Him, there was nothing in the Son of Man to mar the brilliance of His intrinsic and white-hot holiness.

Otherwise, how could He have offered Himself for sinners such as you and me; for though there is no fault in Him, there is no good in us.

The old commentator Matthew Henry correctly observed, "When Pilate declared, 'I find no fault in this man,' he did thereby in effect pronounce the sacrifice without blemish."

"He alone," wrote Jewish scholar Alfred Edersheim, "has exhibited a life in which absolutely no fault could be found; and promulgated a teaching to which absolutely no exception can be taken. Admittedly He is the One perfect Man—the ideal of humanity, His doctrine the one absolute teaching. The world has known none other, none equal."

. . . That He, to Whom no sin was known,
Might cleanse His people from their own.

—Caelius Sedulius, fifth century

For born Son-like, and led forth lamb-like,
and slaughtered sheep-like, and buried man-like,
He has risen God-like, being by nature God and man.

—Melito of Sardis, c. AD 150

September 29

*For You, LORD, are the Most High over **all** the earth;*
*You are exalted above **all** the gods.*

Psalm 97:9

Have you ever noticed that, as a rule, the higher an object's elevation, the more unchanging is its nature? Dr. A. T. Pierson (1837–1911), the brilliant Bible teacher from New York City who filled in for Charles Spurgeon during the latter's illness, wrote:

> That which is "most high" is lifted up above all else. The lower down we are the more perishable everything is. The grass under your foot in the summer is one of the frailest things in nature; it grows and blooms today, it withers and decays tomorrow. You ascend a little higher and you find the trees that last not only for one season but many seasons, till you come to great trees like the Sequoia in the Californian forests, that have been standing for 3,000 or 3,500 years, but even these decay and fall by-and-by. You rise above the level of the trees, and come to the hills that last for ages. . . . You soar above the mountains, and you come to the planets that are constantly changing their places in the sky as they move around the sun in their annual journeys; but far beyond the planets stand the fixed stars that never have changed their place since time began.
>
> So you see that the farther up you go, the nearer you come to that which does not change, and beyond all these is He who is "the same yesterday, and today, and forever." He is the unchanging God and the unchanging friend of His people.

September 30

"My grace is sufficient for you,
for power is perfected in weakness."
*Therefore, I will most gladly boast **all** the more about my weaknesses,*
so that Christ's power may reside in me.

2 Corinthians 12:9

Grace is a five-letter word summarizing all the riches of God on our behalf—His love, power, promises, provision, presence, eternity, availability, and His very Son—all sufficient, more than enough, abundantly provided, and lavishly given. That's why we can *all the more* boast in our weaknesses. When God helps, blesses, and uses us in spite of our infirmities, all the glory is His.

In *Grace Abounding to the Chief of Sinners*, John Bunyan, the seventeenth-century preacher and author of *Pilgrim's Progress*, tells of being so cast down he could hardly function. Then 2 Corinthians 12:9 came to mind, and for several weeks the phrase *My grace is sufficient* stayed in his mind and kept him from despair. When spirits again collapsed, this verse came back with greater force:

> These words did, with great power, suddenly break in
> upon me, "My grace is sufficient for thee, My grace
> is sufficient for thee, My grace is sufficient for thee,"
> three times together; and, oh! methought that every
> word was a mighty word unto me: *My*, and *grace*, and
> *sufficient*, and *for thee* . . . . At which time my under-
> standing was so enlightened, that it was as though
> I had seen the Lord Jesus look down from heaven
> through the tiles upon me, and direct those words
> unto me.[72]

October 1

READING: MARK 13:9–13

*And the good news must first be proclaimed to **all** nations.*
Mark 13:10

When we moved into our house on Pennington Bend eighteen years ago, our little girls found small maple tree seedlings growing in the pots and flower beds. Like a mighty commander-in-chief, a maple tree somewhere in our neighborhood had sent its air force of miniature helicopters across our lawn, and as a result we had little maple sprouts coming up everywhere. Our girls potted and repotted some of them, and by and by they were large enough for planting. Today we have a beautiful grove of maples towering over our back deck. And every spring, they send thousands of little helicopters flying across our lawn. I find scores of tiny little maple trees coming up in all my pots and flowerbeds.

The Lord placed within those trees an enormous and urgent drive to reproduce, and they prolifically scatter their seeds to the four winds.

We, too, are here on this earth to scatter prolifically the gospel seed to the four winds. We've got a message to share with the neighbors and with the nations—to all people and to all countries. We share Christ in attitude, letting others see our joy. We share Him in action, letting others see our lives. But we must also share Him assertively, specifically telling someone else the Good News that Jesus Saves. And when we've finished our task, then He'll return.

*This good news of the kingdom will be proclaimed
in all the world as a testimony to all nations.
And then the end will come.*
Matthew 24:14

October 2

All *my springs are in You.*
Psalm 87:7

When I was a youngster, my parents built a home at the foot of Roan Mountain on the Tennessee and North Carolina border. My dad, who had grown up there, took countless hikes up the hillside looking for marshy ground indicating the presence of a spring. Using dynamite and a shovel, he dug back to the heads of springs, installed reservoirs, and piped the water down to the house. Many times I went with him to clean out the springs, and we were amazed at how these small creeks and brooks could perpetually run underground, never drying up, never exhausted, and always fresh and cool.

Psalm 87 was a psalm of rejoicing for those living in Jerusalem, the Mountain of God. This city wasn't built on a river or lake; it depended on the Gihon Spring for its water supply. But when the psalmist said, "All my springs are in you," he meant that all his innermost resources were found in His ever-flowing and overflowing Lord—all his courage, all his joy, all his resilience, all his optimism, all his hope, all his love, all his wisdom, all his patience.

The Lord Jesus is the source of that which refreshes our personalities and of all that makes our personalities refreshing. As Matthew Henry put it, "There is in Him an all-sufficiency of grace and strength; all our springs are in Him, and all our streams are from Him."

I thirst for springs of heavenly life,
and here all day they rise—
I seek the treasure of Thy love,
and close at hand it lies.

—*Anna Waring*

October 3

*I am able to do **all** things*
through Him who strengthens me.

Philippians 4:13

I don't think Paul spoke this verse with naked literalness, as in: "I can run a mile in six seconds." He was saying, "I can do whatever God calls me to do through Christ who strengthens me."

The context of Philippians 4:13 has something specific in mind. Paul was saying, "I can maintain a good attitude even in difficulty through Christ who strengthens me. Even here in my prison cell in want and destitution, I can be content. I have learned the secret of being content—whether well-fed or hungry, whether in abundance or in need. I am able to do all things through Him who strengthens me."

We don't need to stay angry, depressed, embittered, bereaved, anxious, or alarmed. We can have joy, contentment, and inner restfulness through Him who strengthens us with a good disposition. And if He helps us in our attitudes, He can help us with our actions.

Jesus, I have given myself up to Thy service.
The question with me is where shall I serve Thee?
I learn from Thy word it is Thy holy pleasure that
the Gospel be preached in all the world. My desire is,
O Lord, to engage where laborers are most wanted.
Perhaps one part of the field is more difficult than
another. I am equally unfit for any, but through Thy
strengthening me, I can do all things. O Lord, guide
me in this.

—Robert Morrison,
the first Protestant missionary to China, as a young man

October 4

He will give His angels orders concerning you,
*to protect you in **all** your ways.*

Psalm 91:11

Psalm 91 crops up in missionary biographies so frequently it could almost be called the Missionary's Psalm. For example, Robert Atchison was an alcoholic tramp who, following his conversion to Christ, became a missionary to Asia and traveled thousands of miles on foot, taking the gospel to remote areas. Once he and his wife labored amid the Black Death, but he later wrote: "We wrapped ourselves up in the ninety-first Psalm and continued about the Lord's business."[73]

It was Psalm 91 that persuaded John and Isobel Kuhn to return to China despite the outbreak of war between China and Japan in 1937, as she tells in her memoir *In the Arena.*[74]

Psalm 91 saved the life of missionary Sam James who, in a moment of deadly crisis in Vietnam, recalled its words and gained the presence of mind to outwit a group of Vietcong soldiers bent on his destruction on a dangerous road in the Vietnamese Delta.[75]

When evangelist D. L. Moody faced death on a sinking ship in the Atlantic, he read Psalm 91 to the terrified passengers, calming both them and himself.[76]

But of course, Psalm 91 and its promise of angelic protection isn't just for missionaries. Though we can't see them, God's angelic assistants are hovering about us constantly, meeting more needs than we realize and protecting us from dangers of which we're unaware. You are the "you" of Psalm 91:11: "He will give His angels orders concerning *you,* to protect you in all your ways."

October 5

Sing a new song to the LORD;
*sing to the LORD, **all** the earth.*

Psalm 96:1

I receive a lot of letters because of my book *Then Sings My Soul* on the history of hymns. One man wrote to thank me for helping preserve the stories of the old hymns, but he added, "I just can't stand all this new music with the drums and everything. I love the old songs."

I wrote back and told him I love the old hymns, too, but that if there's ever a generation of believers that doesn't write its own music, Christianity is dead. Every generation expresses their faith with original songs that flow from their hearts. We need to sing the old songs, but we also need the new ones.

The church has always practiced "blended worship," combining old hymns with newer compositions, and it reminds me of Jesus' words in Matthew 13:52: "Every student of Scripture instructed in the kingdom of heaven is like a landowner who brings out of his storeroom what is new and what is old."

The writer of Psalm 96 wrote a new hymn, and he wanted everyone singing it—all the earth. If all the earth were singing the Songs of Zion, all the earth would be happy, at peace, at one with God and each other, and blessed beyond measure.

You and I are included in that phrase "all the earth." So sing a new song to the Lord with all your heart. Or at least sing an old song with new vigor . . .

"For the Lord is great and greatly to be praised."

(v. 4 NKJV)

October 6

He is not God of the dead but of the living,
*because **all** are living to Him.*
Luke 20:38

What if someone asked you to prove from the Old Testament that we are immortal souls with eternal life in Christ, that there is life after death? That's the challenge the Sadducees flung into the face of Christ in Luke 20. It was the final week of our Lord's earthly life, and Jesus was fielding questions in the temple. The Sadducees, who didn't believe in the resurrection, pressed Him with a hypothetical story of a woman who had been repeatedly widowed and remarried: "In the resurrection, whose wife will the woman be?"

Jesus answered their question, then He flew straight to the Old Testament to show how the Sadducees were mistaken in their presuppositions. The passage He quoted was from Exodus 3, when God spoke to Moses from the burning bush and said, "I am the God of Abraham and . . . of Isaac and . . . of Jacob."

That was it. That was our Lord's whole argument and, on this occasion, the entirety of His scriptural proof for eternal life. He rested His case on the tense of the verb. God didn't say, "I *was* the God of Abraham, Isaac, and Jacob," but "I *am* their God—right now, even though they've not walked this earth for hundreds of years. They're still alive, and I am presently and actively their God."

Think of your loved ones in heaven. Think of yourself five minutes after your death.

What death?

God is not a God of the dead, but of the living—for all who are in Christ are alive and enjoying His presence (v. 38).

October 7

*He died for **all** so that those who live*
should no longer live for themselves, but for the One
who died for them and was raised.

2 Corinthians 5:15

This verse (1) begins with the death of Christ: "He died for all"; (2) ends with the resurrection: "and was raised"; and (3) puts you and me right in the middle: "that those who live should no longer live for themselves, but for [Him]." Because of the death of Christ, we have a life *forgiven*. Because of His resurrection, we have a life *forever*. And the coupling that links the two is a life *for Him*. In other words, His death and resurrection gives us:

- *Hope.* Jesus said, "Because I live, you will live too" (John 14:19). The grave itself is just a rest stop on the route to resurrection.
- *Happiness.* When Jesus appeared to His disciples after His resurrection, they were overwhelmed with joy. True 20/20 vision is found in John 20:20—"So the disciples rejoiced when they saw the Lord."
- *Holiness.* None of us can achieve purity through our own efforts, but the holiness of the risen Christ is imputed to us by faith, and in God's sight we are as He is.
- *Heaven.* During my thirty years of pastoring, I've preached three series of sermons on heaven; but as I get older, I'm not sure that once a decade is enough. Revelation 21–22 becomes more precious and vivid every day.
- *Healing.* By His stripes we are healed.
- *And most of all—Him.* Because He lives, we have Him; and with Him we have all the rest.

October 8

READING: 1 PETER 4:10–11

Are you called to be a speaker? . . .
*Do it with **all** the strength and energy that God supplies.*
1 Peter 4:11 (NLT)

A young minister recently asked me how to keep one's morale up when the crowd at church is small. It's one thing to preach to a packed room, but what of those "off Sundays" when the pickings are meager? I told him we mustn't base our morale on the size of our audience, but on the energy in our hearts.

One day the great evangelist George Whitefield preached near Princeton, New Jersey, but the weather was rainy and the room wasn't filled. Whitefield, who normally addressed thousands, was languorous. His restless audience seemed disinterested, and one old fellow sitting near the pulpit nodded off.

Suddenly Whitefield stopped. A series of terrible expressions crossed his face in succession until he bore the appearance of a thunderstorm. "If I had come to speak to you in my own name, you might rest your elbows on your knees and your heads upon your hands and sleep," he said with deliberation. "But I have not come in my own name."

Slamming his hand and his foot at once, he caused the house to ring. The sleeping man woke with a start. "Ay, ay," said Whitefield, eyeing him. "I have waked you up, have I? I meant to do it. I have not come here to speak to sticks and stones; I have come to you in the name of the Lord God of hosts, and I must and I will have an audience." The congregation was fully aroused, and the sermon produced powerful results.[77]

Brethren, pray,
and holy manna will be showered all around.

—*George Atkins, 1819*

October 9

*He comforts us in **all** our affliction,*
so that we may be able to comfort those
who are in any kind of affliction.
2 Corinthians 1:4

Three years ago, I hit something of a low point in ministry due to pressures and problems in pastoring. Katrina and I took a couple of days in Chicago, and I sat each morning in the Hancock Plaza with a cup of coffee and 2 Corinthians. As I read through Paul's autobiographical account, I was startled to see the words he used to describe his labors for Christ. I underlined these phrases: . . . *all our troubles . . . great distress . . . anguish of heart . . . many tears . . . grieved . . . distressed . . . no peace of mind . . . hardships . . . great pressure beyond our ability to endure it . . . despairing even of life . . . not equal to the task . . . not competent . . . deadly peril . . . hard pressed on every side . . . harassed at every turn . . . struck down . . . perplexed . . . downcast . . . beaten . . . flogged . . . shipwrecked . . . sorrowful . . . poor . . . sleepless nights . . . we may seem to have failed . . . conflicts on the outside, fears within.*

And yet the overall tone of 2 Corinthians is not woe-is-me-ism; it's one of praise-the-Lord-ism. Paul's secret was his discovery that God comforts him in all his afflictions, and he had learned to receive that comfort—and to recycle it into the lives of others.

Found in Christ, I will not falter,
Faint, or fail to do His will.
Outwardly I'm growing weaker;
Inward, stronger still!
Day by day His Word renews me
With the Spirit's inner flow
As I look at things eternal,
Not at things below.

—RJM

October 10

READING: ACTS 20:17–32

I commit you to God and to the message of His grace,
which is able to build you up and to give you an inheritance
*among **all** who are sanctified.*

Acts 20:32

This is Paul's great message to the elders in Ephesus. Not expecting to see them on earth again, the great apostle committed them to the Word of God's grace, which could edify them and give them an inheritance with all Christians. He was telling them, in essence, never to give up.

Fanny Crosby wrote a hymn entitled "Never Give Up." Though it's largely forgotten today, Fanny considered it one of her best, saying: "There is a great and wonderful truth embodied in these words. The whole victory of life is in them—'Trust in the Lord and take heart.' That means the exercise of courage, the consciousness of being linked to one mightier than ourselves, and it helps one to keep smiling, to keep sunshiny, and to have not only a song on the lip, but one in the heart."[78]

> Never be sad or desponding,
> If you have faith to believe.
> Grace, for the duties before you,
> Ask of your God and receive.
>
> What if your burdens oppress you;
> What though your life may be drear;
> Look on the side that is brightest,
> Pray, and your path will be clear.
>
> Never give up, never give up,
> Never give up to your sorrows,
> Jesus will bid them depart.
> Trust in the Lord, trust in the Lord,
> Sing when your trials are greatest,
> Trust in the Lord and take heart.

October 11

*I have relied on You **all** my life.*
Psalm 71:6 (TEV)

Once when I was tempted to fret about something, I came to Isaiah 50:10: "Let him who walks in the dark, who has no light, trust in the name of the LORD and rely on his God" (NIV). I've come to appreciate that word *rely*. It's a biblical synonym for *faith* and *trust*, and it's akin to our English word *rally*. There's something about the word *rely* that's very practical to me, and its every recollection rallies my spirit. When I can't solve my problems, I can rely on the Lord who is my all-in-all, all my life.

> *Rely* on the grace of God. . . .
> We were under great pressure, far beyond our ability to endure, so that we despaired even of life. Indeed, in our hearts we felt the sentence of death. But this happened that we might not *rely* on ourselves but on God, who raises the dead. . . .
> Then Asa called to the LORD his God and said, "LORD, there is no one like you . . . . Help us, O LORD our God, for we *rely* on you, and in your name we have come against this vast army. . . ."
> The men of Judah were victorious because they *relied* on the LORD, the God of their fathers. . . .
> I *rely* on You all day long . . . . I have *relied* on you since the day I was born . . . . I have *relied* on you all my life . . . .
> *Rely* on the Lord! Be strong and confident! *Rely* on the Lord![79]

October 12

All who are mature should think this way.

Philippians 3:15

I read the other day about two characters in the United Kingdom who robbed a post office at gunpoint, but when they exited with their loot, their car was gone. They'd left it running, and it had been stolen.

Then there was the twenty-five-year-old man in Portsmouth, Rhode Island, who was arrested in connection with a string of vending machine robberies. It didn't help when he posted his four-hundred-dollar bail in coins.

A man in Seattle tried to steal gasoline from a motor home. He inadvertently attached his siphoning hose, not to the gasoline tank, but to the sewage tank. Police found him writhing in the street, clutching his stomach.

We're drawn to "dumb criminal" stories not only because we need a good laugh but because we relate to them. Few of us are stupid criminals, but we've all done stupid things. After a half century of making plenty of mistakes and observing others, I've noticed that immaturity is as widespread as the human race. Immature people display immature attitudes, cause immature problems, say immature words, and do immature things. They have immature marriages, raise immature children, and live immature lives.

The Bible says, "Are you immature? Learn to be mature. Are you foolish? Learn to have sense" (Prov. 8:5 TEV).

The fast track to maturity is Philippians 3:12–15—taking hold of Christ, forgetting what's behind and reaching forward to what's ahead, and pursuing the upward goal of God's heavenly call in Christ Jesus. "All who are mature should think this way."

October 13

READING: PSALM 34:5–10

Those who look to Him are radiant . . . .
This poor man cried, and the LORD heard him
*and saved him from **all** his troubles.*

Psalm 34:5–6

A recent study of the spending habits of women in the People's Republic of China reported that the average Chinese woman spends one-fourth of her total income on cosmetics and hair design. Another study found the average woman in Shanghai uses twenty different cosmetics every day.

I don't know the figures for Americans, but I did read that men in the United States are catching up with women in the amount spent annually on cosmetics and personal care products.

We all need a little help with our looks. But the best cosmetic is looking to Jesus. Those who look to Him are radiant, and their faces reflect His joy and peace. Our countenances are confident, for we know God hears us when we cry to Him. Our faces are aglow, for we know He saves us from all our troubles.

Ralph Waldo Emerson once said, "The gods we worship write their names on our faces." Our emotions show up on our face, and no amount of cosmetics or cosmetic surgery can hide depression, selfishness, pride, or anger. When Moses met with the Lord on Mount Sinai, his face was aglow, and Proverbs 15:13 says the same is true for us: "A joyful heart makes a face cheerful."

As Spurgeon once said, we should wash our faces every day in a bath of praise.

A man's wisdom illumines him
and causes his stern face to beam.

Ecclesiastes 8:1 (NASB)

October 14

READING: MARK 12:28–34

*Love Him with **all** your heart,*
*with **all** your understanding,*
*and with **all** your strength . . . .*
[This] is far more important
*than **all** the burnt offerings and sacrifices.*

Mark 12:33

The Welsh Revival of 1904 was an outpouring of the Holy Spirit on the churches and people of Wales that spread around the world and can be called the last great revival of global proportions. By some accounts it had its beginning in the village of New Quay, fifteen miles from the nearest railway station. The local pastor, Rev. Joseph Jenkins, had read Andrew Murray's book *With Christ in the School of Prayer*. He began pleading for an awakening in his own heart and in those of others. In that spirit, he assembled the young people of the village for a Sunday morning prayer service. When Jenkins asked for testimonies, a new convert named Florrie Evans stood and said with a tremor in her voice: "I love Jesus Christ—with all my heart."

Those words struck the group like an electrical charge. It was later described as a fire igniting right in the room. Soon those young people, ages sixteen to eighteen, began traveling through Wales as the human conveyers of a burning revival that brought an estimated one hundred thousand people into the kingdom. One young man, Evan Roberts, became the primary vehicle of revival; but the revival spark was provided by young Florrie Evans.

And if we would say her words as earnestly as she said them that day, we'd all have a bit of the Welsh revival in us.

"I love Jesus Christ—with all my heart."

October 15

READING: PROVERBS 3:15–18

Her ways are pleasant,
*and **all** her paths, peaceful.*
Proverbs 3:17

Proverbs 3:17 is talking about Wisdom. Proverbs 3 says that those finding wisdom are happier people, for she is more profitable than silver and her revenue is better than gold. Her ways are pleasant, and all her paths are peaceful.

William Arnot wrote my favorite commentary on Proverbs in the mid-1800s, in which he defined the Proverbs as "laws from heaven for life on earth," and he describes the book of Proverbs as "much matter . . . pressed into little room that it may keep, and carry . . . wisdom in portable form."[80]

God's wisdom in the book of Proverbs is as profound as deepest theology, as vital as scientific research, and as reflective as purest philosophy, but it's also as practical as getting up in the morning. The thirty-one chapters of Proverbs (one chapter for each day of the month) are packed with advice about working hard, eating wisely, watching how much we drink, guarding how much we speak, managing our emotions, avoiding unhealthy friendships and immoral sexuality, handling money well, and making good decisions.

Proverbs is full of pithy verses to memorize, short in length and long in influence—verses that are able to safeguard our behavior like guardrails on a mountain road. The 915 verses in the book of Proverbs represent God's wisdom for the hundreds of situations we step into each day. Her ways are pleasant and all her paths are peaceful.

To my eyes Thy precepts
show wisdom more than sages know.
—*The Psalter, 1912*

October 16

All my best friends despise me,
and those I love have turned against me.
Job 19:19

The Old Testament is as full of Jesus as the New Testament, and every book from Genesis to Revelation gives us insights into the predicted Messiah. For example, the story and character of Job seem to foreshadow Jesus in a number of ways:

- Both Jesus and Job grappled with the problem of suffering and the mystery of evil.
- Both were originally wealthy and blessed beyond belief.
- Both were blameless. Jesus was utterly sinless. Of Job God said, "No one else on earth is like him, a man of perfect integrity, who fears God and turns away from evil" (1:8).
- Both were priests who offered sacrifices for sin.
- Both were intercessors.
- Both were targeted by Satan during a vast cosmic battle between God and the devil.
- Both went through a period of unspeakable suffering. Each became a man of sorrows and acquainted with grief.
- Both were forsaken by God and rejected by their friends. Job 16:9–11 says, "His anger tears at me . . . . They open their mouths against me and strike my cheeks with contempt . . . . God hands me over to unjust men; He throws me into the hands of the wicked."
- Both emerged victorious and resumed the former places of privilege and power.
- Both thwarted Satan, prayed for their friends, and saw the blessings of their troubles.

The book of Job is a microcosm of all the suffering of the world. Job raises the questions—and Jesus provides the answers.

October 17

*He entered the holy of holies once for **all**,*
not by the blood of goats and calves, but by His own blood,
having obtained eternal redemption.

Hebrews 9:12

Unlike the Old Testament priests who offered sacrifices continually, Jesus offered Himself one time for all time, on one
cross for all people. As Hebrews 7:27 put it, "He doesn't need to
offer sacrifices every day, as high priests do—first for their own
sins, then for those of the people. He did this once for all when
He offered Himself." An old Irish bookseller named William
McComb put it this way in his hymn "Chief of Sinners":

> Chief of sinners though I be,
> Jesus shed His blood for me;
> Died that I might live on high,
> Died that I might never die;
> As the branch is to the vine,
> I am His, and He is mine.
>
> O the height of Jesus' love!
> Higher than the Heaven above;
> Deeper than the deepest sea,
> Lasting as eternity;
> Love that found me—wondrous thought!
> Found me when I sought Him not!
>
> Chief of sinners though I be,
> Christ is all in all to me;
> All my wants to Him are known,
> All my sorrows are His own;
> Safe with Him from earthly strife,
> He sustains the hidden life.

October 18

If anyone is in Christ, he is a new creation;
*old things have passed away; behold, **all** things have become new.*
2 Corinthians 5:17 (NKJV)

The writer of the above words was a virulent anti-Christian intellectual who seized, imprisoned, and abused believers. He was a co-conspirator in the murder of the first Christian martyr. He was devout in his religiosity, a Pharisee of the Pharisees. But when he met Jesus, everything changed, and all things became new. He discovered:

- *A new name:* "Then Saul—also called Paul" (Acts 13:9).
- *A new way of looking at himself:* "Paul, a slave of God, and an apostle of Jesus Christ" (Titus 1:1).
- *A new nature:* "the new man . . . created according to God's likeness in righteousness" (Eph. 4:24).
- *A new motto:* "For me, living is Christ and dying is gain" (Phil. 1:21).
- *A new set of friends:* "I have you in my heart, and you are all partners with me in grace" (Phil. 1:7).
- *A new truth:* "I am not ashamed of the gospel, . . . it is God's power for salvation to everyone who believes" (Rom. 1:16).
- *A new lifestyle:* "Just as Christ was raised from the dead by the glory of the Father, so we too may walk in a new way of life" (Rom. 6:4).
- *A new mission:* "I have become all things to all people, so that I may by all means save some" (1 Cor. 9:22).
- *A new future:* "eternal life through Jesus Christ our Lord" (Rom. 5:21).

We have two great truths here: The believer's position—he is "in Christ"—and the believer's character—he is a "new creation."

—*Charles H. Spurgeon*

October 19

Jesus loved him and said to him,
"You lack one thing:
*Go, sell **all** you have and give to the poor,*
and you will have treasure in heaven.
Then come, follow Me."

Mark 10:21

When the rich young ruler came to Jesus desiring eternal life, the Lord told him to liquidate all his assets and give away the family fortune. What if He said that to us?

A key to understanding this story is to realize when it occurred. It didn't happen alongside the Sea of Galilee in the early, refreshing years of Christ's ministry; it occurred just days before Calvary. Jesus was on His final approach to Jerusalem, and the cross overshadowed His way. Satan was going to sift His followers as wheat. Time was short, and earthly possessions were a liability.

I've found 1 Corinthians 7:29–31 a useful cross-reference: "The time is short. From now on those who have wives should live as if they had none; those who mourn, as if they did not; those who are happy, as if they were not; those who buy something, as if it were not theirs to keep; those who use the things of the world, as if not engrossed in them. For this world in its present form is passing away" (NIV).

Because of the urgency of the times, we should live with a certain detachment to the things of this world, as Luther the Reformer told us:

Let goods and kindred go, this mortal life also.
The body they may kill; God's truth abideth still.
His Kingdom is forever.

October 20

*Are they [angels] not **all** ministering spirits sent out
to serve those who . . . inherit salvation?*

Hebrews 1:14

Where the young man came from, I don't know. I never saw him again, but I've wondered many times if he were an angel.

It was on a train in Paris. I was returning from Africa with my daughter, Grace, and we had a short time to get to the airport. I wasn't sure we'd boarded the right train, so I nervously asked everyone in earshot, "Is this the train to Charles de Gaulle?" No one spoke English, and I gave up, studied my maps, and hoped for the best.

When the train stopped at an intermediate station, people began exiting. I sat there glancing at my watch and worried about our connections. Suddenly a voice spoke perfect English: "If you're going to Charles de Gaulle Airport, you're on the wrong train." Sitting across from me was a young man who added, "The train you want is right over there," pointing to the opposite platform.

With a quick "Thanks!" I leaped up and jerked Grace out the door. As we lugged our bags toward the other train, I heard the voice again: "Here!" He tossed me my backpack through the closing doors. In my panic, I'd left it on the seat, and it held our passports, tickets, identification, and money.

I've had a nagging sense all these years that he might have been an angel. At the very least, I believe he could have been angelic. God's angels surround us more than we know—all of them ministering spirits sent to serve His children.

Angels have much more to do with us
than we imagine.

—*Charles H. Spurgeon*

October 21

Carefully consider the path for your feet,
*and **all** your ways will be established.*

Proverbs 4:26

How may we know God's will? He is ever giving many signs and hints as to the way we should take, clear enough to those who are only anxious to know and do the holy and acceptable and perfect will of God.

It is a mistake to seek a sign from heaven; to run from counselor to counselor; to cast a lot; or to trust to some chance coincidence. Not that God may not reveal His will thus; but because it is hardly the behavior of a child with his Father. There is a more excellent way.

Let the heart be quieted and stilled in the presence of God; weaned from all earthly distractions and worldly ambitions. Let the voice of the Son of God hush into perfect rest the storms that sweep the lake of the inner life, and ruffle its calm surface. Let the whole being be centered on God Himself. And then, remembering that all who lack wisdom are to ask it of God, and that Jesus Christ is already made unto us wisdom, let us quietly appropriate Him, in that capacity, by faith; and then go forward, perhaps not conscious of any increase of wisdom, or able to see far in front; but sure that we shall be guided, as each new step must be taken, or word spoken, or decision made.

It is an immense help in any difficulty to say, "I take thee, Lord Jesus, as my wisdom," and to do the next thing, nothing doubting.

—*Dr. F. B. Meyer*[81]

October 22

*Finally **all** hope that we would be saved was disappearing. . . .*
*"God has graciously given you **all** those who are sailing with you."*
Acts 27:20, 24

The shipwreck of Paul is one of the most vivid stories of the New Testament, yet one of the least familiar. As the storm raged, all hope vanished among the passengers and crew; but an angel appeared to Paul, telling him to keep hope alive, for "God has graciously given you all those who are sailing with you." The presence of one apostle gave hope to 276 heartsick souls.

So often my job as pastor is to lift up the spirits of someone about to throw in the towel. Perhaps he relapsed into an addictive habit or feels like giving up on a loved one. Perhaps she is drowning in fear, guilt, or depression. It's wonderful to see a spark of hope return to his or her eyes.

Somewhere I read of a doctor named Rosenow—Dr. Edward Rosenow, I think—who explained why he devoted his life to medicine. While growing up on a Wisconsin farm, his brother became dangerously ill. The doctor was sent for, and Dr. Rosenow, then only a boy, slipped into the room and hid behind a sofa to watch. After treating the sick boy, the doctor turned to his parents, "Have no fear, he is going to get well." The light that came into their faces was wonderful to see, and the boy behind the sofa determined then and there to cause that light to appear in the faces of others.

That's the gift of encouragement, and you'll meet someone today who needs its uplift.

October 23

May your bolts be of iron and bronze;
*may your strength endure through **all** your days!*
Deuteronomy 33:25 (NAB)

As long as God keeps you on this earth, He'll give you strength sufficient for the day. This wonderful blessing represents the final words of Moses. His last comments were directed to the tribe of Asher, but believers of every age have rightly applied the blessing to themselves. As the old King James Version quaintly puts it, "As thy days, so shall thy strength be."

In every condition, in sickness, in health;
In poverty's vale, or abounding in wealth;
At home and abroad, on the land, on the sea,
As thy days may demand, shall thy strength ever be.
—*John Rippen*

Afflicted saint, to Christ draw near—
Thy Savior's gracious promise hear,
His faithful Word declares to thee,
That as thy days thy strength shall be.

Let not thy heart despond and say
"How shall I stand the trying day?"
He has engaged by firm decree,
That as thy days thy strength shall be.
—*John Fawcett*

Oh, ask not thou, How shall I bear
The burden of tomorrow?
Sufficient for today, its care,
Its evil and its sorrow;
God imparteth by the way
Strength sufficient for the day.
—*J. E. Saxby*

October 24

READING: EPHESIANS 6:18–20

*With **all** prayer and petition
pray at **all** times in the Spirit,
and . . . be on the alert with **all**
perseverance and petition for **all** the saints.*

Ephesians 6:18 (NASB)

This is one of the Bible's greatest verses on prayer, notable for it's fourfold "all." We're to use *all* prayers at *all* times with *all* perseverance for *all* saints.

Learn to employ all kinds of prayers—private prayer, corporate prayer, spontaneous prayer, morning prayer, evening prayer, prayers before meals, prayers before trips, walking prayers, written prayer, family prayers, church prayers, silent prayers, spoken prayers.

Learn to pray at all times. In Psalm 3, David prayed when endangered; in Psalm 4, before going to bed; in Psalm 5, before beginning the day; in Psalm 6, when guilty; in Psalm 7, when attacked; in Psalm 8, when impressed with creation's beauty; in Psalm 9, when happy; in Psalm 10, when God seemed far away.

Learn to persevere in prayer. Bishop Joseph Hall states: "It is not the arithmetic of our prayers, how many they are; not the rhetoric of our prayers, how eloquent they may be; nor the geometry of our prayers, how long they may be; nor the music of our prayers, how sweet our voice may be; nor the logic of our prayers, how argumentative they may be; nor the method of our prayers, how orderly they may be; nor even the divinity of our prayers, how good the doctrine may be;—which God cares for. Fervency of spirit is that which availeth much."

And learn to pray for all the saints—as many as possible specifically and by name.

October 25

Whatever your hands find to do,
*do with **all** your strength.*
Ecclesiastes 9:10

Whatever you do . . .

*Commit to the Lord **whatever you do,** and your plans will succeed.*
Proverbs 16:3 (NIV)

*Plan carefully what you do, and **whatever you do** will turn out right.*
Proverbs 4:26 (TEV)

*Work hard at **whatever you do.***
Ecclesiastes 9:10 (TEV)

*Do faithfully **whatever you do.***
3 John 5 (NKJV)

*"**Whatever you do,** do it enthusiastically, as something done*
for the Lord and not for men, knowing that you will receive
the reward of an inheritance from . . . the Lord Christ.
Colossians 3:23

*"**Whatever you do,** in word or in deed, do everything in the name*
of the Lord Jesus, giving thanks to God the Father through Him.
Colossians 3:17

*"Remember that God is going to judge you for **whatever you do.**"*
Ecclesiastes 11:9 (TEV)

*Therefore, whether you eat or drink, or **whatever you do,***
do everything for God's glory.
1 Corinthians 10:31

October 26

Go and stand in the temple complex,
*and tell the people **all** about this life.*

Acts 5:20

As a young man, Demosthenes tried to speak before the Assembly in Athens but was laughed off the stage. In despondency, he traveled to the coast where he shaved the beard off half his face so he wouldn't be tempted to go out in public, and he started practicing. He used the crashing of the ocean as a sounding board to strengthen his voice. He spoke with pebbles in his mouth to improve his enunciation. He shouted his speeches running uphill to improve his lung capacity. He wrote the speeches of Thucydides word for word to learn the construction of sentences. The day came when he spoke again in the Athenian Assembly, and as Demosthenes finished his address, the audience was on its feet, shouting, "Yes! We shall follow this man! We shall do as he says!"[82]

As a young man, Benjamin Disraeli addressed the British Parliament, but his speech was so poor he was shouted down. Taking his seat, he swore: "I sit down now, but the time will come when you will hear me." He went to work developing his positions on issues, his vocabulary and speech patterns, his delivery; and the day did come when Parliament and the entire world listened to him.[83]

Anyone can be a soul-winner who is willing to pay the price.
All the things we need to be a success—the promises of God,
the power of God, and the preparation of God—
are available to the Christian who seeks them.

—Dr. Robert L. Sumner[84]

October 27

*Be strong, **all** you people of the land . . . .*
Work! For I am with you.

Haggai 2:4

In her book *I Was Winston Churchill's Private Secretary*, Phyllis Moir described how diligent her boss was about his work. Before becoming prime minister, Churchill was anxious about the Nazi threat, but he also had a series of book deadlines. On the day Prague fell, he was hurrying to complete a three-hundred-thousand-word history of the English people. He said after supper, "It's hard to take one's attentions off the events of today and concentrate on the reign of James II—but I'm going to do it." And he did.

"When a job of writing has to be done," said Moir, "Mr. Churchill sits down to it whether he is in the mood or not and the effort generates his creative power."[85]

It reminds me of what basketball star Jerry West said: "You can't get much done in life if you only work on the days when you feel good."[86]

The prophet Haggai upbraided the people for resting in their paneled homes when the Lord's temple was in disrepair and the Lord's work needed to be done.

There are times when we need to relax our minds and bodies, but God didn't make us to waste our time or to sit around being endlessly entertained. Jesus said, "My Father works and I work." We only have a few years to accomplish all that God wants us to do. Let's be about our Father's business, so one day He'll say to us in glory, "Well done, good and faithful servant."

October 28

*Avoid **all** perverse talk;*
stay far from corrupt speech.
Proverbs 4:24 (NLT)

Recently I read through Proverbs, circling every verse about our words and our speech patterns. When I finished, I found that every circled verse fit into one of three categories that summarize how we should use our tongues.

One set of verses tells us, bluntly, *to shut up*, to close our mouths, and to be cautious about what we say. Proverbs 10:19 says: "When there are many words, sin is unavoidable, but the one who controls his lips is wise." Proverbs 17:27 says, "The intelligent man restrains his words," and Proverbs 17:14 adds, "To start a conflict is to release a flood; stop the dispute before it breaks out." According to Proverbs 11:12, "A man with understanding keeps silent." Someone once said, "Never miss an opportunity to keep your mouth shut." It's not necessary to state our opinion on every subject, to have the last word in every argument, or to defend ourselves against every criticism.

Other proverbs, however, tell us *to build up*, to use our words to edify and encourage others. Proverbs 10 says, "The mouth of the righteous is a fountain of life . . . . The tongue of the righteous is pure silver . . . . The lips of the righteous feed many" (vv. 11, 20, 21).

A third set of verses tells us *to speak up*. In Proverbs 31:8, we read, "Speak up for those who have no voice, for the justice of all who are dispossessed." That includes speaking up for the Lord when the occasion arises.

True wisdom is knowing when to shut up, when to build up, and when to speak up.

Lord, give us that wisdom!

October 29

This Book of the Law shall not depart from your mouth,
but you shall meditate in it day and night,
*that you may observe to do according to **all** that is written in it.*
For then you will make your way prosperous,
and then you will have good success.

Joshua 1:8 (NKJV)

When I became serious about following Christ as a sophomore at Columbia International University, a dorm buddy gave me Joshua 1:8 as a verse to memorize. It's been an anchor for my thinking ever since. Here the Lord gives us three necessary steps for Bible study.

First, read it. Keep reading God's Word aloud. Don't stop reading and repeating it.

Then meditate on it day and night. Meditation is the missing link in getting the words from the pages of the Bible into our bloodstream. When I memorize a verse and then think about it while showering or shaving, my mind begins to absorb it as my body absorbs food. I remember hearing speaker Bill Gothard once say that meditation is the process of memorizing, visualizing, and personalizing Scripture. I've found that some of my best insights come when I take a long walk in the park and mull over some passage I've been studying, or when I turn off my car radio and really think through a verse while driving.

Third, obey it and do all that it says. Bible study is worthless if it doesn't lead to application and obedience.

That includes, of course, being obedient to Joshua 1:8. I encourage you to meditate on some rich portion of Scripture day and night this week.

October 30

He is like a tree planted by streams of water
that yields its fruit in its season,
and its leaf does not wither.
*In **all** that he does, he prospers.*

Psalm 1:3 (ESV)

It seems to me that King David discovered Joshua 1:8 (see yesterday's devotion) and put it to practice—memorizing, visualizing, and personalizing it. Out of those meditations came Psalm 1:3, a picturesque passage about the person who meditates on the Word of God day and night. As we meditate on God's Word, our thoughts increasingly reflect His thinking and wisdom. As that occurs, we make better decisions and speak wiser words—and as a result, in all we do we prosper.

One way of meditating on Scripture is to sit down with a notepad or computer screen and literally rewrite it in our own words, either as a paraphrase or as poetry. For example, here's how one diligent student of Scripture rewrote Psalm 1:1–3 for the 1927 Psalter Hymnal:

Blest is he who loves God's precepts,
Who from sin restrains his feet,
He who will not stand with sinners,
He who shuns the scorners' seat.

Blest is he who makes the statutes
Of the Lord his chief delight,
In God's law, divinely perfect,
Meditating day and night.

He is like a tree well planted
By the flowing river's side,
Ever green of leaf and fruitful:
Thus shall all his works abide.

October 31

*Then Hezekiah encouraged **all** the Levites
who performed skillfully before the Lord.*

2 Chronicles 30:22

When Lou Gehrig was starting his baseball career, he went into a slump and almost quit. He doubted his talent and ability, and his spirits collapsed. A friend named Paul Krichell heard about it and took a train to Hartford, Connecticut, to find Lou. He invited his friend to join him for a steak dinner at the Bond Hotel, and Lou poured out his frustrations. Paul spent the evening telling Lou that all hitters go through slumps, that the best ones—even Ty Cobb—fail to get hits six or seven out of every ten tries. But eventually good hitters start hitting again, and, said Paul, you're a good hitter. After dinner, Gehrig walked with Paul to the train station and thanked him for coming. The next day, Lou started blasting the ball again, and over the next eleven games he had twenty-two hits, including six home runs—and his career took off. "I decided not to quit after all," he said.[87]

Sometimes we need to take a train, track someone down, buy them a steak, and encourage them, as King Hezekiah did for the spiritual leaders and singers of Israel.

Our children especially need encouragement. Their self-image is based, in large measure, by their perceptions of what we think of them. We need to find ways to affirm their strengths and express our love and admiration for them. Husbands and wives need encouragement more than they need harping criticism. Our co-workers and leaders and friends and neighbors need to be built up.

Who can you encourage today?

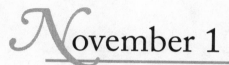

November 1

*Every athlete exercises self-control in **all** things.*
They do it to receive a perishable wreath,
but we an imperishable.

1 Corinthians 9:25 (ESV)

In his book *Power Living: Mastering the Art of Self-Discipline*, former Navy SEAL Michael Janke defines self-control as "the ability of the individual to adhere to actions, thoughts, and behaviors that result in personal improvement instead of instant gratification."[88] He suggests that our ability to be self-managed casts a long shadow on our children and grandchildren. When we begin to use self-discipline to control our emotional highs and lows, our appearance, our work ethic, and our commitment to physical exercise, we are providing an example and leaving a legacy for those who follow us.

Galatians 5:22–23 teaches that the fruit of the Spirit is . . . self-control. Paul taught that people should be married whenever possible lest Satan tempt them due to their lack of self-control (1 Cor. 7:5). In Acts 24:25, as he presented the gospel to Governor Felix, Paul discoursed on righteousness, self-control, and the judgment to come. The Bible asserts that God hasn't given us a spirit of fear, but of power, love, and self-control (2 Tim. 1:7 ESV). In his second epistle, Peter tells us to make every effort to add to our faith goodness, knowledge, and self-control (1:5–6).

When we detect an area in our lives needing mastery, the Lord's grace is sufficient to bring it under self-control as we walk in the Spirit and commit ourselves to obedience. After all, if athletes discipline themselves in all things just to win a wreath that wilts away, shouldn't we do the same for a prize that lasts forever?

November 2

*In Him **all** the treasures of wisdom and knowledge are hidden.*
Colossians 2:3

Jesus Christ, being God, is omniscient, possessing total knowledge. He knows thoroughly and completely the most minute fact about every microscopic organism in the deepest sea, and the exact chemical composition of the largest star in the universe. He knows the future as perfectly as the past, and we can hide nothing from Him. Nothing can happen to us He does not see. He knows what's on the surface and what's out of sight. He knows our thoughts, motives, hurts, circumstances, feelings, and needs. He cannot learn anything for He already knows everything, being both infinite and intimate.

- He knows my name (Ps. 91:14).
- He knows the way I have taken (Job 23:10).
- He knows the secrets of my heart (Ps. 44:21).
- He knows what I am made of (Ps. 103:14).
- He knows better than I what I need (Matt. 6:8 MSG).
- He knows what is in the darkness, and light dwells with Him (Dan. 2:22).
- He knows everything (1 John 3:20 NIV).

You know how true it is that in Him are hid
all the treasures of wisdom and knowledge. . . .
But if you have not seen Christ, then you know nothing yet
as you ought to know. . . . What good will it do you in hell
that you knew all the sciences in the world, all the events
of history, and all the busy politics of your little day?

—*Robert Murray McCheyne*[89]

November 3

*All a man's ways seem right in his own eyes,
but the LORD weighs the motives.*

Proverbs 16:2

In 1914, Archduke Franz Ferdinand, heir to the Austro-Hungarian throne, visited Bosnia. The archduke was an impulsive man who, ignoring warnings, insisted on riding through Sarajevo despite assassination threats. Someone tossed a bomb into his car and the archduke deftly batted it away, but it exploded in the street and injured his aide. The enraged archduke, acting on impulse, insisted on visiting his aide in the hospital. But the archduke's driver became disoriented en route, and, acting on impulse, took a wrong turn down a street. An official shouted, "That's the wrong way," and the car stopped in front of a high school student named Gavriol Princip, who also acted on impulse. He drew a pistol and fired. Within minutes, Archduke Ferdinand, his wife Sophia, and their unborn child were dead, sparking the conflagration we call World War I, which cost the lives of millions and set the stage for World War II, in which another fifty million perished.

The same sort of things can happen in miniature in our own lives unless we learn to control our impulses. By nature we're stubborn, impulsive, and determined to have our own way. We can be hardheaded, opinionated, and immature, while all the time insisting we're right.

But the Lord weighs our motives. A desire to glorify Him helps us rein in our passions, subdue our stubbornness, and bless (rather than mar) the lives of others.

Take my hands, and let them move
at the impulse of Thy love.

—*Frances Havergal, 1874*

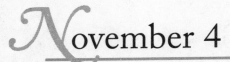

November 4

Have you noticed My servant Job?
He is the finest man in **all** *the earth—*
a man of complete integrity.
He fears God and will have nothing to do with evil.

Job 1:8 (NLT)

The sun never set on the British empire during the days of Queen Victoria. It was England's golden age, a time of extraordinary British literary output, spiritual revival, social reform, international trade, and economic progress. Among the reasons for English supremacy was the far-famed honesty of her merchants. The historian R. C. K. Ensor explained: "If one asks how nineteenth-century English merchants earned the reputation of being the most honest in the world (a very real factor in the nineteenth-century primacy of English trade), the answer is: because hell and heaven seemed as certain to them as tomorrow's sunrise, and the Last Judgment as real as the week's balance-sheet. This keen sense of moral accountability had also much to do with the success of self-government in the political sphere."[90]

That's a good analysis of Job's life too. Job was the finest man on earth, but his integrity didn't come from an inherited disposition or a politically correct viewpoint. It was his reverence for God that kept him from evil.

Our ethics are determined by our God-choices. As followers of Jesus Christ, we become honest men and women, not because it comes naturally (it doesn't) or because it's the social norm (it isn't), but because we have a holy God. Heaven and hell are as certain as tomorrow's sunrise, and the last judgment is as real as this week's balance sheet.

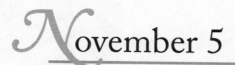# November 5

She rewards him with good, not evil,
***all** the days of her life.*
Proverbs 31:12

Only once in my life have I had the courage to preach about Proverbs 21:9: "Better to live on the corner of a roof than to share a house with a nagging wife." But I buffered my remarks by saying, truthfully, that we could easily substitute the word *husband*. The importance of family congeniality is emphasized in Proverbs with a series of *better* statements.

- "*Better* a little with the fear of the LORD than great treasure with turmoil" (Prov. 15:16).
- "*Better* a meal of vegetables where there is love than a fattened calf with hatred" (Prov. 15:17).
- "*Better* a dry crust with peace than a house full of feasting with strife" (Prov. 17:1).
- "*Better* to live on the corner of a roof than to share a house with a nagging [spouse]" (Prov. 21:9).
- "*Better* to live in a wilderness than with a nagging and hot-tempered [spouse]" (Prov. 21:19).
- "*Better* to live on the corner of a roof than in a house shared with a nagging [spouse]" (Prov. 25:24).

In short, we need to be congenial at home. Sometimes we treat total strangers better than we treat our own family members. We all have days when we're out of sorts, and we all have to work on our attitudes all the time; but it is hard to live with an ill-tempered, irritable, sulking, unpleasant person. As Christians, we shouldn't be hard to live with. We should reward our loved ones with good, not ill, all the days of their lives.

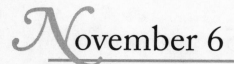

November 6

All the people took note of this, and it pleased them.
In fact, everything the king did pleased them.

2 Samuel 3:36

Frances Havergal wrote a children's book in 1881 titled *Morning Bells* that contains some insights on this verse, which, in the King James Version, says, "Whatsoever the king did pleased all the people." The verse is referring to how Israel felt about King David, but Havergal pointed out it should be true of us toward our King too:

> Do you take notice of what your King does? Does it please you to hear and read of what He has done and is doing? It must be so if He really is your King.
>
> But the "whatsoever" is a little harder; and yet, if it is once really learnt, it makes everything easy. For if we learn to be pleased with the "whatsoever" our King Jesus does, nothing can come wrong to us.
>
> Suppose something comes today which is not quite what you would have liked; heavy rain, for instance, when you wanted to go out,—recollect that your King Jesus has done it, and that will hush the little murmur, and make you quite content.
>
> Ask Him this morning to make you so loving and loyal to Him, that whatsoever He does, all day long, may please you because it has pleased Him to do it.

How wonderful to learn this in childhood, yet most of us are still in the schoolhouse of faith. He does all things well, He works all things for good, and whatever He does should please us day by day.

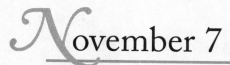# November 7

*Above **all**, be strong.*
Joshua 1:18

It's a shame we're as weak as we are, for the Bible says, "Above all, be strong," and "Finally, be strengthened by the Lord and by His vast strength" (Eph. 6:10). He has promised that as our days, so shall our strength be (Deut. 33:25).

We may not be strong in ourselves, but the Lord is our strength and He strengthens us in our inner beings out of the riches of His grace (Ps. 28:7, Eph. 3:16). We can't always be physically strong, but we should always have a spiritual toughness and emotional fortitude that reflects the joy of the Lord, which is our strength (Neh. 8:10).

One of Bible's most convicting verses to me is Proverbs 24:10 (NIV): "If you falter in times of trouble, how small is your strength!" It's even more convicting in Peterson's paraphrase: "If you fall to pieces in a crisis, there wasn't much to you in the first place." Or the Living Bible: "You are a poor specimen if you can't stand the pressure of adversity."

Sometimes the Bible is pretty blunt! But after all, we have the promises of God. We have the presence of Christ. We have the certainty of heaven. We have the indwelling Holy Spirit. We have the power of prayer and the joy of the Lord.

So above all, be strong!

God is our Refuge and our Strength,
Our ever present Aid,
And, therefore, though the earth remove,
We will not be afraid.

—Psalm 46:1–2
from the Scottish Psalter, 1650

November 8

*The One who descended is the same as the One who ascended far above **all** the heavens, that He might fill all things.*

Ephesians 4:10

Jesus ascended *above all* the heavens.

"For the Lord is great and is highly praised; He is feared *above all gods*" (1 Chron. 16:25). His name is "exalted *above all* blessing and praise" (Neh. 9:5). He is "exalted *above all* the nations" (Ps. 113:4), and Jesus is "the One who comes from *above*" and "is *above all*" (John 3:31).

Because He is *above all*, I should keep Him *above all* in my heart.

- "*Above all*, be strong and very courageous to carefully observe the whole instruction My servant Moses commanded you. Do not turn from it to the right or the left, so that you will have success wherever you go" (Josh. 1:7).
- "*Above all*, fear the Lord and worship Him faithfully with all your heart, considering the great things He has done for you" (1 Sam. 12:24).
- "Guard your heart *above all* else, for it is the source of life" (Prov. 4:23).
- "*Above all*, put on love—the perfect bond of unity" (Col. 3:14).
- "*Above all*, keep your love for one another at full strength, since love covers a multitude of sins" (1 Pet. 4:8).

Maybe that's what Oswald Chambers meant by his phrase "My utmost for His highest."

One there is, above all others,
Well deserves the name of Friend;
His is love beyond a brother's,
Costly, free, and knows no end.

—John Newton, 1779

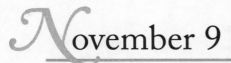# November 9

*This is **all** that I have learned:*
God made us plain and simple,
but we have made ourselves very complicated.
Only the wise know what things really mean.

Ecclesiastes 7:29–8:1 (TEV)

Rev. C. Evans of Bristol, England, sent word to a poor congregation in a small village that he would be passing through and would be glad to preach for them. The people hesitated for some time, but finally permitted him to preach. He noticed the mood was glum before his sermon, but happy and joyful afterward. Asking the reason for their change of disposition, he was told: "Why, sir, to tell you the truth, knowing that you were a very learned man, and that you were a teacher of young ministers, we were much afraid we should not understand you; but you have been quite as plain as any minister we ever hear."

"Ay, ay," replied Evans. "You entirely misunderstood the nature of learning, my friend. Its design is to make things so plain that they cannot be misunderstood."

I began my ministry preaching in a church beside a home for neglected children, and I had to learn early to make my messages simple. Since then, I've learned that the greatest minds present the deepest truths in the simplest terms.

As another old divine once put it, "How much learning, my brethren, is required to make these things plain!"[91]

Simplicity is the ultimate sophistication.

—*Leonardo da Vinci*

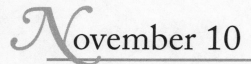

November 10

*My house will be called
a house of prayer for **all** nations.*
Mark 11:17

The Lord wants us to pray for all nations, and for kings and for all in authority. We can exercise knee-based influence over leaders whom we may never meet. Here's an example: Prince Edward VII of England was well known for his drinking and immorality. When his mother, Queen Victoria, died in 1901, Edward assumed the throne at age fifty-nine and reigned for nine years.

In 1910, a prayer warrior named Joe Evans was vacationing in the New York mountains, away from newspapers and interruptions. One morning he felt a burden to intercede for Edward, and the burden became so intense he anguished in prayer for the king's conversion. The following day came the news, "Edward is dead."

Years later, Joe shared dinner with Dr. J. Gregory Mantle of England. Dr. Mantle said, "Joe, did you know that Edward VII was saved on his deathbed?"

He went on to explain: "The king was in France when he was taken ill. He was brought to England and there was hope that he might recover. However, there came a turn for the worse. At that time, His Majesty called one of his lords-in-waiting and ordered him to go to Paternoster Row and secure for him a copy of a tract that his mother, Queen Victoria, had given to him when he was a lad. It was entitled "The Sinner's Friend." After much searching, the lord-in-waiting found the tract, brought it to His Majesty, and upon reading it, King Edward VII made earnest repentance and received the Lord Jesus as his Savior."[92]

I urge . . . prayers . . . for kings.
1 Timothy 2:1–2

November 11

*We proclaim Him, warning . . . with **all** wisdom.*

Colossians 1:28

On Christmas night 1776, George Washington's Continental Army was freezing, underfed, underclothed, discouraged, sick, and miserable. Yet they crossed the treacherous ice-swollen Delaware River to attack the Hessians at Trenton. The Hessian commander, Colonel Johann Rall, was attending a Christmas party that night, not dreaming the American forces were on the move. A warning was brought to him, but Colonel Rall, who was playing cards, just stuffed the note in his pocket without reading it.

When Washington's men attacked, Rall was caught by surprise and mortally wounded. As the doctor cut away his clothes, the note fell from his pocket. Rall scanned it and said, "If I had read this, I would not be here."

He ignored the warning, lost the battle, and lost his life.

Every sermon, every Bible lesson, every word of testimony, and every verse of Scripture is a warning, calling us to repentance and revival. Our God is a consuming fire, and a day of judgment is coming. We must not neglect the warning, and today's church must not forget that our message includes the ministry of warning.

Paul said, "We proclaim Him, warning . . . with all wisdom."

Oh! that I had a trumpet voice to warn you.
Oh! while you are dying, while you are sinking into perdition,
may I not cry to you; may not these eyes weep for you!
Take to heart, I beseech you, the realities of eternity.
Oh, turn, turn! Why will you die?
Believe on the Lord Jesus Christ, and ye shall be saved.

—Charles H. Spurgeon
at Exeter Hall on Sunday morning, February 26, 1869

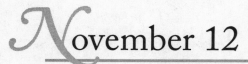

November 12

The LORD your God will bless you
in all your produce and in all the work of your hands,
and you will have abundant joy.
Deuteronomy 16:15

Deuteronomy 16 lists the holidays of ancient Israel, one of which was the Festival of Booths. It was a time to thank God for the blessings of the harvest and to rejoice in His blessings on all their produce and in all the work of their hands.

The Lord also blesses our efforts in whatever we do for His glory, and we should thank Him with joy and serve Him with gladness. A happy temperament is the key to an exuberant life, but a depressed spirit is an unnecessary burden to bear continuously.

Sherwood Wirt, founding editor of *Decision* magazine, decided one day to take down his concordance and look up the word *joy*. He later said that after studying awhile, he felt like shouting, "Eureka! I have found the cave of Aladdin." Dr. Wirt counted 542 references to joy in the Bible, including 141 references to gladness, 85 references to delight, 70 references to pleasure, 40 references to laughter, 30 references to merry, 27 references to happiness, and a host of references in newer versions to exuberance, jubilation, merriment, rapture, bliss, and other synonyms for joy.

"The Bible," exclaimed Wirt, "is a book of joy."[93]

The Lord expects us to be joyful. That should be our foundational attitude, and it should show up in our faces, in our voices, and in our attitudes. As evangelist Billy Sunday once said, we should have a joy that is fireproof, famine-proof, and devil-proof.

November 13

Joshua said to them,
"Do not be afraid or discouraged.
Be strong and courageous,
*for the LORD will do this to **all** the enemies you fight."*
Joshua 10:25

Years ago in the South African town of Ladysmith, a man was reportedly arrested and convicted of the crime of being a discourager. It was during the Boer War, and he moved up and down the lines of soldiers demoralizing the troops.

I've met some of his kin, but there's never a reason to listen to them. Joshua 10:25 commands us not to be afraid or discouraged, but strong and courageous. The Lord will fight on our behalf against all our adversaries and adversities.

In 1 Chronicles 28:20, David told Solomon, "Don't be afraid or discouraged, for the LORD God, my God, . . . won't leave you or forsake you until all the work for the service of the LORD's house is finished."

When King Jehoshaphat was facing catastrophic invasion, the prophet Jahaziel said, "Listen carefully, all Judah . . . . This is what the Lord says: 'Do not be afraid or discouraged because of this vast multitude, for the battle is not yours, but God's'" (2 Chron. 20:15).

King Hezekiah told his people, "Be strong and courageous! Don't be afraid or discouraged before the king of Assyria or before all the multitude with him, for there are more with us than with him. He has only human strength, but we have the LORD our God to help us and to fight our battles" (2 Chron. 32:7–8).

Oh, to be neither discouraged or a discourager!

All discouragement is from the devil, but all encouragement is from the Lord.

November 14

*Let **all** who seek You rejoice and be glad in You;*
let those who love Your salvation continually say,
"The LORD is great!"

Psalm 40:16

While speaking in Japan last year, I took an early morning walk through a park. The sun was fresh and bright, and the dew was evaporating from the grass and vaporizing from the ground. In the park was an old Japanese fellow with his dog. The man wore a cap and jacket and a heavy pair of shoes. The animal was a medium-sized black-and-white mutt. But if ever a dog was smiling, that one was. He was running in circles around his master, his eyes locked on him.

When I drew near, the dog glanced at me but was not distracted. The man had a tennis ball. When he threw it into the air, the dog would leap up, catch it, bring it back, and drop it at the man's feet, all without breaking stride in his endless loops around his master. I watched from a distance, and then I walked on thinking that old dog had more sense than I had. Though just an animal, he knows that the greatest thing in life is his time with his master.

The psalmist said that all who seek the Lord should rejoice and be glad in Him. We should exclaim continually, "The Lord is great!"

When was the last time we said that!

Lord, make us as devoted to you as a faithful dog to his master. Let all who seek You rejoice and be glad in You.

November 15

*We always thank God for **all** of you,*
remembering you constantly in our prayers.
1 Thessalonians 1:2

As a child, I memorized 1 Thessalonians 5:17 (KJV)—"Pray without ceasing"—because it was one of the shortest verses in the Bible and easy to learn. But it wasn't so easy to understand. Children think in literal terms, and I couldn't see how anyone could really pray continuously.

Now I realize that the Bible isn't talking about continuously occurring prayer, but prayer that is consistently recurring. Last year, while reading through this epistle, I noticed that Paul refers to the concept of consistently recurring prayer several times.

He began his letter by saying, "We always thank God for all of you, remembering you constantly in our prayers." The word *constantly* in 1 Thessalonians 1:2 is exactly the same Greek word as "without ceasing" in 1 Thessalonians 5:17.

Then in chapter 2, verse 13, Paul wrote, "This is why we constantly thank God." This, too, is a rendering of the exact same word.

In 1 Thessalonians 3:10, the apostle said, "We pray earnestly night and day to see you." And there we have a definition of the phrase *without ceasing*. It means to pray night and day, to pray perpetually, to pray with great frequency and regularity, to pray at the drop of a hat, to pray during our regular times of intercession, but also to go around praying, as it were, under our breath.

So how and when do prayer warriors ply their trade? Always . . . all . . . constantly . . . without ceasing . . . night and day.

November 16

*Grace be with **all** who have undying love for our Lord Jesus Christ.*

Ephesians 6:24

Ephesians 6:24 is the final sentence of the book, and Paul leaves us with two concluding thoughts: (1) Oh, that we might have undying love for our Lord Jesus Christ; and (2) Jesus-lovers are blessed with the vastness of His grace.

One man who believed this was Thomas Vincent, a seventeenth-century Puritan preacher who penned a small book quaintly titled *The True Christian's Love to the Unseen Christ: A Discourse Chiefly Tending to Excite and Promote the Decaying Love of Christ in the Hearts of Christians.* In the preface, Vincent noted:

> The life of Christianity consists very much of our
> love to Christ . . . . Without love to Christ we may
> have the name of Christians, but we are wholly with-
> out the nature. We may have the form of godliness,
> but are wholly without the power . . . .
>
> Christ knows . . . the . . . affections of His disciples
> for Him; that if He has their love, their desires will
> be chiefly after Him. Their delights will be chiefly in
> Him; their hopes and expectation will be chiefly from
> Him; their hatred, fear, grief, anger, will be carried
> forth chiefly as sin as it is offensive unto Him.[94]

When He is our All in All, we are His through and through and we love Him day by day; in the process, His grace meets our every need.

> O Love that wilt not let me go,
> I rest my weary soul in Thee;
> I give Thee back the life I owe,
> That in Thine ocean depths its flow may richer, fuller be.

—*George Matheson, 1882*

November 17

*Now the God of **all** grace,*
who called you to His eternal glory in Christ Jesus,
will personally restore, establish, strengthen,
and support you after you have suffered a little.

1 Peter 5:10

What a strange and wonderful promise! He is God of all grace. He gives us eternal glory in Christ Jesus. He will personally tend to us, though we may go through patches of suffering.

When I think of this verse, I'm reminded of a story that came from the pen of Pastor Ichabod Spencer of Brooklyn, New York. Spencer told of visiting the bedside of a dying woman who was bolstered up in bed, gasping for breath, and the whole bed shook as she convulsed with heart palpitations. "I am dying," she told him and the gathered friends.

"And are you ready to die?" he asked.

Gasping for every word, she said, "God knows I have taken Him at His Word and I am not afraid to die."

Spencer quoted Scriptures and prayed with her, but as he turned to leave, she caught his hand. "I wanted to tell you," she gasped, "that I can trust in God while I am dying. You have often told me He would not forsake me. Now I find it is true."

Spencer left the house to plan her funeral, but the woman did not die. To everyone's surprise, she recovered and lived for many years. But no one ever forgot her "dying" testimony: "I have taken the Lord at his Word. I can trust God while I'm living and while I'm dying. He will never leave me or forsake me."[95]

Between here and heaven,
every minute that the Christian lives
will be a minute of grace.

—*Charles H. Spurgeon*

November 18

*And **all** of you clothe yourselves with humility toward one another,*
because God resists the proud, but gives grace to the humble.

1 Peter 5:5

Andrew Murray is one of the few people who could have written a credible book on the subject of humility. Born in South Africa in 1828, his was a lifelong ministry of prayer, preaching, and writing. In his early fifties, Murray contracted a mysterious throat ailment that left him almost voiceless. For those two years of silence he pondered the subject of humility. He later developed a series of twelve messages on this subject, which were published in 1895 under the title *Humility: The Beauty of Holiness.*

"Jesus found His glory in taking the form of a servant," wrote Murray. "There is nothing so divine and heavenly as being the servant and helper of all. Humility, the place of entire dependence on God, is, from the very nature of things, the first duty and the highest virtue of the creature, and the root of every virtue. . . . Humility is the only soil in which the graces root; the lack of humility is the sufficient explanation of every defect and failure. Humility is not so much a grace or virtue along with others; it is the root of all, because it alone takes the right attitude before God and allows Him as God to do all."

Brother, are you clothed with humility?
Ask your daily life. Ask Jesus. Ask your friends. Ask the world.
And begin to praise God that there is opened up to you
in Jesus a heavenly humility of which you have hardly known,
and through which, a heavenly blessedness you possibly
have never yet tasted, can come to you.

—Andrew Murray

November 19

*This gospel has been proclaimed
in **all** creation under heaven,
and I, Paul, have become a minister of it.*

Colossians 1:23

Our English word *gospel* comes from the old Anglo-Saxon term *God's spell* or *God's story.* The Greek word on which it's based means the "good message" or the "good news." If you take the Greek word and transliterate it—that is, you just replace the Greek letters for corresponding English letters—you get the word *evangel.* The prefix *ev* means "good" and look at the stem word: *angel*—literally, "message" or "messenger."

This word occurs a few times in Matthew, Mark, Luke, John, and Acts. But it explodes in Paul's writings. He used the word *gospel* sixty-eight times! According to Paul, the gospel is something to be proclaimed in all creation under heaven. Even a child can do it.

Last year I visited a couple who had attended our church in the early 1980s, Gary and Teresa Smith. Their twenty-nine-year-old daughter, Heather, is active in campus evangelism and mission trips. Gary told me how Heather had come to Christ.

When our own daughter, Victoria, was five years old, she prayed to become a Christian. In her excitement, she told Heather, who was six. Heather asked her parents about being a Christian, and the next Sunday she came forward and was saved at the altar. It was a case of a five-year-old leading a six-year-old to Christ—decisions that have made the fundamental difference in their lives ever since. If a five-year-old can be the means of leading someone to Christ, don't you think we should do the same?

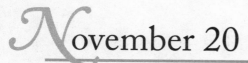

November 20

*Count it **all** joy*
when you fall into various trials,
knowing that the testing of your faith produces patience.
James 1:2–3 (NKJV)

When evangelist Samuel Logan Brengle was old and infirm, he wrote, "My old eyes get dimmer. The specialist says the light will fade altogether. So I gird myself for darkness, quote James 1:2 to 4, shout Hallelujah, and go on!"[96]

James 1:2 is well worth quoting in times of difficulty, for it tells us to count it all joy.

The term for count is *hegéomai,* to make a decision after weighing all the facts. That's why some translations use the word *consider.* We don't automatically jump for joy in the face of misfortune. We have to think things through from the perspective of Scripture. When we have a problem, our first reaction may be painful. We have to work it out in our minds, pray about it from every angle, and consider it in the light of God's promises.

The word *joy* is the Greek term *chará,* which is used only one other time in this epistle. In James 4:8–9, we're told: "Cleanse your hands, sinners . . . . Your laughter must change to mourning and your joy to sorrow." If we aren't right with the Lord, we have no reason to stay happy; we have sorrow. If we are right with the Lord, we don't have reason to stay gloomy; we cultivate joy.

In Christ, we can count it all joy—whatever happens—for God will turn it to good and in the process teach us the lessons of perseverance.

So gird yourself with James 1:2, shout Hallelujah, and go on.

November 21

READING: LUKE 17:11–19

*Jesus asked, "Were not **all** ten cleansed?*
Where are the other nine?"
Luke 17:17 (NIV)

As we gear up for Thanksgiving, it's important to realize that our Lord's question in Luke 17:17 implies an expectation. He had healed ten lepers, and He expected all ten to thank Him with joyful gratitude; but only one did so.

That one, I think, had cultivated a different attitude in all of life. While the other nine had cursed their fate, he had worked hard to keep a good attitude. While the other nine had complained about their sickness, he had found ways of looking on the bright side. While the other nine had awakened each morning in a bad mood, he had noticed the sunrise. While the others had gobbled down whatever food they found, he had bowed his head in thanksgiving. While the other nine wore expressions of scorn and cynicism, he had learned to smile.

Thanking Jesus was more natural to him than to the others that day, for he had worked on it. Thanksgiving is never an isolated act; it's the expression of a cultivated attitude.

> Ten met the Master in a field,
> Called to Him, agonized, were healed.
> Nine hastened on their various ways.
> One only, cleansed, returned to praise,
> Lettered in gratitude and grace,
> Meeting His Master face to face.
>
> Let me give thanks! O number me
> Among the lesser company.
>
> —*Mabel Munns Charles*

November 22

*God was pleased . . . through him to reconcile to himself **all** things, . . .
by making peace through his blood, shed on the cross.*
Colossians 1:20 (NIV)

I was in Mrs. Richardson's fifth grade class on this day in 1963. It was Friday afternoon, and I was excited because my dad was picking me up early from school to spend the weekend with my Aunt Louise. Going to the office to sign out, we found the principal hovering over a radio. Looking up, she said gravely, "President Kennedy's been shot." I remember my dad saying, "There are dangers in every profession." An hour later, arriving at my aunt's office, I asked if the president had died, to which Aunt Louise nodded gravely.

President Kennedy's death was a defining moment in the twentieth century, but two thousand years ago, a greater than JFK died; and His death was *the* defining moment in *all of history*. His blood was the means by which God was pleased to reconcile all things to Himself.

Not long ago a commuter train derailed in Los Angeles, causing eleven deaths and two hundred injuries. One man, napping in the double-decker car, woke up to find himself trapped under the debris and covered with blood. Realizing he was badly injured, he used the blood oozing from his body to write a note with his finger, telling his family he loved them.[97]

Now, Christ's blood speaks, too.
His blood cries . . . "Peace! Pardon!
Forgiveness! Mercy! Acceptance!"

— *Charles H. Spurgeon,
preaching at Royal Surrey Gardens,
August 29, 1858*

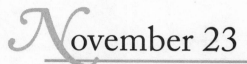

November 23

When they saw Him walking on the sea,
they thought it was a ghost and cried out;
*for they **all** saw Him and were terrified.*
Immediately He spoke with them and said,
"Have courage! It is I. Don't be afraid."

Mark 6:49–50

At three o'clock in the morning, the disciples, straining at their oars, could not see Jesus, who was praying on the hillside; but He saw them. Wending down the mountain, He spread an invisible carpet-runner across the waves, and by sunrise, all was well.

The faith that pleases Jesus is the faith that adopts a sunrise attitude amidst a midnight storm. The Lord is pleased with a faith-attitude that knows in the darkness that Jesus is on His way.

> Exhausted and frightened, they battled the rain,
> The wind, the waves, enduring the strain,
> Till finally their nerves could stand it no more;
> And their strength was all gone,
> And their muscles were sore.
>
> But up on the mountain Jesus could see,
> Every white-capping wave on the rough Galilee.
> And treading the billows like a carpet of sod,
> He came to their aid
> With the power of God.
>
> They worshipped Him then, with rejoicing and awe
> For the marvels He did, and the wonders they saw.
> But better to praise Him with the storm at its worst;
> By remembering His power
> And promises first.

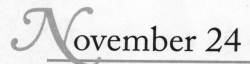ovember 24

The Pharisees, who were lovers of money,
*were listening to **all** these things and scoffing at Him.*
Luke 16:14

At Edward and Abby Robinson's dinner table, the conversation was always about money, and their daughter, Hetty, took it all in. She learned to read the financial papers by age six, and when she was thirteen, she became the family bookkeeper. When her parents died, she inherited a fortune and increased it by making shrewd investments. Hetty was the first woman in American history to make a substantial impact on Wall Street and became America's richest woman. But she was so frugal she bought secondhand clothes, ate in the cheapest restaurants, and didn't live anywhere long enough to pay property taxes. She never turned on the heat or used hot water. She rode in an old carriage, and every afternoon she went to Wall Street to count her cash while munching on baked onions. She was so surly and miserly that she was dubbed the "Witch of Wall Street."

The Bible extols the virtues of wise saving and generous giving, but it's easy to love money too much. In the New Testament, the Pharisees were the strictest adherents of Judaism, yet they loved money and scoffed at all that Jesus said. Making money is good; saving it is better; giving it is best of all.

John Wesley had the capacity of making a vast amount of money, yet he lived on a shoestring and gave most of his income away. His famous Trilateral about money is hard to beat: "Gain all you can. Save all you can. Give all you can."

November 25

*They were **all** trying to intimidate us, saying,*
"They will become discouraged in the work, and it will never
be finished." But now, my God, strengthen me.

Nehemiah 6:9

George Liele, an American slave, became a courageous preacher who eventually settled in Kingston, Jamaica, where his fearless preaching rankled white slave owners. When he was thrown into jail in 1797, his work was carried on by one of his converts, Moses Hall.

Hall, in turn, had nurtured a young slave named David who led prayer meetings. One day a group of slave owners burst into a prayer meeting, seized David, murdered him, cut off his head, and placed it on a pole in the center of town. Marching Moses Hall up to the macabre site, they demanded, "Moses, whose head is that?" He said it was David's.

"Do you know why he is up here?"

"For praying, sir."

"No more of your prayer meetings," they charged. "If we catch you at it, we shall serve you as we have served David."

Then in front of the crowd, Moses dropped to his knees beside the pole and said, "Let us pray." Other blacks joined in as they prayed for the salvation of the murderers. The challengers could do nothing but walk away.[98]

Nehemiah, too, faced deadly enemies, all of whom tried to intimidate him into stopping the work, but he prayed ("Now, my God, strengthen me") and persevered and prevailed.

That's the biblical model of courage.

Press onward, press onward, your courage renew;
The prize is before you, the crown is in view.

—*Fanny Crosby*

November 26

These men who have caused trouble
***all** over the world have now come here.*

Acts 17:6 (NIV)

The first Christians were walking torches who weren't afraid to share their faith, spread their news, praise their Lord, and set their world on fire. They'd discovered a secret that had turned them inside out. Gone were their inhibitions, failures, sins, and temporal concerns. The risen Christ was living within them, walking among them, and working through them. They were filled with the Spirit and they shared the Word with boldness, though it sometimes brought the lash down on their backs and the government down on their heads.

They didn't expect to be here long, so they made the most of every opportunity.

It was said of them, "These men who have turned the world upside down have come here too." It was an unintended compliment.

There are still Christians like that, but the majority of us are content with being middle-of-the-roaders whose lukewarm Laodicean faith won't even cause the world to tilt a little.

The gospel isn't going to turn the world upside down until it turns us inside out and right-side up, and we'll not set others on fire until we ourselves become walking torches.

The Christians who have turned the world upside down
have been men and women with vision in their hearts
and the Bible in their hands.

—*T. B. Maston*[99]

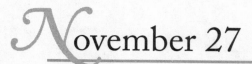

READING: ZEPHANIAH 3:14–20

*Be glad and rejoice with **all** your heart . . . .*
I will bring you back, yes,
at the time I will gather you.
I will make you famous and praiseworthy
*among **all** the peoples of the earth.*

Zephaniah 3:14, 20

Isobel Kuhn's books are largely autobiographical as she openly
shares the struggles she faced as a missionary in Asia. On one
occasion, for example, she and her husband were directed where
she didn't want to go. Isobel's passion was with the Lisu people
on the border of China and Burma. When their mission directed
them elsewhere, Isobel grew angry and disgruntled, and she knew
that was unhealthy.

"For some years it had been my habit to fast and pray one
morning a month for my own spiritual needs, the church's needs,
and world revival," she wrote. "My diary records that while I was
waiting before the Lord on this occasion, some verses in Zephaniah 3 were given me."

Those verses assured Isobel that God would deal with all her
concerns and that He would soon take her back to the Lisu work:
"Rejoice with all your heart . . . . I will bring you back."

"I cannot tell you the joy and victory that flooded me," she
wrote, ". . . although I told no one, not even my husband." And in
time she did return to work with the Lisu with great results.

We become angry, anxious, disgruntled, and dissatisfied so
easily, but it's a sin to remain in such an attitude. When we learn
to bring our concerns to the Lord, to wait before Him in prayer
and perhaps in fasting, and to find the verse or verses we need,
then we've gained the victory.

November 28

*David and **all** Israel danced before God with great enthusiasm.*
1 Chronicles 13:8 (NAB)

Years ago I gave my wife a book entitled *Enthusiasm Makes the Difference!* A day or two later, I came home to find her exhausted. She explained, "That book was so motivating that I jumped out of bed this morning with enthusiasm. I did my errands with enthusiasm. I rushed through the grocery store with enthusiasm. I washed and ironed and cooked and cleaned with enthusiasm. Enthusiasm made the difference all right. Enthusiasm Wore Me Out!"

According to etymologists, the word *enthusiasm* has a Christian origin. When people in the early church came to Christ, they were filled with a joy, zeal, and power they'd never known before. Since no one term described all these things, they put together the Greek words for "in"—*en*—and "God"—*Theos,* creating the term *en-theos-ist:* enthusiast.

Oswald Chambers described enthusiasm as being "intoxicated with God." If that sounds too impious, remember that the first Christians were so excited about the Lord they were accused of being drunk! Not all of us are comfortable dancing before the Lord as David did, but how much better to be enthusiastic than lethargic.

It's remarkable how we can change our mood when we decide to be enthusiastic.

Work with enthusiasm, as though you were working
for the Lord rather than for people.
Ephesians 6:7 (NLT)

I have had a real burst of enthusiasm for Christ today.
—*Hannah Whitall Smith*[100]

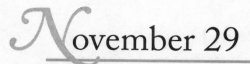

November 29

*Behold, I make **all** things new.*
Revelation 21:5 (NKJV)

The last two chapters of the Bible are a travel brochure with literal, vivid, wonderful descriptions of what's ahead for God's children. At the dawn of eternity, Jesus will make all things new. There will be a new universe, a New Earth, a New Jerusalem, and a new order of things, for the old order will pass away.

The word *city* occurs twelve times in Revelation 21–22. By any definition, a city is a literal place with people, streets, trees, buildings, parks, and cultural venues, all subject to a common government. Christ rose literally, bodily from the grave, so heaven must be a literal, physical, bodily place.

It will be an immense city of light, constructed out of a translucent gold and illumined by the glorious presence of the Lord Jesus Christ. God's throne will occupy the city center, and the Crystal River will flow down the middle of the main boulevard and through a park containing the tree of life.

The Lord deliberately concluded His Book with these two chapters because He wants us to know, to anticipate, and to visualize what's ahead. He will make all things new!

George McDonald, the Scottish preacher, was trying to describe heaven one day to his son, and the boy looked at his father and said, "It seems too good to be true." McDonald smiled and replied, "Nay, it is just so good that it must be true."

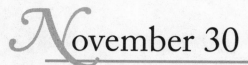

November 30

*If I donate **all** my goods to feed the poor . . .*
but do not have love, I gain nothing.

1 Corinthians 13:3

The Love Chapter of the Bible, 1 Corinthians 13, tells us that nothing we do is commendable in God's eyes if our motives are wrong. Even giving all our goods to feed the poor is worthless if we don't do it out of genuine love. As Proverbs 21:2 says, "All the ways of a man seem right to him, but the LORD evaluates the motives."

On the other hand, when we support the Lord's work out of a Spirit-fueled love, our gifts are crowned with eternal rewards.

Years ago, a member of the Swedish Royal Family, Princess Eugenie, longed to build a hospital for incurables. She was already supporting many charities, and it seemed impossible to raise more funds. But recognizing the pressing need for such a hospital and after prayer, she sold her diamonds and proceeded to build the hospital.

After the hospital opened, Eugenie visited often, going from patient to patient. She was particularly concerned about an older woman who had suffered greatly from disease. The princess spent time with the woman, seeking to lead her to faith in Christ, but the woman resisted. One day, however, as the princess approached the woman's bed, the woman cried out, "I thank God that the blood of Jesus Christ His Son cleanses me from all my sin."

In tears, the princess stood alongside the woman and said, as if to herself, "I have seen my diamonds again."[101]

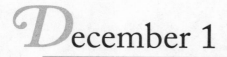

December 1

*These **all** died in faith without having received the promises,*
but they saw them from a distance, greeted them,
and confessed that they were foreigners
and temporary residents on the earth.

Hebrews 11:13

Hebrews 11, with its list of biblical heroes, teaches the value of godly biography. Christians didn't just appear on this planet in the twenty-first century. We've had four thousand years of histories and heroes, and we should know something of those who have passed the gospel down to us like living links in a chain of grace.

The biblical stalwarts are summarized in Hebrews 11, and the notables of Christian history are sitting on the biography shelves of our homes and libraries.

One of my favorite heroes is Dwight Moody (1837–99), who was saved as a teenager in the back of a Boston store, started working with Sunday school children in Chicago, and eventually became the greatest evangelist in the nineteenth century. Despite scant education and no training, Moody possessed an inexhaustible passion for souls and an extraordinary spiritual anointing.

Someone once asked him how he managed to remain so close to Christ. Moody replied, "I have come to Him as the best friend I have ever found, and I can trust Him in that relationship. I have believed He is Savior; I have believed He is God; I have believed His atonement on the cross is mine, and I have come to Him and submitted myself on my knees, surrendered everything to Him, and got up and stood by His side as my friend, and there isn't any problem in my life, there isn't any uncertainty in my work but I turn and speak to Him as naturally as to someone in the same room, and I have done it these years because I can trust Jesus."

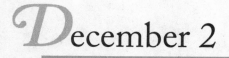

December 2

*My love be with **all** of you in Christ Jesus.*
1 Corinthians 16:24

Most know Julia Child from her television show *The French Chef*. In real life, Julia was a tall, opinionated, likeable woman with a distinctive voice who had served in the OSS in China under "Wild Bill Donovan." During World War II, she met Paul Child, and in 1948 he was assigned to the American Embassy in Paris.

One evening they had a conversation about the "rude Frenchmen." Many people are offended by French officials and storekeepers. Paul told Julia that in the 1920s he had found 80 percent of the people difficult and 20 percent charming. Now the reverse was true—80 percent of the Parisians were charming and only 20 percent were rude.

But Paul admitted the difference wasn't in the people. His own attitude had changed. "I am less sour now than I used to be," he said. "It's because of you, Julia."[102]

We're prone to be sour by nature, and people upset us, get on our nerves, and exasperate us. The apostle Paul had lots of problems with those in Corinth, and as we read his two letters, we hear the aggravation in his voice toward some in the church who were causing problems. Yet he could end his letter saying, "My love be with all of you in Christ Jesus."

We can even like those who are rude, but not because of them. It's our own attitude that changes. We should all be able to say, "I'm less sour now than I used to be. It's because of You, Jesus."

December 3

Be glad in the LORD and rejoice, you righteous ones;
*shout for joy, **all** you upright in heart.*

Psalm 32:11

Once several years ago, God convicted me of disobeying a prepositional phrase. I was working day and night, wearing myself out trying to win people to Christ and grow a church. At length, my emotional energy gave out. I still kept going physically, but the joy and enthusiasm and radiance had seeped out of my soul like air out of a tire. Then one day I read Psalm 100:2: "Serve the LORD with gladness."

I was obeying the first three words of that verse as well as I knew how, but I was disobeying the qualifying phrase "with gladness." Then I saw an even starker warning about it in Deuteronomy 28:47–48: "Because you didn't serve the Lord your God with joy and a cheerful heart, even though you had an abundance of everything, you will serve your enemies."

Then there was this question I came across in Galatians 4:15 (NIV): "What has happened to all your joy?"

That was many years ago, and I've learned to get more sleep at night, to pace myself more carefully, to replenish my inner soul with solitude and prayer and Bible study, and to work on my attitude.

Every one of us bears this responsibility, for a joyless believer is a sorry recommendation for the Christian faith. Be glad in the Lord, rejoice, and shout for joy—all you who are upright.

If you have no joy,
there's a leak in your Christianity somewhere.

—Billy Sunday

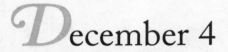

December 4

*In **all** things I gave you an example,*
that so laboring ye ought to help the weak,
and to remember the words of the Lord Jesus,
that He Himself said,
"It is more blessed to give than to receive."

Acts 20:35 (ASV)

Paul ended his sermon to the Ephesian elders in Acts 20 by asking them to follow his example in all things, especially by working hard to help the weak. Then he quoted Jesus: "It is more blessed to give than to receive." That statement by our Lord isn't found in the Gospels, but somehow Paul knew of it and slipped it into the Scriptures as the "Almost Forgotten Beatitude."

The word *blessed* occurs many times in the Bible, but this is the only time in Scripture we find the phrase *more blessed.*

Jesus was really describing two great blessings—receiving and giving. He didn't indicate one was a curse and the other a blessing. He indicated that both were blessings, but one is greater than the other.

It's wonderful to receive, especially when the giver is God Himself. His mercies come morning by morning, every good gift comes from above, and from the fullness of His grace we receive one blessing after another. Could anything be better than receiving?

Just one—giving.

The reason is that when we receive, we're acting like ourselves; but when we give, we're acting like God. Having an attitude of giving allows us to move into the divine realm and do something that God Himself delights to do; and that is the greater blessing.

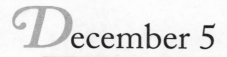ecember 5

*My hand made **all** these things,*
*and so they **all** came into being.*
This is the LORD's declaration.
I will look favorably on this kind of person:
one who is humble, submissive in spirit,
and who trembles at My word.

Isaiah 66:2

I've never been around many great people—almost none—but I have on several occasions been in close proximity with Billy Graham, and this is what has impressed me most about him. His voice, which is so authoritative and powerful in public, is soft and gentle in private, and it seems to me that his favorite word is *Certainly.*

"Dr. Graham, can I have a moment with you?"—Certainly. "Dr. Graham, may we have a picture?"—Certainly. "Dr. Graham, would you do this or that?"—Certainly.

He has a servant's heart, and that's why God has so used him.

Isaiah 66 opens with God's assertion that heaven is His throne and earth is His footstool. His hand made all these things. He is the Creator and our Lord. We are the creation and His servants. And He looks favorably on those who are humble.

There aren't many books or sermons on the subject of humility, and the reason is obvious. Anyone—certainly me—who writes or speaks on this subject is automatically a hypocrite. Whenever we talk about humility, we do so hypocritically because all of us are sinners by nature and choice, and the essence of sin is pride.

Humility is an attitude we choose and a grace God cultivates in us over a period of time. But great people learn to be humble people, submissive to God and reverencing His Word.

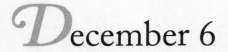

December 6

Repentance for forgiveness of sins
*would be proclaimed in His name to **all** the nations,*
beginning at Jerusalem.
You are witnesses of these things.

Luke 24:47–48

It's nearly 2:00 a.m. on a sleepless night. As I've worked on this manuscript, an e-mail came from one of my church members who evidently isn't in bed either. Her name is Tracy, and she knows that people from all the nations are flooding into America, and we don't always have to travel overseas to reach internationals. Her e-mail said:

> Three weeks ago in the English class I teach at the local college, my Kurdish student, Gula, was upset. The hospital had billed her $7,000 for a visit to the emergency room. She was so distraught that after class it came natural for me to pray with her. Yes, I stood right in the classroom and prayed for her. She wept and I did as well.
>
> Tonight I had a party at my house for my ESL students.[103] Gula came up to me and said, "Remember you prayed with me? Do you know what happened? The hospital told me my balance is zero. They told me a nice person had given money for those needing financial help. You prayed and look what God did!"
>
> And then, no lie, this Muslim Kurd excitedly said, "I want to go to your church with you sometime." I couldn't believe my ears. So Gula with her three children is going with me to church this Sunday. Look what God is doing! Wow. He amazes me.

December 7

The grace of the Lord Jesus Christ,
and the love of God,
and the fellowship of the Holy Spirit
*be with **all** of you.*

2 Corinthians 13:13

A *benediction* is a prayer of blessing at the end of a worship service, or, in this case, at the end of a book in the Bible. It comes from the Latin word *benedictus*, which is made up of a prefix meaning "well" coupled with the verb "to speak." Though the word *benediction* doesn't occur in Scripture, benedictions do occur. There are a number of prayers in which the priests of the Old Testament or the writers of the New Testament bless God's people.

The Apostolic Benediction in 2 Corinthians 13:13 is Trinitarian in nature. Each Member of the Trinity wants to bless us—Father, Son, and Holy Spirit.

God the Son wants to bless us with grace. Grace is a word employed by the New Testament writers to summarize the totality of God's gifts and blessings to us in Christ.

God the Father wants to bless us with love. How comforting to fall asleep every night and awaken each morning knowing that the God of heaven and earth loves us!

God the Spirit wants to bless us with fellowship. We walk with God via the Holy Spirit, and it's the Spirit that unites us with the body of Christ as in a loving family.

> May the grace of Christ our Savior
> And the Father's boundless love
> With the Holy Spirit's favor,
> Rest upon us from above.
>
> *—John Newton, 1779*

December 8

The grace of God has appeared,
*with salvation for **all** people.*

Titus 2:11

The word *grace* ranks high in the Christian vocabulary. It's the translation of the Greek word *charis*, and there are several layers of meaning. It was used in secular Greek writings during biblical times, meaning "something that delights." In Plato's writings, for example, it was used to mean good pleasure, goodwill, favor, pleasure, something that pleases.

As time went by, *charis* was particularly used to describe favor shown by rulers, as when a king or governor presented someone with a gracious gift. Suppose, for example, you were invited to the White House, and during your tour you visited the president in the Oval Office and he gave you a gift—maybe an ink pen used to sign an important document. You'd be delighted and you would treasure it.

Well, the apostles and the writers of the New Testament took this word and packed it full of theological meaning. Dr. J. I. Packer says in his book *God's Words:* "Rightly understood, this one word 'grace' contains within itself the whole of New Testament theology . . . . Grace is the sum and substance of New Testament faith . . . . [It] is the key that unlocks the New Testament; and it is the only key that does it."[104]

Grace is the basis of justification and the source of all our other benefits. Someone said that it's the heart and the hand of God. There's an old acronym that can't be beat. It's easy to remember and doctrinally accurate: G.R.A.C.E. is God's Riches At Christ's Expense.

December 9

READING: ACTS 10:34–43

He sent the message to the sons of Israel,
proclaiming the good news of peace through Jesus Christ—
*He is Lord of **all**.*

Acts 10:36

In this passage, Peter is opening the doors of evangelism to the Gentiles as he takes the gospel to the household of Cornelius in the seaside city of Caesarea, which Herod the Great had built on the Israeli coast to headquarter the occupying Roman government. Cornelius was a Roman centurion who was eager to learn of Jesus Christ. Peter's sermon was brief because it was interrupted by the immediate conversion of his listeners (v. 44), but it can be summed up in verse 36: "Peace through Jesus Christ—He is Lord of all."

Because Jesus Christ is Lord of all, He gives us peace with God and the ensuing peace of God in our hearts. We have peace in every way because He is Lord over everything.

In her book *An Uninvited Guest*, Jeana Floyd relates her battle with breast cancer, and she gives us a marvelous definition of God's peace, using P.E.A.C.E. as a simple acrostic to describe how a cancer patient can find relief from the stresses brought on by the disease. The acrostic works for those facing other challenges too.[105]

P = Pray.

E = Enjoy each day.

A = Accept this as "Father-filtered."

C = Center your thoughts on Him and His will for your life—study His Word, the Bible.

E = Expect to see God's hand move in your life during this time.

Lord of all to Thee we raise
This our hymn of grateful praise.

—*Folliot S. Pierpoint*

December 10

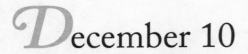

READING: JAMES 3:7–13

Their own tongues work against them.
All *who see them will shake their heads.*

Psalm 64:8

Basil Manly Jr. grew up in a parsonage in Charleston, South Carolina, where his father was pastor of First Baptist Church. He was converted at age fourteen while reading a biography of Jonathan Edwards. That same year, Basil's father was appointed president of the University of Alabama, and Basil enrolled there, graduating in 1844. After further studies, he followed in his father's footsteps both as a pastor and an educator. He was one of four founding faculty members of the Southern Baptist Theological Seminary, eventually becoming its president. He's also remembered as the first president of the Southern Baptist Sunday School Board.[106] Manly left behind many great theological works as well as a number of profound hymns. But perhaps his simplest and most practical work was a little poem written in 1866, titled "Kind Words."

> Words are things of greatest worth,
> Though often lightly spoken;
> Thoughtless fleeting words of mirth,
> May wound the heart that's broken;
> Or words that pass forgotten by,
> May prompt to deeds that cannot die.
>
> Kind words quell the angry soul,
> But bitter railings never;
> Love can soothe with sweet control,
> And kindle love for ever.
>
> Watch well your words,
> Both old and young,
> For life and death hang on the tongue.

December 11

Should you then seek great things for yourself?
*Seek them not. For I will bring disaster on **all** people,*
declares the LORD, but wherever you go
I will let you escape with your life.
Jeremiah 45:5 (NIV)

Jeremiah 45 was written for Baruch, Jeremiah's assistant, warning him that the Babylonian Empire was about to overwhelm Israel and no one would be unaffected. Don't seek power or wealth, advised the Lord, for all will be lost. Instead, humbly serve the One who will watch over your life.

Dr. J. Oswald Sanders coveted a certain job in a Christian organization, and he almost lobbied some influential friends for it. But walking through downtown Auckland, New Zealand, these words came to him with authority: "Seekest thou great things for thyself? Seek them not!" (KJV). Consequently, he didn't seek the position, but it later opened to him on its own in God's timing.

When Charles Spurgeon was eighteen, he applied to Regent's Park College. An interview was set and Spurgeon rose early and set out. But through a misunderstanding he missed his appointment and was not admitted. Crestfallen, Charles walked through the countryside trying to calm down. Suddenly Jeremiah 45:5 came to mind: "Seekest thou great things for thyself? Seek them not!" Spurgeon never made it to college, but he went on to become the most famous preacher in England.

It's proper to seek God's will for your life and to seek great things for His sake, but one day the Lord will bring judgment on all flesh. Worldly power, popularity, and prestige will be swept away. Seek great things for thyself? Seek them not.

December 12

READING: 2 KINGS 5:1–14

Aren't Abana and Pharpar, the rivers of Damascus,
*better than **all** the waters of Israel?*
Could I not wash in them and be clean?

2 Kings 5:12

General Naaman of Syria was a great warrior, but he was a leper and there wasn't a doctor in Damascus who could help him. A little Israeli servant girl in his household—we don't know her name—recommended he consult the prophet Elisha, who, in turn, sent him to dip seven times in the Jordan River. Naaman was disgusted. "Aren't my hometown rivers better than all the waters of Israel?" he asked. But he went anyway, and his skin was restored like that of a child.

The Chickamauga is a river in North Georgia, and it's also a battlefield. The Battle of Chickamauga was fought between the Army of Tennessee and the Army of the Cumberland in September of 1863, and some historians say that it represented the last real opportunity for the Confederacy to win the Civil War. There were thirty-five thousand casualities and more than four thousand fatalities. The ironic thing is that *Chickamauga* is a Cherokee word. It means, literally, "the River of Blood."

If we want forgiveness and everlasting life, we have to go to God's Chickamauga—the River of Blood—and there we can wash away our guilt and stain.

O Fount of grace redeeming,
O River ever streaming,
From Jesus' wounded side.

—From an ancient Latin hymn

December 13

*We have this treasure in jars of clay
to show that this **all**-surpassing power
is from God and not from us.*

2 Corinthians 4:7 (NIV)

The apostle Paul is talking about the treasure of God's glorious message about Jesus: "We are not proclaiming ourselves but Jesus Christ as Lord . . . . He has shone in our hearts to give the light of the knowledge of God's glory in the face of Jesus . . . . Now we have this treasure in clay jars" (4:5–7).

In Bible times, there were no banks or safe repositories, so people buried their treasures in the earth or hid them in caves using clay jars. This is how the famous Dead Sea Scrolls were preserved in caves near the village of Qumran, south of Jerusalem. These priceless scrolls were housed in jars of clay. Likewise, we are God's depositories for His treasure, though we're fragile, breakable, and easily damaged. The Lord could have made us into vaults of steel or chests of titanium, but He made us clay jars, and He did so for a reason: "to show that this all-surpassing power is from God."

The word *all-surpassing* is the Greek word from which we get our English term *hyperbole*. It means "throwing beyond, excess, extraordinary amount, to an extreme degree."

Since the all-surpassing power that fuels our lives is from an external source—from God Himself—we can be resilient in the face of discouragement. It's God's power that keeps us going; therefore, nothing short of God can shut us down. We may be jars of clay, but we contain the treasure of Christ and His ministry, and His all-surpassing power is flowing through us.

December 14

The rain and snow come down from the heavens
and stay on the ground to water the earth.
They cause the grain to grow,
producing seed for the farmer and bread for the hungry.
It is the same with my word.
I send it out, and it always produces fruit.
*It will accomplish **all** I want it to,*
and it will prosper everywhere I send it.
Isaiah 55:10–11 (NLT)

Our joy is to share the Word as best we can and to leave the results with God. It's not by might or power. It's not by personality or persuasive ability. It's not by oratorical skills or intellect. The power is in the Scripture itself. God has sent down His message like raindrops and snowflakes onto a parched world, and just as a refreshing rainstorm will revive a desert, so the Word of God will revive His people and convert the lost. We may not see all the results, but as long as we're faithful to proclaim the Word, our labor in the Lord is not in vain (1 Cor. 15:58).

Johann Sebastian Bach was one of the greatest musicians of all time, and his skills on the organ were without equal. Once when an acquaintance praised Bach's rendition of a particular work, he replied like this: "There is nothing very wonderful about it," he said. "You have only to hit the right notes at the right moment and the instrument does all the rest."[107]

Martin Luther similarly explained: "I simply taught, preached, wrote God's Word . . . otherwise I did nothing . . . . The Word did it all."[108]

December 15

You son of the Devil,
*full of **all** deceit and **all** fraud,*
*enemy of **all** righteousness!*

Acts 13:10

Missionary Isaac D. Colburn of Burma told of a group of Burmese Christians who gathered for an outdoor baptism. Many curious locals showed up to watch, and among them were two men, father and son, who detested the gospel.

As the Burmese pastor opened the poolside service, the father and son interrupted the proceedings with blasphemous words, curses, and obscene gestures. Just as the pastor was about to plunge his first disciple into the water, the two antagonists stripped and plunged naked into the water, where they conducted their own mock baptism, jeering and uttering profanities alongside the name of the Trinity.

Also present that day was a native evangelist named Sau Wah, who, before his conversion, had fiercely opposed the gospel. Now he rose and called to the men in the water, "O full of all deceit and all fraud, you son of the devil, you enemy of all righteousness, will you not cease perverting the straight ways of the Lord?"

These words seemed to strike the two blasphemers like electrical bolts. They raced out of the water, but before going many yards they both fell to the ground. The father was found dead. The son recovered consciousness and was carried to the village, but within a few months he, too, died.

God is a God of love, but He's also a God of judgment. The Bible contains many warnings to the unrighteous, telling us that it's a fearful thing to fall into the hands of the living God. He is to be feared, honored, reverenced, and obeyed.[109]

December 16

READING: ROMANS 8:31–35

What then shall we say about these things?
If God is for us, who is against us?
He did not even spare His own Son,
*but offered Him up for us **all**,*
how will He not also with Him grant us everything?

Romans 8:31–32

When I was a boy, my Aunt Louise came to our house on Christmas Eve with a car full of presents. I don't remember what she gave me that evening, but I remember very well what she gave my sister, who was, as I recall, about five years old. It was a huge walking doll. It was really too tall for my sister to handle, but she and I spent many wonderful days playing in the large box that contained the present.

As we approach the Christmas season, we're prone to forget the Baby and focus on the wrappings and trappings of the season. The onslaught of preparation is well-nigh overwhelming. But in Romans 8, the Bible reminds us that God gave His Son to us all at Christmas and at Calvary. If He gave us this ultimate blessing, will He not also give us all other things needed for daily happiness and everlasting joy?

Yes, yes, He will freely give us all things.

∽

How shall He not?
Can it be imagined that He should do the greater
and not do the less? That He should give so great a gift
for us when we were enemies, and should deny us any
good thing now that through Him we are friends and children?

—*Matthew Henry*

December 17

READING: LUKE 2:25–34

*You have prepared it
in the presence of **all** peoples.*

Luke 2:31

Simeon spoke those words as he took the Christ child in his arms, and the "it" refers to salvation. Simeon said, in essence, "O Lord, in giving us this Baby you have given us the salvation You have prepared in the presence of all peoples."

So it's remarkable how "all peoples" can avoid and even try to rid themselves of Jesus, even at Christmas.

I was asked by a magazine to collaborate on a series of articles about Charles Dickens' book *A Christmas Carol*. Finding an oversized, illustrated copy, I enjoyed reading it again; but something was missing. *A Christmas Carol* makes virtually no mention of Christ.

Dickens himself attended the Church of England, but his beliefs were Unitarian. He believed in a benevolent God and felt the Bible contained good maxims. But he had no creed, and like our modern holiday celebrations, he managed to capture the mood of Christmas while neglecting the manger.

Ebenezer Scrooge was "converted" and his life was changed—but not by Christ. He was transformed from cold miser to warmhearted philanthropist by the power of his dreams. It was the so-called Christmas spirit, not the Holy Spirit, that got hold of him.

Christmas is a tender time for remembering how Almighty God, from eternity past, planned and provided for our salvation, and He did it openly in the sight of all peoples. As the apostle Paul said in Acts 26:26, "This thing was not done in a corner."

Let's keep Jesus front and center in our hearts this season. And may God bless us every one!

December 18

READING: JOHN 1:6–13

*But to **all** who did receive Him,*
He gave them the right to be children of God,
to those who believe in His name.

John 1:12

The prologue of John is one the greatest preambles to any book in the history of publishing. In the first eighteen verses of John, the great evangelist covers all the themes of his book and succinctly brings us face-to-face with the Living Word who became flesh and lived among us. It's the Christmas story from John's perspective, but also the story of the ages. In the middle of this prologue, John describes:

- *The greatest perplexity in the world:* "He was in the world, and the world was created through Him, yet the world did not recognize Him. He came to His own, and His own people did not receive Him" (vv. 10–11). Perhaps the greatest mystery of history is the inexplicable fact that the Jewish Messiah arrived in perfect fulfillment of hundreds of Jewish prophecies, yet He was unrecognized and rejected by the very people He came to save.
- *The greatest privilege in the world:* "But to all who did receive Him, He gave them the right to be children of God" (v. 12).
- *The greatest person in the world:* "The Word became flesh and took up residence among us. We observed His glory, the glory as the One and Only Son from the Father, full of grace and truth" (v. 14).

O come to my heart, Lord Jesus,
There is room in my heart for Thee.

—*Emily Elliott, 1864*

December 19

READING: MATTHEW 2:1–6

When King Herod heard this he was disturbed,
*and **all** Jerusalem with him.*

Matthew 2:3

When Hitler rose to power in Germany, he wanted to take over the German church and dictate the nation's religion. Falsely accusing clergymen of various crimes, he had churchmen arrested and religious publications stopped. He encouraged marriage ceremonies to be conducted by state officials rather than by the church. In 1935 he outlawed obligatory prayer in schools, and he tried to replace Bibles with Nazi propaganda.

He had greater difficulty with the religious holidays because Germans had faithfully observed Easter and Christmas for centuries; so he set out to reinterpret their meaning. Easter became a holiday heralding the arrival of spring, and Christmas was turned into a pagan festival. Carols and nativity plays were banned from the schools in 1938, and even the name Christmas was changed to Yuletide.

Hitler failed, but the same sort of attempts are being made now in America as our society tries to strip Christmas of its meaning and outlaw its traditional observances in the public square.

Two thousand years ago, King Herod tried the same thing. Though he was one of the greatest builders of antiquity—leaving behind such fabulous ruins as Caesarea, Herodium, and the Temple Mount in Jerusalem—he couldn't stop Christmas. For all his power and paranoia, he couldn't overcome a Baby's influence.

No power on earth can stop you from worshipping Jesus this season. Satan has tried from the beginning, but his efforts always fail. After all, we cannot spell Christmas without Christ—and with a capital *C* at that!

December 20

But you, O Bethlehem Ephrathah,
*are only a small village among **all** the people of Judah.*
Yet a ruler of Israel will come from you,
one whose origins are from the distant past.

Micah 5:2 (NLT)

It's getting harder to visit Bethlehem because of ongoing political tensions, but visitors to Israel still trek that way; and many are surprised at how close this little town is to Jerusalem—only about five miles away, and so small—"only a small village among all the people of Judah."

Sometimes we think our place is too small, and we're disappointed at our meager lot. Perhaps we're in a small church, a small town, a small ministry, or a small house. Don't underestimate how greatly Jesus uses small things.

Historian David Hackett Fischer points out that, compared to the great battles of history, Washington's crossing of the Delaware was a very small event. But the outcome saved the United States of America.

French Jesuit Father Jean Nicolas Grou once wrote, "Let your aim be to please our dear Lord perfectly in little things."

If your place is a small one, remember Bethlehem. Of all the cities of Judah, God chose this little town as the birthplace of the Messiah and as the junction of time and eternity.

Jesus bids us shine
With a pure, clear light,
Like a little candle
Burning in the night.
In this world of darkness
So let us shine—
You in your small corner,
And I in mine.
—*Susan Warner*

December 21

We have been rescued from our enemies' clutches,
to serve Him without fear in holiness and righteousness
*in His presence **all** our days.*
Luke 1:74–75

Luke 1 records Zechariah's song celebrating the birth of his son, John, the forerunner of the Messiah. According to Zechariah, the Christ child would rescue us from the enemy's clutches and enable us to enjoy God's presence all our days.

The Bible presents an entire body of material about the Lord's presence within and among His people, and several sets of verses are especially meaningful.

The *Omnipresence* Verses speak of God's limitless presence filling heaven and earth. God is not measurable, and the essence of His person fills the galaxies and extends beyond the limits of the universe. Solomon said in 1 Kings 8:27 that the heavens and the earth cannot contain God. He inhabits eternity, yet He's always with us because He is always everywhere.

The *Presence* Verses are passages that speak of our Lord's presence with His people. The Lord told Moses, "My presence will go with you, and I will give you rest" (Exod. 33:14). Psalm 16:11 says, "In Your presence is abundant joy."

Other verses are *Nearness* Verses. "The Lord is near the broken-hearted . . . . The Lord is near all who call out to Him . . . . Draw near to God, and He will draw near to you" (Pss. 34:18, 145:18; James 4:8).

And don't forget the *With You* Verses, such as "Do not fear, for I am with you" (Isa. 41:10) and "Remember, I am with you always" (Matt. 28:20).

Visualize Him beside you all day today, for in His presence is fullness of joy.

December 22

*She came up and began to thank God
and to speak about Him to **all** who were looking forward
to the redemption of Jerusalem.*

Luke 2:38

During medieval days, December 25 was a pagan holiday with religious overtones. It fell in the dark and cold of winter, just as Europeans needed an outlet for their frustrations and appetites. It was common for mobs to storm wealthy homes, demanding food and drink: "O bring us some figgie pudding . . . . We won't go until we get some." In London, Christmas was a day when women and children didn't leave their homes, a day of drunkenness, rioting, and indulgence.

But one place on the globe changed the way Christmas was celebrated everywhere—Martin Luther's Germany. Luther loved Christmas, and in sparking the Reformation, he took full advantage of the story of Christ's birth. Germany responded with a plethora of wholesome holiday traditions.

Centuries later, Queen Victoria married Prince Albert of Germany, who brought all the hallowed celebrations with him to Windsor Castle. Christmas there became a wonderful time of beautiful trees, gift-giving, songs, and worship. These traditions were picked up and practiced across England, and Christmas began to take shape as we know it today.

Anna of Jerusalem had the right idea all along. When baby Jesus was brought to the temple, she began to thank God and to speak about Him to everyone, giving us a cue as to how Christmas should be observed. Among the traditions you celebrate this year, don't forget the oldest ones—thank God for His Son and speak about Him to everyone.

December 23

"Don't be afraid,
for look, I proclaim to you good news of great joy
*that will be for **all** the people."*

Luke 2:10

On December 19, 1814, Samuel Marsden stepped off the *Active* onto the shores of New Zealand, well aware of the fate of recent travelers. Years before, French explorer Marion du Fresne and his crew were captured and eaten. In 1809, eighty-seven of the crew of the *Boyd* were killed and eaten. In 1816, another crew met the same fate. In 1820, a whaling ship was cast ashore, and its crew consigned to the ovens and dinner tables.

But Marsden brought a horse from the ship and mounted it; and the cannibals, who had never before seen a horse, were awed to silence. That night, the missionary slept among them, and the next day he began his labors.

Christmas Day dawned, and Marsden had a rude pulpit erected. As the islanders gathered in curiosity, the missionary preached from Luke 2:10, about good news of great joy for all people—even cannibalistic savages. That event is remembered as the first Christian service in New Zealand.

For years there were few results, but finally a harvest swept through the island, and when Marsden finally left the island for the last time at age seventy-two, weak and frail, he was carried on the shoulders of strong young men who had grown up to be warriors instead of cannibals. Thousands gathered to say good-bye, and as he viewed the shores of New Zealand for the final time he exclaimed in amazement: "What hath God wrought!"

Gloria in excelsis Deo

December 24

*They reported the message they were told about this child,
and **all** who heard it were amazed at what the shepherds said to them.*

Luke 2:17–18

They were all amazed . . . . When the whole crowd saw Him, they were amazed . . . . All who heard it were amazed . . . . They were all speaking well of Him and were amazed by the gracious words that came from His mouth . . . . They were all struck with amazement . . . . They were all astonished at the greatness of God. . . . Everyone was amazed at all the things He was doing."[110]

The Son of God by the Father without a mother,
the Son of man by the Mother without a father;
the Word who is God before all time,
the Word made flesh at a fitting time.

—*St. Augustine*

I am far within the mark when I say that
all the armies that ever marched, all the navies that ever sailed,
all the parliaments that ever sat, all the kings that ever reigned,
put together, have not affected the life of man on earth
as has that One Solitary Life.

—*Phillips Brooks*

Jesus is God spelling Himself out
in language that man can understand.

—*Samuel D. Gordon*

No other God have I but Thee;
Born in a manger, died on a tree.

—*Martin Luther*

December 25

*But Mary was treasuring up **all** these things in her heart and meditating on them.*

Luke 2:19

In my kitchen I have a funnel, and from time to time I pull it out of the drawer and use it when I need to pour liquid—oil or vinegar or honey—from a large container into a smaller one. I don't use it often, but I'm thankful for it when I need it.

Think of Christmas as a massive funnel. Above all the universe is the immensity and eternity of God Himself—His perfect holiness, His illimitable glory, His endless infinity, His matchless wisdom, His unfailing love, His omnipresence and omnipotence and omniscience. He fills the universe to the edges of reality and beyond and dwells in inapproachable light.

Yet in the womb of Mary, the eternal God—God the Son, the Second Person of the Trinity—was funneled into the human race. God became flesh and dwelt among us.

Who better than Mary to show us how to celebrate Christmas? It's too much for our minds to quickly absorb, so we, like Mary, have to treasure these truths in our hearts and meditate on all of them. That's the essence of worship and that's the joy of Christmas.

Most certainly, the mystery of godliness is great:
He was manifested in the flesh.

1 Timothy 3:16

Of the Father's love begotten, ere the worlds began to be,
He is Alpha and Omega, He the source, the ending He,
Of the things that are, that have been,
And that future years shall see, evermore and evermore!

—*Aurelius Prudentius*

December 26

READING: 1 TIMOTHY 3:13–16

*The shepherds returned, glorifying and praising God
for **all** they had seen and heard.*

Luke 2:20

I've preached about Christmas each December for thirty years, and last year I wondered if there was anything new I could say. Asking God for insight, I read through the accounts of our Lord's birth again, and this time I saw something new. Everyone intimately acquainted with the coming of the Christ child responded with great worship and high thanksgiving. There was a universality of praise among all involved.

- When *Elizabeth* heard the news, she was filled with the Holy Spirit and exclaimed her wonderment with a loud voice. Even her unborn child leaped in the womb (Luke 1:41).
- When *Zechariah* finally spoke, he was filled with the Holy Spirit and proclaimed, "Praise the Lord, the God of Israel" (Luke 1:67–68).
- *Mary's* response was: "My soul proclaims the greatness of the Lord, and my spirit has rejoiced in God my Savior" (Luke 1:46–47).
- The *angels* sang, "Glory to God in the highest heaven!" (Luke 2:14).
- *Simeon* in the temple took the Christ child in his arms and praised God (Luke 2:28).
- Old *Anna* saw the Babe, thanking God and speaking about Him (Luke 2:38).
- The *magi* were "overjoyed beyond measure," and falling to their knees, worshipped Him (Matt. 2:10–11).
- And the *shepherds* glorified and praised God for all they saw and heard (Luke 2:20).

So what should our response be to Christmas?

December 27

All those who take refuge in Him are happy.
Psalm 2:12

It's important to be happy.

We can't live on an emotional high all the time, of course, nor should we. Not even our Lord did that, for on one occasion He wept, on another He said His soul was troubled, and on another He cried, "My God, My God, why . . . ?"

Still, the "default setting" for the Christian's attitude should be one of deeply contented joy, and it's very unbiblical to go around all the time with an unhappy attitude. Our happiness is as deep as His care and as perpetual as His peace. It comes from taking refuge in Him.

No matter what may happen to me day by day, I'm safe in His hands, and He is working all for good. Based on that, we choose happiness. After the holidays, some of us tend toward the blues. Let your "blues" be the blue skies of God's blessings as you gear up for a New Year of exploring God's grace.

A man is as unhappy
as he has convinced himself he is.

—*Seneca*

A person is about as happy
as they make up their mind to be.

—*Abraham Lincoln*

I feel it my duty to be as happy
as the Lord wants me to be.

—*Robert Murray McCheyne*

December 28

READING: DEUTERONOMY 15:7–11

Give to him [to the poor],
and don't have a stingy heart when you give,
and because of this the LORD your God
*will bless you in **all** your work*
and in everything you do.

Deuteronomy 15:10

In *None of These Diseases*, Dr. S. I. McMillen discussed the financier John D. Rockefeller. As a young man, Rockefeller was strong and husky, and he drove himself like a slave. He was a millionaire by age thirty-three. By forty-three he controlled the largest business on earth. By fifty-three, he was the world's only billionaire. But he developed a disease called alopecia, in which he lost hair from his head, eyebrows, and eyelashes. His digestion was terrible, and he lost weight until he looked like a dead man. The newspapers began compiling his obituary.

One night Rockefeller realized he couldn't take one dime into the next world. All his accomplishments were sand castles, doomed by the inevitable tide. For the first time he realized money was not a commodity to be hoarded but to be shared. He began transforming his money into blessings for others. He gave hundreds of millions to universities, hospitals, and missions. He led efforts to rid the South of hookworm and in the development of penicillin. The focus of his life changed from getting to giving. The result? He didn't die in his fifty-third year, or in his fifty-fourth. He lived to be ninety-eight.

Whether or not Rockefeller was a born-again believer, I don't know. But he did discover one of the moral laws God has placed in the universe: Giving is good for us. It enriches our lives.

December 29

READING: JOB 38:18–24

Have you comprehended the extent of the earth?
*Tell Me if you know **all** this.*

Job 38:18

Near the end of the book of Job, the Lord peppers Job with questions like: "Where were you when I created the earth? Do you feed the wild animals? Have you comprehended the extent of the earth? Tell Me if you know all this." The point being—the Lord is great enough to be trusted with our perplexities. His fabulous creation is assurance that He is intelligent, powerful, caring, and able to rule over all.

That's why, until it was kidnapped by atheistic philosophers, the scientific community understood it was investigating the wonders of God's creation. For example, Robert Boyle, the Father of Modern Chemistry, was a dedicated Christian who avidly studied the Bible and promoted missions.

Today is the anniversary of Boyle's conversion. On December 29, 1640, Boyle, age thirteen, gave his heart to Jesus following a tempestuous night. Loud claps of thunder shook his house, he later recounted, "and every clap was both preceded and attended with flashes of lightning so frequent and so dazzling that [I] began to imagine them the sallies of that fire that must consume the world."

"The next morning came," wrote Boyle, "and a serene cloudless sky returned." He then and there gave himself to the Lord Jesus, to study the Bible, and to consecrate his scientific work as a witness to God's creation.

∞

> There's not a plant or flower below,
> But makes Thy glories known,
> And clouds arise, and tempests blow,
> By order from Thy throne.
>
> *—Isaac Watts*

December 30

I was glad when they said to me,
"Let us go to the house of the LORD."...
***All** the people of Israel—the LORD's people—*
make their pilgrimage here.

Psalm 122:1, 4 (NLT)

Someone sent me this e-mail:

> I had a "drug" problem when I was young. I was
> "drug" to church on Sunday morning. I was "drug"
> to church on Sunday night. I was "drug" to church
> on Wednesday night. I was "drug" to Sunday school
> every week and to Vacation Bible School every sum-
> mer. Those "drugs" are still in my veins, and I don't
> think I'll ever kick the habit.

That could be my testimony. My parents took me to church the
first Sunday of my life, and I haven't missed many Sundays since.
The first Bible verse I memorized was in Mrs. Bailey's junior class,
and it was Psalm 122:1: "I was glad when they said to me, 'Let us
go to the house of the Lord.'"

I've heard countless excuses for neglecting church, and I can
agree with most of them. Yes, I am sometimes tired on Sundays.
Yes, there are hypocrites in church. Yes, sometimes the sermons are
boring. But God's people have always been churchgoers. Meeting
weekly to celebrate Jesus with songs, prayers, worship, and fellowship is important.

It's that time of year now when we think about making some
new resolutions. What about this one? This year, I resolve to drag
myself to church!

He went to Nazareth, where he had been brought up, and on the
Sabbath day he went into the synagogue, as was his custom.

Luke 4:16 (NIV)

December 31

The grace of the Lord Jesus
*be with **all** the saints. Amen.*
Revelation 22:21

Just as Genesis is the book of beginnings, Revelation is the book of endings, bringing the Bible full circle. Scripture begins and ends in Paradise. The devil isn't in the first or last two chapters of Scripture, but the Tree of Life is. In Genesis 1, God creates the heavens and the earth; in Revelation 21–22, He recreates them. In the Bible's opening scenes, humanity is perfect, sinless, happy, immortal, and in constant fellowship with God—and so in the final ones.

Between the beginning and ending of Scripture are 1,185 chapters that tell us the story of the ages—how sin and suffering entered the human race and how God loved us and became a man to save us through the shed blood of the Lamb. Though written in sixty-six installments by forty-plus authors over fourteen hundred years in three languages on three continents, the Bible's story is consistent and cohesive, unfolding like the master plot of a novel, and centered around one person, the Lord Jesus Christ.

When we come to the final paragraph of Revelation, we have the closing credits of Scripture: the Last Blessing (v. 14), the Last Invitation (v. 17), the Last Warning (vv. 18–19), the Last Promise (v. 20), the Last Prayer (v. 20), and the Last Benediction: "The grace of the Lord Jesus Christ be with all the saints. Amen."

The word *saints* encompasses everyone washed in the blood of Christ, the word *all* affirms its all-inclusiveness, and the final *Amen* punctuates it with a divine exclamation point. There is no better ending for a book, so . . .

The grace of the Lord Jesus be with you!
Amen.

otes

1. Sometimes, the word *all* is used as hyperbole in Scripture. As I worked my way through the 5,675 occurrences of the word, I tried to exclude these from this devotional study. I've selected only those "alls" that I feel are intended as literal.

2. Amy Carmichael, *Edges of His Ways* (Fort Washington, PA: Christian Literature Crusade, 1955, 1975, 1998), 8.

3. R. Laird Harris, Gleason L. Archer Jr., and Bruce K. Waltke, *Theological Wordbook of the Old Testament*, electronic ed. (Chicago: Moody Press, 1999, c1980) 101.

4. A. W. Tozer, *The Knowledge of the Holy* (New York: Harper & Row, 1961), 61.

5. David B. Diebel and Harold G. Koenig, *New Light on Depression* (Grand Rapids: Zondervan, 2004), 20.

6. Adapted from W. F. Weiherman, *That Reminds Me* (St. Louis: Concordia Publishing House, 1955), 21.

7. Related by David Michell in *A Boy's War* (Singapore: OMF Books, 1988), 139.

8. Quoted by David L. Larson in *The Company of Preachers* (Grand Rapids: Kregel Publications, 1998), 622–23.

9. C. C. Ryrie, *What You Should Know About Inerrancy* (Willow Grove, PA: Woodlawn Electronic Publishing 1998, c1981).

10. Richard Wurmbrand, *Tortured for Christ* (Bartlesville, OK: Diane Books, 1967), 45.

11. Philip Schaff, *History of the Christian Church, Vol. 2: Ante-Nicene Christianity* (Grand Rapids: Eerdmans Publishing Co., 1910), 20–21.

12. Clive Anderson, *Travel with C. H. Spurgeon: In the Footsteps of the "Prince of Preachers"* (Epsom, Surrey: Day One Publications, 2002), 53–54.

13. Personal letter to the author. Used with permission.

14. William Zinsser, *Writing About Your Life* (New York: Marlowe & Company, 2004), 31–32.

15. D. M. Field, *Van Gogh* (Edison, NJ: Chartwell Books, Inc., 2005), 19, 35.

16. Quoted by Steve Turner, *Amazing Grace: The Story of America's Most Beloved Song* (New York: HarperCollins Books, 2002), 72.

17. Deuteronomy 4:29; Deuteronomy 6:5; Deuteronomy 10:12; Deuteronomy 30:2, 10; Joshua 22:5; Joshua 23:14; 1 Samuel 7:3; 1 Samuel 12:24; Proverbs 3:5–6; Acts 8:37.

18. Adapted from the author's book *The Promise: How God Works All Things Together for Good* (Nashville: B&H Publishing Group, 2008).

19. Mary W. Tileston, *Daily Strength for Daily Needs*, installment for December 14.

20. William Law: *A Serious Call to a Devout and Holy Life* (Grand Rapids: William B. Eerdmans Publishing Company, 1966, reprinted from the edition printed in 1898 by Macmillan and Co.), 172–73.

21. Colossians 3:15; Ephesians 5:4; Colossians 3:17; Psalm 136:1, 3; Psalm 107:8; Psalm 100:4; Colossians 2:6–7; Ephesians 1:16; 1 Corinthians 15:57; 2 Corinthians 9:15.

22. Mount Moriah is in Jerusalem (2 Chron. 3:1).

23. Calvin Miller, *Jesus Loves Me* (New York: Warner Books, 2002), 54–55.

24. I made slight alterations to Spurgeon's original text to increase its readability to the modern eye.

25. Adapted from the author's book *The Promise: How God Works All Things Together for Good* (Nashville: B&H Publishing Group, 2008).

26. Abridged from Henry Parry Liddon's sermon, "The Power of His Resurrection."

27. Elie Wiesel, *Night* (New York: Hill and Wang, 2006), 57–58.

28. See entry for March 14.

29. Isaiah 32:17–18, John 14:27, Leviticus 26:6, Isaiah 66:12, Psalm 4:8, Romans 8:6, Galatians 5:22, Psalm 29:11, Psalm 119:165, Isaiah 9:6, Isaiah 53:5, Luke 24:36–39, Ephesians 2:14.

30. David Brinkley, *A Memoir* (New York: Alfred A. Knopf, 1995), 86.

31. *The Kneeling Christian* is my favorite book on prayer, written by Albert Ernest Richardson. My copy was printed by Zondervan Publishing House and is undated. This reading is from the first chapter.

32. J. Edwin Orr, *Always Abounding: An Intimate Sketch of Oswald J. Smith of Toronto* (London: Marshall, Morgan, & Scott, Ltd., 1940), chapter 1.

33. This story is in an old volume with a missing title page. On the spine are the words: *Anecdotes Christian Ministry*. The last page has this attribution: *Religious Tract Society: 1799*. This story is found on pages 15–16.

34. Charles Haddon Spurgeon, "God's Providence," at http://www.spurgeon.org/sermons/3114.htm, accessed on March 10, 2007.

35. This story was frequently told by Dr. Robert C. McQuilkin and is included in his biography, *Always in Triumph: The Life of Robert C. McQuilkin* by Marguerite McQuilkin, published in 1956 by the Bible College Bookstore of Columbia Bible College in Columbia, South Carolina. I repeated this story in a prior book, *From This Verse,* published by Thomas Nelson Publishers in 1998.

36. This story is told in an old volume in my library with a missing title page. On the spine are the words: *Anecdotes Christian Ministry*. The last page has this attribution: *Religious Tract Society: 1799*. This story is found on page 25.

37. Jeremiah 32:26–27; Genesis 18:14; Mark 10:27; Mark 14:36; Hebrews 7:25; Ephesians 3:20; 2 Corinthians 9:8; Jude 24; Luke 18:27; Luke 1:34, 37; Jeremiah 32:17; 2 Kings 3:18.

38. For more about Alexander Mackay and King M'tesa, see the entry for July 31.

39. Juliann DeKorte, *Ethel Waters: Finally Home* (Old Tappan, NJ: Fleming H. Revell Company, 1978), 67.

40. See the devotion for November 21.

41. *The Gideon,* "The Witch Doctor," April 2006, 5.

42. Thomas à Kempis, *Consolations for My Soul, A Contemporary Translation by William Griffin* (New York: The Crossroad Publishing Company, 2004), 34.

43. Paul L. Maier, *Eusebius: The Church History* (Grand Rapids: Kregel Publications, 1999), 265–66.

44. F. W. Boreham, *Shadows on the Wall* (New York: The Abingdon Press, 1922), 22–26.

45. Albert Ernest Richardson, *The Kneeling Christian* (Grand Rapids: Zondervan, undated), 88.

46. *Voices of the Faithful*, with Beth Moore; Kim P. David, compiling editor (Franklin, TN: Integrity Publishers, 2005), 67.

47. Colossians 1:11, Ephesians 3:16, Deuteronomy 33:25, Ephesians 6:10, Isaiah 27:5, Psalm 28:7, Psalm 29:11, Isaiah 40:30–31.

48. Henry David Thoreau, *Walden* (New York: Barnes & Noble Books, 2004), 345.

49. An archaic term for "boundary" or "destination."

50. This story is told in an old volume in my library with a missing title page. On the spine are the words: *Anecdotes Christian Ministry*. The last page has this attribution: *Religious Tract Society: 1799*. This story is found on pages 15–16.

51. J. Edwin Orr, *This Promise Is for You* (London: Marshall, Morgan, & Scott, 1935), 79–84.

52. "Hundreds of Coins Found in Patient's Belly," CNN, February 18, 2004.

53. G. M. Alexander, *Changes for the Better,* vol. 1 (W. Yorks, England: Zoar Publications, 1976), 7–10.

54. Amy Carmichael, *Thou Givest . . . They Gather* (Fort Washington, PA: Christian Literature Crusade, 1958), 3.

55. This verse was adapted from Daniel 7:10 that says, "Thousands upon thousands served Him; ten thousand times ten thousand stood before Him."

56. Isabel Fleece, *Not By Accident: What I Learned from My Son's Untimely Death* (Chicago: Moody Press, 1964/2000), 17–18.

57. Quoted by Mary W. Tileston in *Daily Strength for Daily Needs,* entry for March 6.

58. Ibid., entry for July 11.

59. Mark Joyella and Elaine Chan, "Stress Mess in U.S.," the *New York Post*, October 25, 2007, http://www.nypost.com/seven/10252007/news/nationalnews/stress_mess _in_u_s_.htm (accessed October 25, 2007).

60. Charles Haddon Spurgeon, *John Ploughman's Talks* (New York: Sheldon & Company, nd), 139.

61. For more about Alexander Mackay, see the entry for June 5.

62. Darlene Deibler Rose, *Evidence Not Seen: One Woman's Faith in a Japanese P.O.W. Camp* (Carlisle, UK: M Publishing, 1988), 45–46.

63. Morris L. West, *The Devil's Advocate* (New York: Dell, 1959), 334–35.

64. 1 John 1:9, 1 John 1:7, Psalm 103:3, Isaiah 38:17, Psalm 51:9, Jeremiah 33:8.

65. Jill Briscoe, *A Little Pot of Oil* (Sisters, OR: Multnomah Publishers, 2003), 29–32.

66. Matthew 15:25, Psalm 119:147, Psalm 40:13, Psalm 60:11, Hebrews 2:18, Luke 18:7, Psalm 121:1–2, Psalm 145:14, Isaiah 41:13, Psalm 146:5–6, Hebrews 4:16.

67. Margaret Truman, *First Ladies* (New York: Random House, 1995), 99.

68. Nino Lo Bello, *The Incredible Book of Vatican Facts and Papal Curiosities* (New York: Barnes & Noble Books, 1998), 108–09.

69. Frank L. Houghton, *Amy Carmichael of Dohnavur* (Fort Washington, PA: Christian Literature Crusade, 2000), 354.

70. John W. Peterson with Richard Engquist, *The Miracle Goes On* (Grand Rapids: Zondervan Publishing House, 1976), 141–42.

71. F. B. Meyer, *The Christ Life for Your Life* (Chicago: Moody Press, u.d.), 24–25.

72. John Bunyan, *Grace Abounding to the Chief of Sinners* (Grand Rapids: Baker Book House, 1986), 96.

73. Carl F. H. Henry, *The Pacific Garden Mission* (Grand Rapids: Zondervan Publishing House, 1942), 56.

74. Isobel Kuhn, *In the Arena* (Singapore: OMF International, 1995), 59–60.

75. Sam James, *Servant on the Edge of History* (Garland, TX: Hannibal Books, 2005), chapter 4.

76. William Moody, *The Life of Dwight L. Moody* (Murfreesboro, TN: Sword of the Lord Publishers, u.d.), chapter 35.

77. This story is told in an old volume in my library with a missing title page. On the spine are the words: *Anecdotes Christian Ministry*. The last page has this attribution: *Religious Tract Society: 1799*. This story is found on pages 50–52.

78. Bernard Ruffin, *Fanny Crosby* (Cleveland, OH: United Church Press, 1976), 191.

79. Acts 13:43 (NLT); 2 Corinthians 1:8–9 (NIV); 2 Chronicles 14:11 (NIV); 2 Chronicles 13:18 (NIV); Psalm 25:5 (NET); Psalm 22:10 (TEV); Psalm 71:6 (TEV); Psalm 27:14 (NET)

80. William Arnot, *Studies in Proverbs* (Grand Rapids: Kregel Publications, 1978; reprint of the 1884 edition published by T. Nelson London under the title "Laws from Heaven for Life on Earth"), 16.

81. F. B. Meyer, *Christian Living* (Philadelphia: Henry Altemus Company, u.d.), 17–19.

82. Richard Bewes, *Speaking in Public—Effectively* (Great Britain: Christian Focus, 1998), 9–11.

83. Hesketh Pearson, *Dizzy: The Life and Personality of Benjamin Disraeli Earl of Beaconsfield* (New York: Grosset & Dunlap, 1951), 66.

84. Robert L. Sumner, *Biblical Evangelism in Action* (Murfreesboro, TN: Sword of the Lord Publishers, 1966), 120.

85. Phyllis Moir, *I Was Winston Churchill's Private Secretary* (New York: Wilfred Funk, Inc., 1941), 100, 164.

86. Quoted by John Maxwell in *Success: One Day at a Time* (Nashville: J. Countryman, 2000), 9.

87. Jonathan Eig, *Luckiest Man: The Life and Death of Lou Gehrig* (New York: Simon & Schuster, 2005), 48–49.

88. http://self-discipline.8m.com/, accessed September 22, 2005.

89. Clyde E. Fant and William M. Pinson, *A Treasury of Great Preaching* (Waco, TX: Word Publishing, 1995).

90. Quoted by David L. Larsen, *The Company of Preachers* (Grand Rapids: Kregel Publications, 1998), 449.

91. This story is told in an old volume in my library with a missing title page. On the spine are the words *Anecdotes Christian Ministry.* The last page has this attribution: *Religious Tract Society: 1799.* This story is found on page 64.

92. This story is found in *Out of My Life* by Dr. V. Raymond Edman, who was at the conversation between Evans and Mantle (Grand Rapids: Zondervan, 1961), 103–06.

93. Sherwood Wirt, *The Book of Joy* (New York: McCracken Press, 1994), 8–9.

94. Republished in 1993 by Soli Deo Gloria Publications

95. Ichabod Spencer, *A Pastor's Sketches* (Vestavia Hills, AL: Solid Ground Christian Books, 2001), 58.

96. Quoted in *Samuel Logan Brengle: Portrait of a Prophet* by Clarence W. Hall (Atlanta: The Salvation Army Supplies and Purchasing Dept., 1933), 247.

97. "Train Passenger Recalls Blood Message" by Greg Risling (AP) in North-West Cable News, at http://www.nwcn.com/sharedcontent/nationworld/nation/020 405ccjccwNatTrainBlood.75ec0d82.html, accessed November 7, 2005.

98. Account from various written and electronic sources.

99. A version of this devotion first appeared in the April 2008 issue of *Turning Points* magazine, of which the author of this book is a principal writer.

100. Hannah Whitall Smith, *The Christian's Secret of a Holy Life: The Unpublished Personal Writings of Hannah Whitall Smith,* Melvin Easterday Dieter (Oak Harbor: Logos Research Systems, Inc., 1997), December 10.

101. Adapted from J. Allen Blair, "Don't Bring Leftovers," an undated tract published by Glad Tidings, Inc., P. O. Box 18824, Charlotte, NC 28218.

102. Julia Child and Alex Prud'homme, *My Life in France* (New York: Alfred A. Knopf, 2006), 25.

103. ESL, English as a Second Language

104. J. I. Packer, *God's Words* (Downers Grove, IL: InterVarsity Press, 1981), 94–95.

105. Tammi Reed Ledbetter, "Despite Breast Cancer, I Was Not Alone" in *Baptist Press,* October 22, 2007.

106. This publishing house, B&H Publishing Group, is the shortened form of Broadman & Holman. Its original name, Broadman Press, was formed by combining the names of John Broadus and Basil Manly Jr.

107. Patrick Kavanaugh, *The Spiritual Lives of Great Composers* (Nashville: Sparrow Press, 1992), 13.

108. David L. Larson, *The Company of Preachers* (Grand Rapids: Kregel, 1998), 155.

109. Dr. A. J. Gordon, *The Holy Spirit in Missions* (F. H. Revell Co., 1893). A version of this story also appeared in the author's previous book, *From This Verse.*

110. Mark 1:27, Mark 9:15, Luke 2:18, Luke 4:22, Luke 4:36, Luke 9:43.